Postmodernism in Educational Theory:
Education and the Politics of Human Resistance

edited by
Dave Hill, Peter McLaren,
Mike Cole and Glenn Rikowski

the Tufnell Press

ii

the Tufnell Press,

47 Dalmeny Road,
London, N7 0DY

First published 1999

British Library Cataloguing-in-Publication Data
A catalogue record for this book is
available from the British Library

ISBN 1 872767 81 8

Printed in England by Da Costa Print, London

Contents

Notes on the contributors

Michael W. Apple is John Bascom Professor of Curriculum and Instruction and Educational Policy Studies at the University of Wisconsin, Madison, USA. A former elementary and secondary school teacher and past-president of a teachers union, he has written extensively about the relationship between education and differential power. He has worked with educators, unions, dissident groups, and progressive movements throughout the world to democratize educational research, policy, and practice. Among his recent books are *Official Knowledge* (Routledge 1993), *Cultural Politics and Education* (Teachers College Press 1996), *Power/Knowledge/Pedagogy* (Westview Press 1998), and *Democratic Schools* (OUP 1995), and *Power, Meaning and Identity* (Peter Lang, 1999).

Jenny Bourne is a sociologist, who has written and lectured on the sociology of race relations, and an activist in the women's and anti-racist movements. She was a member of Women Against Racism and Fascism and Women in Black and has written *Towards an anti-racist feminism* and *Homelands of the mind: Jewish feminism and Identity Politics.* She is a founder member of the Collective that produces the anti-racist bimonthly, *CARF.* She has acted as consultant to educational initiatives on anti-racism from those of the GLC and the Central Council for Education and Training in Social work to the *HomeBeats* CD Rom. She works as senior researcher at the Institute of Race Relations.

Mike Cole is research and publications mentor and senior lecturer in education in the School of Education at the University of Brighton. He has written extensively on equality issues; in particular, equality and education. In more recent years he has engaged in critiques of postmodernism, globalisation and education. With Dave Hill he co-founded the Hillcole Group of Radical Left Educators in England. He edited *Bowles and Gintis revisited* (Falmer Press 1988), *The Social Contexts of Schooling* (Falmer Press 1989) and *Education for Equality* (Routledge 1990). His most recent publications include the co-written (with the Hillcole Group), *Rethinking Education and Democracy* (Tufnell Press 1997) and the co-edited collections *Promoting Equality in Primary Schools* (Cassell 1997), *Promoting Equality in Secondary Schools* (Cassell 1999) and *Migrant Labour in the European Union* (Berg 1999). He is the editor of *Human Rights, Education and Equality* (Falmer Press 1999), and *Professional Issues for Teachers and Student Teachers* (David Fulton 1999).

Ramin Farahmandpur is a doctoral student at the Graduate School of Education and Information Studies at the University of California, Los Angeles. His current areas of interests include the impact of global capitalism on multicultural education, and the representation and reproduction of minority and indigenous cultures in the mainstream media, popular films, and school textbooks.

Ted Hankin received a Degree in Education from Trent Polytechnic and a PhD in philosophy from the University of Birmingham, where he studied the base and superstructure question in Marxist theory. On a national level Ted supports the Leninist metanarrative. He has written fairly extensively for sections of the Leninist press. On a local level, he has been involved with a claimants action group for some time. He is currently working on (i) a materialist account of the demise of the Soviet Union, concentrating on the failure to continually revolutionise the forces of production partly, with reference to Mao's late economic writings and (ii) notes towards a dialectical theory of truth.

Dave Hill teaches at University College Northampton. He is a former Labour Parliamentary candidate (in 1979 and 1987), former Labour Group Leader on East Sussex County Council, Regional higher education Chair of NATFHE, the lecturers' Union, leader of various regional political campaigns and mobilisations and a local leader of the Anti-Nazi League. He has advised the Labour Party on teacher education from a radical Left perspective. With Mike Cole, in 1989, he co-founded the Hillcole Group of Radical Left Educators. He has written a number of Hillcole Group booklets on Teacher Education, has co-written the two Hillcole Group books *Changing the Future: Redprint for Education* (Tufnell Press 1993) and *Rethinking Education and Democracy* (Tufnell Press 1997), has co-edited *Promoting Equality in Primary Schools* and *Promoting Equality in Secondary Schools* (Cassell 1997; 1999). He is editing *Education, Education Education: Capitalism, Socialism and 'the Third Way'* (Cassell, forthcoming).

Jane Kelly is Principal lecturer in the School of Art and Design History at Kingston University where she teaches nineteenth and twentieth century Art History and Theory. She is Field leader for the BA in the History of Art, Architecture and Design and also for the MA in Art History. Her current research interests are in Critical Theory and Methodology, including modernism, postmodernism, Marxism and feminism. She has written several articles on the relationship between feminism and postmodernism, as well as on feminist Art history and contemporary art and practice. At present she is researching the relationship between Marxism and Feminism. She has been active in the Women's Liberation Movement, feminist and other political developments since the 1970s.

Peter McLaren is a professor in the Division of Urban Schooling in the Graduate School of Education and Information Studies, University of California, Los Angeles. He is the author, editor, and co-editor of over thirty books and monographs on the politics of education, critical ethnography, cultural studies, and Marxist social theory. A political activist and leading exponent of critical pedagogy, Professor McLaren lectures worldwide on the politics of liberation. His most recent books are *Critical Pedagogy and Predatory Culture* (Routledge, 1995), (with Henry Giroux, Colin Lankshear and Mike Peters) *Counternarratives: Cultural Studies and Critical Pedagogies in Postmodern Spaces* (Routledge, 1997) *and Revolutionary Multiculturalism: Pedagogies of Dissent for the New Millennium* (Westview Press, July 1997). His works have been published in eleven languages.

Michael Neary is a lecturer in the Department of Sociology at the University of Warwick, Coventry. He previously worked with the young unemployed and young offenders on projects in South London, which included being Director of Wandsworth Youth Development and Education Officer for the Inner London Probation Service. His most recent publications include *Money and the Human Condition* (with Graham Taylor) (Macmillan, 1998) and *Youth, Training and the Training State: the Real History of Youth Training in the Twentieth Century* (Macmillan 1997). His *Global Humanization: Studies in the Manufacture of Labour* (Mansell) is forthcoming in 1999.

Glenn Rikowski is a Research Fellow in Post-Compulsory Education & Training in the School of Education at the University of Birmingham. He previously taught at Epping Forest College and other further education (FE) and higher education institutions and schools in London and Essex. Dr. Rikowski's research has included work on: working students; higher education aspirations of FE students; continuing vocational education; FE funding; FE student retention; and the British horological industry. He is a member of the Hillcole Group of Radical Left Educators and has been active in various trade union and anti-cuts campaigns.

Mike Sanders teaches English and media and Popular Culture at University College Northampton, where he is on the Executive Committee of the lecturer's union, NATFHE. He has also taught English at the Universities of Exeter and Aberystwyth, and was a shopworker and USDAW shop steward prior to entering higher education. His current research interests include Chartist poetry, and Women and Radicalism in the early nineteenth century.

Geoff Whitty has been the Karl Mannheim Professor of Sociology of Education at the London University Institute of Education since 1992 and became Dean of Research there in September 1998. He publishes widely in academic and professional journals. Among his books are *Sociology and School Knowledge* (Methuen 1985), *The State and Private Education* (Falmer Press 1989) (with Tony Edwards and John Fitz), *Specialisation and Choice in Urban Education* (Routledge 1993) (with Tony Edwards and Sharon Gerwitz). His most recent book with Sally Power and David Halpin, is *Devolution and Choice in Education: the School, the State and the Market* (Open University Press 1998). His main areas of research and scholarship are in the sociology of the school curriculum, education policy, teacher education and health education. He has directed ESRC-funded research projects on the impact of education policies, and is frequently engaged by local education authorities and health authorities to evaluate policies at local level. These currently include a health promoting school initiative and a pilot education action zone.

CHAPTER 1

Postmodernism in Educational Theory
Glenn Rikowski and Peter McLaren

Postmodernism in educational theory

In many parts of the capitalist world postmodernist politics still lays claim to contemporary relevance. Indeed, it claims to be the only politics available. The authors of this book collectively discern a need to clear the decks of such junk theory and debilitating 'political' posturing because of the urgent tasks ahead for socialists. We also, in various ways, stress the significance of education and training as resources for constructing a future based on the struggle against capital, the social forms and institutions it engenders and the social inequalities that arise from its market mechanisms.

Some 'Left' postmodernisms, or 'postmodernisms of resistance' appear to hold out prospects for a fruitful consummation of postmodernist and Marxist outlooks. We aim to dispel that illusion. Education has a crucial role to play in the struggle for a future where social, economic and political options are not *closed* by the domination of capital and its value-form of labour.

Postmodernism is an obstacle to the formation of open and radical perspectives which challenge inequalities and the deepening of the rule of capital in all areas of social life. As Raduntz (1999, p. 14) notes, postmodernism 'constitutes a sterile theoretical cul-de-sac with no political program for transformative change'. In recent years, postmodernism has assumed an educational form—as educational theory, postmodernised modes of 'reflective' teacher practice, postmodern educational research methods and so on. Hence, it poses a particular challenge to those viewing education as a resource for social equality and democracy.

The incursion of postmodernism into UK educational circles has been a relatively recent phenomenon. It appears to have followed what has been described as the 'cultural turn' in social theory: a focus on symbolic meaning after decades of research dominated by structural, functionalist and empirical approaches within the human sciences. Stronach and MacLure (1997) note that the *British Education Index* had no postmodern entries between 1986-1991. There was one for 1992, two for 1993 and fifteen for 1994 (p. 32). Thus, 1994 seems to be a significant milestone for British educational postmodernism, and the publication of Usher and Edwards' *Postmodernism and Education* in that year heralded the 'arrival' of postmodernism in the British educational *milieu*. Stronach and MacLure's (1997) *Educational Research Undone* and

Stuart Parker's *Reflective Teaching in the Postmodern World* (1997) consolidated the position of postmodernism within educational research and pedagogy respectively in the British context. In the United States, postmodernism appeared in educational theory and research much earlier and much more extensively. The late 1980s and early 1990s saw an explosion of education books and articles written from postmodernist perspectives (Aronowitz and Giroux, 1990; Lather, 1991—as leading examples), the first being Peter McLaren's critique of postmodernism, *Postmodernity and the Death of Politics: A Brazilian Reprieve* (1986). During this period, some American education journals became clearing houses for educational postmodernism.

Attempts to 'define' postmodernism and 'educational postmodernism' are fraught with difficulty. Daring to spell out differences between postmodernism and postmodernity (as in Cole, Hill and Rikowski, 1997; and Fielding and Rikowski, 1996) easily brings down accusations of oversimplification and crassness from postmodernists (cf. Blake, 1997). Even taking Usher and Edwards' (1994, pp. 1-2) rendering of postmodernism, as a certain 'attitude' towards 'life', or a certain 'state of mind'; ironical, self-referential posture and style, a different 'way of seeing'—still begs the question of why this *particular* 'attitude' is superior, more relevant or politically 'cool' than any other. For us, a commitment to social justice which seeks to end social inequalities is a better 'attitude' to adopt.

At the popular level, postmodernism reflects a certain celebration of aimless anarchism, captured by Martin Jay as 'a world in which Beavis and Butt-head have replaced Horkheimer and Adorno as the reigning champions of negation' (1998, p. 108). As a social-theoretical project, 'postmodernism' is excessive; within the realm of 'discourse' (which functions as a parallel universe) it knows no bounds. In the social universe, the real world (which, for us, incorporates 'discourse'), on the other hand, collectively and individually, we face structural constraints on our form of life; constraints sets by capital and its social relations (Postone, 1996). For postmodernists, all concepts are decentred (fragmented, splattered) and all dualisms (such as the Marxist notion of two major social classes) deconstructed. The search for 'meaning' within texts/discourse becomes infinitive; comprising endless academic work for postmodernists. As Cole, Hill and Rikowski (1997) show through a critique of the work of Blake (1996), postmodernism, 'as excessive social-theoretical practice', attempts to negate the Enlightenment project, and with it reason and rationality, along with any attempts to secure 'knowledge'. Meta-narratives, ethics and value, and any appeals to 'truth' are also scuppered. The effects of postmodernism are predictable: relativism, nihilism, solipsism, fragmentation, pathos, hopelessness. Worse, it acted as obfuscation and veil for the projects of the Radical Right (Hill and Cole, 1995; Cole and Hill, 1996), and continues to obscure their continuing project under the guise of the 'Third Way' (Hill, 2000).

Of course, postmodernists might argue that their object and purpose is just 'playfulness'. Blake (1996, 1997) claimed that he was merely appraising and assessing postmodernism's value for educational philosophy. Waite (1996), on the other hand, holds that such indulgences can more accurately be viewed as acts invoking *self destruction*. Facing the harsh rule of capital, we need to build ourselves up, find similarities between us (as opposed to emphasising differences and fractured, hybrid identities) and to enhance our strengths based on *labour in and against capital* (Neary, 1997). We need to become a social and political force of substance; not virtual forces in the ethereal realm of 'discourse'. And while it is true that in some respect there is a materiality to discourse as a form of practice, postmodernists fail to make the necessary connections between discursive materiality and social relations of production.

It is the political uselessness and debilitating effects of postmodernist discourse which jar most. This can be best illustrated through an example. At the 1997 British Association's Annual Festival of Science, Alan Smithers indicated that some education research efforts were 'a desperate waste of time' (Barnard, 1997; Halpin, 1998, p. 1). To illustrate the general point, Smithers picked on Nigel Blake's (1996) article, *Between Postmodernism and Anti-Modernism*. Educational research in general, and postmodernist educational perspectives in particular, continued to take a battering, the critics spurred on by Chris Woodhead from the UK Government's Office for Standards in Education (Ofsted).

In an article in the *Times Education Supplement* (Blake and Smith, 1997) Blake struck back through arguing that 'discussions about [educational] policy and practice can be informed by *rational argument* and critique' (our emphasis). However, Blake's appeal to rational discourse as arbiter of the value of education research flies in the face of both the postmodernist and his own tendency (Blake, 1996) to be sceptical about, or to undermine, 'Western' or Eurocentric notions of 'reason' and rationality. After attempting to rescue himself with the enemy's poison, Blake then confusedly argues that *postmodernist* perspectives on educational research can be of value (Blake and Smith, 1997). This indicates that not only is postmodernism useless as a basis for self defence, *even for postmodernists*, but as a resource for defending the poor, informing class struggle and arguing against the reality of social inequality it is likely to be even more unhelpful.

Identity politics and contemporary crises

Postmodernist 'politics', such as it is, largely rests upon the concepts of identity and difference. As Jenny Bourne shows (this volume), the 'politics of identity and difference [are] being clearly used to justify the break with class politics'. The problem with basing a 'Left' politics on notions of identity and difference is that these concepts, when driven through the mill of postmodernism, become an *anti-politics*, a kind of 'game of despair' (Cole and Hill, 1995). This is because, in pointing towards the fragmentation of 'selves' and a corresponding lack of a *core* to personhood, the hybridity of 'identities' (we are legion), and the infinite play of *difference* based on social context, perspective, infinite interpretation and variegated relations to the Other—we are left with *little or nothing in common* upon which to build a politics of resistance to capital. This applies to a prospective politics of gender, 'race', disability and sexuality as much as it does for a politics based upon class struggle. Postmodernists reflect what Peter Sloterdijk calls 'cynical reason', which is an 'enlightened false consciousness' or:

> [a] hard-boiled, shadowy cleverness that has split courage off from itself, holds anything positive to be a fraud, and is intent only on somehow getting through life. (1988, p. 546)

The hyper-tech cousins of the postmodernists, the post-human and transhuman theorists who emphasise our march towards the cyborg (fused human-machine entity), add another layer of thought which throws a politics of *commonality* off-balance; though some (Pepperell, 1997) hold out prospects for a new *cyberpolitics* based on our shared evolutionary destiny (Haraway, 1988, 1991). However, what postmodernists and post/trans-human theorists[1]— protagonists for a cyborg future—blatantly ignore or deny is that our lives and 'selves' are, after all, very much centred: by *capital*, as social force and social relation. As capital is a social force which exists as a range of contradictory social drives and flows through capitalist social relations, and insofar as we become capital, then *our everyday lives are lived through and express these contradictions*. Our lives *are* fragmented, shattered and unbalanced—and postmodernism reflects this, though only at the level of 'discourse' and the 'text'—but this strikes a chord only because the 'human' has historically become capital, human-capital (Rikowski, this volume). Thus, as well as causing havoc *externally* to individuals, capital is also the 'horror within' personhood; we live our lives through its forms (money, value, state, commodity and so on) and its contradictions. As Rikowski (this volume) indicates, the struggle against the 'horror within' cannot be undertaken 'internally'—through some form of 'Marxist psychotherapy'. Rather, the need is for a politics aimed at the abolition of the value-form of labour—the dissolution of capital itself—and this involves our *uniting* as labour against capital.

Beyond our fragmented selves, international capital is going through a severe crisis. As McLaren and Farahmandpur (this volume) and McLaren (1998b) note, the outcomes of the current crisis of capital accumulation include the redistribution of income from poor to rich; the erosion of welfare benefits; the socialisation of risks to capital; the suppression of labour incomes; the re-enforcement of absolute surplus-value extraction (longer working hours); a raft of anti-labour laws in many Western countries; increased casualisation, job insecurity and flexibilisation of labour (temporary contracts, part-time and low-paid McJobs in the service sector); and increasing social division within the working class, accompanied by profound weaknesses within labour movements in many countries. Furthermore, many Governments have reacted to the crisis by seeking to give businesses within their national capitals a competitive edge in the global market place by reforming education and training systems (e.g. in the context of the ideologies of globalisation and modernisation, see Cole, 1998). In the UK in particular, human capital theory (largely implicitly, but increasingly explicitly) is at the foundation of education and training policy development. Reform 'mania' has resulted, powered by a generalised drive to raise the quality of human capital (labour-power) throughout British capital. This is certainly the case with respect to current U.S. school reform efforts too (McLaren and Farahmandpur, this volume). The special emphasis on labour-power quality results from the (erroneous) perception of Governments that they can at least control *this* commodity, if no other.

There is a need for a socialist response to these developments. One of the aims of this book is to provide a range of such responses. But we are not just reacting against the poverty of postmodern theory and current economic and educational crises. Our project aims to go further and much deeper. The various contributions in the book highlight the contradictory roles of education and training in capitalism. Education and training are implicated in the social production of labour-power, and in social inequalities and divisions on the one hand, but can become critical forces for change on the other. With respect to the latter, McLaren (1997) emphasises the critical, revolutionary and contraband role that pedagogies can play. Michael Neary (chapter 5) and Mike Sanders, Dave Hill and Ted Hankin (chapter 6) make clear that education and training have significant roles to play in strategies of human resistance to the rule of capital in everyday life and struggles for social justice and social equality.

Outline

This book incorporates two major themes: the appraisal and critique of postmodernism within educational theory; and the explication of Marxist and socialist-feminist alternatives to postmodernism which highlight human resistance to capital and its associated forms of inequality. With respect to education and training, the focus is fourfold: first, there is an emphasis on the degeneration of educational theory through the 'postmodern turn' (and the effects for educational politics, policy and perspectives); second, attention is given to the ways capitalist education and training are implicated in the social production of labour-power, the living commodity on which the whole capitalist system rests; third, a range of educational inequalities are analysed and theorised, and various implications for the struggle for equality within education are drawn out; finally, and most importantly, the subversive, critical and emancipatory aspects of education are explored, with an emphasis on *critical, revolutionary and contraband pedagogies*—pedagogies that run against the grain of capitalist educational and social life.

With these themes and foci in view, the book is organised into two main sections. The first section concentrates on postmodernism in educational theory, but also in politics and policy developments. The second section brings education as a form of human resistance to capital and social inequalities and divisions to the fore, whilst also expanding on *specific* aspects of the critique of postmodern educational theory and research (e.g. Kelly on feminism and postmodernism, Bourne on 'race' and postmodernism, Sanders, Hill and Hankin on social class).

In chapter 2, **Michael Apple and Geoff Whitty** argue that the pendulum has swung too far away from social and educational theories and traditions informing change in curriculum and pedagogy. Postmodernist and poststructuralist alternatives, although superficially 'cool', have sometimes merely thrown up old forms of social and educational outlooks where social control becomes the dominant *leitmotif*. Apple and Whitty advocate a shift from a postmodernist obsession with *meaning* in educational discourse towards a concern with *critical action*. They call for a re-emphasis on the *political economy of education*, though not to the neglect of cultural aspects of contemporary social and educational life. The chapter provides analyses of educational 'reforms' of the last ten years (mainly in a British context, but also with examples from the USA and New Zealand) and asks the question: can these be characterised as instances of *postmodern* educational reforms? Apple and Whitty argue that analysis of changes in capitalist accumulation processes is a more useful starting point for exploring these 'reforms'. Whilst they point towards some positive effects of postmodern theory, they are critical of its excessive moments and flights of fancy.

The main target of chapter 3, by **Mike Cole and Dave Hill**, is 'postmodernisms of resistance'. They contrast these false pretenders with straightforwardly reactionary forms of postmodernism. Fashionable 'postmodernisms of resistance' seek to provide an alternative to Marxist educational perspectives. The authors provide trenchant criticisms of postmodernist thought in general, and 'postmodernisms of resistance' in particular before showing how *all* forms of postmodernist discourse disempower those aiming to uncover and struggle against a range of social and educational inequalities. Finally, they provide arguments which indicate that postmodernist educational research and writing gloss over the major division within capitalist society: the social class divide.

In chapter 4, **Glenn Rikowski** indicates that a politics of human resistance to the rule of capital faces a particular problem: *we are capital*. Most of the article is taken up with demonstrating how we become capital, and in what ways 'human' life is capitalised. Criticisms of fashionable trans/post-human theories are provided *en route*. Special emphasis is given to the social production of labour-power in capitalism, and the parts that education and training play in the formation of human-capital; humanity *as* capital. Finally, the chapter points towards the role that critical pedagogy can play in understanding and resisting our predicament as human-capital.

Michael Neary (chapter 5) problematises the concept of 'youth', and *inter alia*, the sociology of youth and youth cultural studies. By delving deeply into Marxist theory, Neary provides an innovative critique of conventional theories of human resistance. Through focusing upon some of Marx's basic structuring concepts—*value, labour, labour-time* and so on—Neary expresses how capital is 'an impersonal form of social domination' created by labour itself and which takes the form of abstract labour. In this analysis, Neary exposes some weak points within capitalist domination. He then proceeds to explore these vulnerabilities through an historical account of the 'production of a specific form of human sociability: youth, through a particular form of regulation: training'. Neary does this through an examination of the UK Employment and Training Act of 1948. Through this account, he shows how the resultant 'training culture' *was set against human resistance* (to capital's domination). Neary's exploration of the 1948 Act and the post-War and contemporary youth condition shows how we can theorise resistance beyond orthodox accounts of working class struggle, and in a way which shows that human resistance to capital 'cannot be contained'.

In chapter 6, **Mike Sanders, Dave Hill and Ted Hankin** provide compelling arguments for a 'return to class analysis' as a basis for a rejuvenated educational theory and politics. These authors show how we still live in a class-divided society and unearth some of the key facts regarding social class differences. They then go on to show the deleterious effects of postmodernist discourse on contemporary educational debate and politics. The main part of the chapter is taken up with working through problems and issues in class analysis, prior to showing the relevance of social class to a range of contemporary policy developments. They end with an argument for reinvigorating the secondary curriculum through a pedagogy which enlightens young people about the (capitalist) nature of the society in which they live and which provides resources for critical analyses of contemporary society.

Jenny Bourne (chapter 7) critiques postmodernist and poststructuralist 'positions' on 'race'. She shows how these perspectives have de-radicalised the study and politics of 'race', whilst simultaneously undermining social class analysis. Bourne provides an account of the rise of postmodernist theory through its beginnings in Cultural Studies to its eventual flowering in the hokum of New Times and theories of identity and identity 'politics'. She shows how we can reclaim radical 'race' perspectives, pinpointing criticisms within culturalism and positions which make positive claims for a 'politics of identity/ difference', and showing how 'Left' postmodernists have betrayed the oppressed. Bourne concludes with a critique of the work of Phil Cohen on youth and education. This critique functions as an illumination of the poverty of postmodern perspectives. Postmodernism, argues Bourne, is useless as a basis for understanding and resisting racism.

In chapter 8, **Jane Kelly** critically surveys postmodernist and poststructuralist feminisms. She charts the development of these theories within feminism and then exposes their incoherence. For Kelly, 'postmodernised feminism' is on a road to nowhere: bereft of political direction, imbued with theoretical drift. Through an historical and empirical analysis of the position of women in Britain, Kelly finds that there is still much about which to be angry. The position of women on a range of issues—from pay, to working conditions and beyond—requires clear theoretical analysis which can function as guide to effective political action for changing women's lives for the better. The preoccupations of postmodernism are elsewhere. Postmodernism is not only excessive in its effects, but is a form of self-indulgence, argues Kelly.

Peter McLaren and Ramin Farahmandpur (chapter 9) begin with a wide-ranging critique of neo-liberal ideology which pinpoints some of the contemporary attacks on workers and oppressed groups committed in its name. Whilst McLaren and Farahmandpur acknowledge some positive aspects of postmodern theory, they note its failure to become a force for effective opposition to neo-liberal policy drives. They develop critical positions on globalisation and the marketisation of social life, and then go on to demonstrate the 'naughtiness' of postmodernism through pointing out its collusion and synergy with neo-liberalism. Following a 'return to class analysis' and a extensive review of the relevance of social class to understanding key aspects of capitalist inequalities, McLaren and Farahmandpur set about 're-enchanting the project of critical educational theory' through developing a contraband pedagogy.

In the Concluding chapter, **McLaren, Hill and Cole** focus on the notion of 'human resistance', and show how the various chapters in this volume inform and theorise this issue. They explore concrete ways through which we can resist the degenerative tendencies of contemporary capital, and examines where education fits into strategies for human resistance. At this juncture, the authors make a case for forms of critical and revolutionary pedagogy and explicate the roles they can play in an anti-capitalist politics of human resistance.

Acknowledgements

This is to acknowledge the welcome contributions of Mike Cole and Dave Hill to this chapter.

Notes

1. Post-human and post transhuman theory are outlined and discussed in Rikowski (this volume).

CHAPTER 2

Structuring the Postmodern in Education Policy
Michael W. Apple and Geoff Whitty

Education policy and the conservative restoration

There has been a breakdown in the accord that guided a good deal of educational policy since World War II. Powerful groups within government and the economy, and within 'authoritarian populist' social movements, have been able to redefine-often in very retrogressive ways—the terms of debate in education, social welfare, and other areas of the common good. No longer is education even seen as part of that fragile social alliance which combined many 'minority' groups, women, teachers, community activists, progressive legislators and government officials, and others who acted together to propose (limited) social democratic policies for schools (e.g. expanding educational opportunities, limited attempts at equalizing outcomes, developing special programs in bilingual and multicultural education, and so on). A new alliance has been formed, one that has increasing power in social and educational policy. This power bloc combines multiple fractions of capital, neo-conservative intellectuals, authoritarian populist religious fundamentalists—which in the USA are increasingly powerful—and a particular fraction of the management oriented new middle class. Its interests are less in increasing the life chances of women, people of colour, or labour. (These groups are obviously not mutually exclusive). Rather, in general, it aims at providing the educational conditions believed necessary both for increasing international competitiveness, profit, and discipline and for returning us to a romanticized past of the 'ideal' home, family, and school (Apple, 1993; Apple, 1996a).

In essence, the new alliance in favour of the conservative restoration has integrated education into a wider set of ideological commitments. The objectives in education are the same as those which serve as a guide to its economic and social welfare goals. They include the expansion of that eloquent fiction—the 'free market'—the drastic reduction of government responsibility for social needs, the reinforcement of intensely competitive structures of mobility, the lowering of people's expectations for economic security, and the popularization of what is clearly a form of Social Darwinist thinking, as, for example, the recent popularity of Herrnstein and Murray's The Bell Curve (1994) in the United States so clearly and distressingly indicates.

The political right in the United States and Britain has been very successful in mobilizing support against the educational system and its employees, often exporting the crisis in the economy onto the schools. Thus, one of its major achievements has been to shift the blame for unemployment and underemployment, for the loss of economic competitiveness, and for the supposed breakdown of 'traditional' values and standards in the family, education, and paid and unpaid workplaces from the economic, cultural, and social policies and effects of dominant groups to the school and other public agencies. 'Public' is now the center of all evil; 'private' is the center of all that is good (Apple, 1996a).

Unfortunately, major elements of this restructuring are rendered virtually invisible in discussions among some of the groups in the critical and 'progressive' communities within education itself, especially by some (not all) of those people who have turned uncritically to postmodernism and poststructuralism. What we shall say here is still rather tentative, but it responds to some of our intuitions that a good deal of the academic debate over the politics of one form of textual analysis over another or even whether we should see the world as a 'text,' as discursively constructed, for example, is at least partly beside the point and that 'we' may be losing some of the most important insights generated by, say, other critical traditions in education and elsewhere.

In what we say here, we hope that we do not sound like unreconstructed reductionists. We simply want us to remember the utterly essential—not essentialist—understandings of the relationships (admittedly very complex) between education and relations of power which we need to consider but seem to have forgotten a bit too readily.

Between neo and post

The growth of the multiple positions associated with postmodernism and poststructuralism is powerful and important. It is indicative of the transformation of our discourse and understandings of the relationship between culture and power. The rejection of the comforting illusion that there can (and must) be one grand narrative under which all relations of domination can be subsumed, the focus on the 'pragmatic' and on the 'micro-level' as a site of the political, the illumination of the utter complexity of the power-knowledge nexus, the extension of our political concerns beyond the 'holy trinity' of class, gender, and race, the stress on multiplicity and heterogeneity, the idea of the decentered subject where identity is both non-fixed and a site of political struggle, the focus on the politics and practices of consumption, not only production—all of this has been important, though not totally unproblematic to say the least (Clarke, 1991; Best and Kellner, 1991).

With the growth of postmodern and poststructural literature in critical educational and cultural studies, however, we have tended to move too quickly away from traditions that continue to be filled with vitality and provide essential insights into the nature of the curriculum and pedagogy that dominate schools at all levels. Thus, for example, the mere fact that class does not explain all can be an used as an excuse to deny its power. This would be a serious error. Class is of course an analytic construct as well as a set of relations that have an existence outside our minds. Thus, what we mean by it and how it is mobilized as a category need to be continually deconstructed and rethought. Thus, we must be very careful when and how it is used, with due recognition of the multiple ways in which people are formed. Even given this, however, it would be wrong to assume that, since many people do not identify with or act on what we might expect from theories that link, say, identity and ideology with one's class position, this means that class has gone away (Aronowitz, 1992).

As we indicated above, we are certainly cognizant of the fact that there are multiple relations of power—not only that 'holy trinity' of race, class, and gender. We also recognize that conflicts not only among these relations but within them as well are crucial and that power can also be productive. While we don't totally agree with Philip Wexler (1992) that in schools and the larger society class difference is always the overriding organizing code of social life, we are deeply worried that issues of class have been marginalised in critical work in education. It took so long for questions about class and political economy to come to the fore in our understanding of educational policy and practice—especially in the USA where class discourses have been much more muted than in Europe (Fraser and Gordon, 1994; Apple, 1995)—that it would be a tragic circumstance if, just when a fuller understanding of these dynamics is needed the most, they were marginalised (Apple, 1996b). The neo-liberal and neo-conservative economic and ideological offensive that is being felt throughout the world demonstrates how very important it is that we take these dynamics seriously.

The same must be said about the economy. Capitalism may be being transformed (and perhaps not totally in the ways suggested by 'post' theorists), but it still exists as a massive structuring force. Many people may not think and act in ways predicted by class—essentialising theories, but this does not mean that the structures of the racial, sexual, and class divisions of paid and unpaid labour have disappeared; nor does it mean that relations of production (both economic and cultural, since how we think about these two may be different) can be ignored if we do it in non-essentialising ways (Apple, 1996a).

We say all this because of the very real dangers that now exist in critical educational studies. While there has been great and necessary vitality at the 'level' of theory, a considerable portion of critical research has often been faddish, moving rapidly from theory to theory. The rapidity of its movement through recent French cultural theory and its partial capture by an upwardly mobile fraction of the new middle class within the academy—so intent on mobilizing its cultural resources within the status hierarchies of the university that it has lost any but the most rhetorical connections with the multiple struggles against domination and subordination at universities, schools, and elsewhere—has as one of its effects the denial of gains that have been made in other traditions. Sometimes, it merely re-states them in new garb, without acknowledgement of the intellectual work that has gone before. At worst, it may actually move backwards, as in the reappropriation of, say, Foucault as just another (but somewhat more elegant) theorist of social control, a discredited and a-historical concept that denies the power of social movements and historical agents (Zipin, 1998). Unfortunately, in the rush to poststructuralism and postmodernism and in the supposed rejection of 'the' Enlightenment project, many of us may have forgotten how very powerful the structural dynamics are in which we participate. In the process, cynical detachment often replaces our capacity to be angry.

We want to stress again that, though sometimes overstated, there are significant parts of what are sometimes called 'postie' approaches that are insightful and to which we need to pay close attention. These include particularly the focus on identity politics, on multiple and contradictory relations of power, on non-reductive analysis, and on the local as an important site of struggle. These positions have taught us and continue to teach us a good deal. However, the way they have been introduced into education has sometimes involved stylistic arrogance and a blatant stereotyping of other approaches. There is sometimes too, amongst 'posties' in education, a concomitant certainty that they have 'the' answer to issues we have all been struggling with for years, a cynical lack of attachment to any action in real schools, and a trendy rhetoric that when unpacked often says some rather commensensical things that reflective educators have known and done for as long as we can remember. Let us hasten to add that this is true for only a portion of these approaches; but all of this gives cause for concern.

Thus, there is a fine line between necessary conceptual and political transformations and trendiness. Unfortunately, the latter sometimes appears in the relatively uncritical appropriation of postmodernism by some educational theorists. For example, as one of us has argued at greater length elsewhere and as we shall go into more detail in the second half of this chapter, there certainly are (too many) plans to turn schools over to market forces, to diversify types of schools and give 'consumers' more choice. Various commentators, such as Stephen Ball, have claimed to see in these new forms of schooling a shift from the 'Fordist' school of the era of mass production to the 'post-Fordist school'

(Ball, 1990). The emergence of new and specialised sorts of school may be the educational equivalent of the rise of flexible specialization driven by the imperatives of differentiated consumption, and taking the place of the old assembly-line world of mass production. This certainly has a postmodern ring to it, although it also contains elements of a correspondence theory oddly similar to that which underpinned earlier arguments about the relationship between education and the economy and which were highly questionable even wheb first proposed (see, e.g. Bowles and Gintis, 1976 and Cole (ed.), 1988).

Yet, in many of the new reforms being proposed, there is less that is 'postmodern' than meets the eye. Even in those that are self consciously marketed as 'new schools for new times', there is usually 'an underlying faith in technical rationality as the basis for solving social, economic, and educational problems.' Specialization is just as powerful as—perhaps even more powerful than—any concern for diversity (Whitty, Edwards, and Gewirtz, 1993, pp. 173-174). Rather than an espousal of 'heterogeneity, pluralism, and the local'—athough these may be the rhetorical forms in which some of these reforms are couched—what we also may be witnessing is the revivification of more traditional class and racial hierarchies. An unquestioning commitment to the notion that 'we' are now fully involved in a postmodern world may make it easier to see surface transformations (some of which are undoubtedly occurring) and yet at the same time may make it that much more difficult to recognize that these may be new ways of reorganizing and reproducing older hierarchies (Whitty, Edwards, and Gewirtz, 1993, pp. 180-181). The fact that postmodernism as a theory and postmodernity as a set of experiences may not be applicable to an extremely large part of the population of the world should also make us a bit more cautious (Said, 1993).

Thus, it is important not to evacuate a critical (and self-critical) structural understanding of education. While being cautious of economic reductionism, this does require that we recognize that we live under capitalist relations. Milton Friedman and the entire gamut of privatisers and marketisers who have so much influence in the media and in the corridors of power in corporate board rooms, foundations, and our governments at nearly all levels, spend considerable amounts of time praising these relations. If they can talk about them, why can't we? These relations do not determine everything. They are constituted out of and reconstituted by race, class, gender and multiple other relations, but it seems a bit odd to ignore them. There is a world of difference between taking economic logics and dynamics and the state seriously and reducing everything down to a pale reflection of them. While, some postmodern and poststructural analyses in education do in fact place emphasis on the state, too often it is treated as if it floats in thin air (See, especially, Hunter, 1994).

We are fully cognizant that there are many dangers with such a structural approach, no matter how flexible it is. It has as part of its history attempts to create a 'grand narrative,' a theory that explains everything based on a unitary cause. It can also tend to forget that not only are there multiple and contradictory relations of power at both 'macro' and 'micro' levels in nearly every situation, but that the researcher herself or himself is a participant in such relations (Roman and Apple, 1990; Gitlin, 1994). Finally, structural approaches at times can neglect the ways our discourses are constructed out of, and themselves help construct, what we do and the very power relations under scrutiny. These indeed are issues that need to be taken as seriously as they deserve. Poststructural and postmodern criticisms of structural analyses in education have been fruitful in this regard, especially when they have come from within the various feminist and post-colonial communities (McCarthy and Crichlow, 1993). Although it must be said that some of these criticisms have created wildly inaccurate caricatures of the neomarxist traditions.

Yet, even though the 'linguistic turn,' as it has been called in sociology, education, and cultural studies, has been immensely productive, it is important to remember that the world of education and elsewhere is not only a text. There are gritty realities out there, realities whose power is often grounded in structural relations that are not simply social constructions created by the meanings given by an observer. Part of our task, it seems to us, is not to lose sight of these gritty realities in the economy, in the state, and cultural practices, at the same time as we recognize the dangers of reductive and essentialising analyses.

Our point is not to deny that many elements of 'postmodernity' exist, nor is it to deny the insights of aspects of postmodern theory. Rather, our point is to avoid substituting one grand narrative for another. The grand narrative of class barely existed in the United States for example, since as we mentioned class, state, and political economy only recently surfaced in critical educational scholarship there and were only rarely seen in the form found in Europe where most postmodern and poststructural criticisms of these explanatory tools were developed. It would help if it was remembered that the intellectual and political histories of the United States and many other nations were very different than that castigated by some postmodern critics. Reductive analysis comes cheap and there is no guarantee that postmodern positions, as currently employed by some in education, are any more immune to this danger than any other position.

To put it in a polemical way, one of the main problems on which a critical analysis of education should focus is not only 'meaning and its [supposedly] non-existent foundations, as poststructuralists would, by inversion, have it, but action and its consequences, in particular the structuration of opportunities to act, including to signify and make meanings' (Green and Whitty, 1994, p. 21). Structural conditions 'cannot simply be thought 'away,' they must be thought 'through' in order to be 'acted away,' and our 'thinking' will never be fully up to the task' (Green and Whitty, 1994, p. 21). We need, then, to continue to 'think through' the complicated structural and cultural conditions surrounding schools, to uncover the cracks in these conditions, and in doing so to find spaces for critical action.

Between structure and agency

A focus on critical action is of immense importance here. In any analysis that retains a core of critically reflective structural concerns, ordinary people are not 'crushed' by structural forces. They are actors, individually and collectively, historically and currently. Of course, our very language and perspectives may cause us to miss this, especially the language of efficiency, cost-benefit analysis, and human capital on the right and the language of people as puppets of structural forces or as being totally formed out of 'discourses' and hence having no real agency within some parts of the more 'progressive' academic communities.

Of course, it is the former language—of bureaucracy, of the colonization of all of our lives by the metaphors of markets, profit, and the accountant's bottom line, and so on—that circulates more widely. It leads to what can only be called a loss of memory, an assumption that such approaches were and are neutral technical instrumentalities that if left alone will ultimately solve all of our problems in schools and the larger society (on the terms of dominant groups, of course).

Take the case with our current fascination with management systems and cost cutting within the conservative restoration to make us all 'more efficient and productive.' These things are not neutral techniques. Efficiency, bureaucratic management, employing economic models to understand everything—all of these are ethical constructs. Adopting them involves moral and political choices. Their institutionalization needs to be understood as an instance of cultural power relations. 'Where the origin of social arrangements in political, cultural, and moral choices has disappeared or has come to appear as a neutral technical matter ... one faces a situation of cultural and political hegemony' (Curtis, 1992, p. 175). Yet, in order for these forms of understanding and organization to become dominant, those in dominance have had to engage in the hard work (and it is and has to be hard work) of eliminating or marginalising any serious alternatives (Curtis, 1992, p. 175).

Bruce Curtis reminds us that,

> No bureaucracy can function unless those subject to it adopt specific attitudes, habits, beliefs, and orientations; attitudes toward authority, habits of punctuality, regularity, and consistency, beliefs about the abstract nature and legitimacy of authority and expertise: orientations to rules and procedures. These attitudes, habits, beliefs, and orientations do not spring into existence out of technical necessity; they are the products of complex and protracted conflicts. (Curtis, 1992, p. 8)

Relations of dominance, and of struggles against them, are not theoretical abstractions, then, somewhere out there in an ethereal sphere unconnected to daily life. Rather, they are based on and built out of an entire network of daily social and cultural relations and practices (Curtis, 1992, p. 121). In understanding this, it is dangerous to assume that they are not also partly produced out of the structural positions that people occupy. Dominance depends on both leadership and legitimation. That it is not simply an imposition is a key part of any Gramscian analysis. Dominance also partly relies on 'an element of moral obligation between rulers and ruled, through which both make sense and come to terms with relations of domination.' Such an obligation 'does not imply simple acceptance, but rather offers a set of justifications for political relations and defines the limits of legitimate dominance.' Because of this, for political, economic, and cultural leadership to be successful, those who speak for the most powerful groups in society must engage in serious 'intellectual work.' Such intellectual work involves attempting both to anchor dominant understandings in a particular reading of history and to point toward a 'better future' if the way forward generated out of this way of understanding is followed (Curtis, 1992, p. 102).

Take as an example today's powerful movements toward educational 'reform' such as national testing and marketisation. The forms of understanding underlying these efforts are based on economic discourse as the primary (only?) way to act on the world. The path toward a better future we are constantly told involves making closer connections between all of our social and cultural institutions and an economy in crisis so that 'we' are more competitive nationally and internationally. A contradictory and paradoxical combination of policies such as those on education for employment, tight control over official or legitimate knowledge, and 'choice' are what we need to 'go forward into the 21st Century.' Yet, who is the 'we' who will be helped by this combination of neo-liberal and neo-conservative policies? This is one of the most important questions to ask, since as is shown elsewhere, such policies are immensely destructive both nationally and internationally (Apple, 1996a). But, the task of changing our commonsense (a fully Gramscian concept) so that freedom equals the market, so that failure is only the result of individual character flaws, and so that democracy is simply guaranteeing the unattached individual a choice among consumer products has been more than a little successful (Apple, 1996a).

All of this clearly is occurring within an economic context, but not in any simple 'correspondence' way. And we believe that anything that diminishes our understanding of the economic and ideological context within which such policies are situated also needs to be very carefully thought through. However, when we say this we want to be cautious of not overstating the case. We need to stress again that these conditions are not caused by this context in any linear, unidimensional way. But, to ignore this context as a very powerful set of forces in moving societies in particular directions is to live in a world divorced from reality.

We live in a society in which we are expected, in the words of John Major, 'to condemn a little more and understand a little less' (Ball, 1994, p. 13). Unleashing the 'free market' will be the solution. If the poor still are poor after this society is radically transformed around 'the private' then we'll know that they got poor the old-fashioned way; they earned it. If it wasn't so damaging a set of policies, the assertions would be laughable.

Talking about the extension of market principles into education, Stephen Ball puts it this way:

> The market offers a powerful response to a whole set of technical, managerial, and ideological problems. It appears to give power to all parents, while systematically advantaging some and disadvantaging others, and effectively reproducing the classic lines of the social and technical division of labour. It plays its part in the reformulation generalized ... And it serves to generalize the commodity form, a basic building brick of capitalist culture and subjectivity. (Ball, 1994, p. 10)

This emphasis on individual choice, seen by some rightist commentators as the very essence of democracy, facilitates a denial of the importance of structural disadvantage. It invites us to focus our attention on examples of individuals who, for example, have 'escaped' or been 'rescued' from failing schools as a result of choice policies, without paying attention to the continuing relative disadvantages of working class and black communities as a whole.

In the process of doing this, an understanding of society as a collection of possessive individuals is revivified and any serious sense of the common good is marginalised. The ideological effects of this have been damaging. Our very idea of democracy has been altered so that democracy is no longer seen as a political concept, but an economic one. Democracy is reduced to stimulating the conditions of 'free consumer choice' in an unfettered market (Apple, 1993). The world becomes a vast supermarket. The metaphor of the market is an apposite one, for just as in the real world of the supermarket some people have the resources to go inside and purchase anything they desire, while many, many people must stand outside, looking through the windows and consuming with their eyes only. It is these people who engage in 'postmodern consumption'; they can only consume the image. In a world in which we are moving increasingly toward a double-peaked economy, where the gap between the affluent and the poor grows larger and larger, where worsening conditions within our inner cities and rural areas should be the cause for national embarrassment (Apple, 1996a), we instead reinstall a belief that the possessive individual—the 'consumer'—is the solution. The common good will somehow take care of itself.

From this, it should be clear that there is a cultural project as well as an economic project at work here. One of the goals of the rightist coalition is to separate national identity from origin and ethnicity, to divide history from politics, and to pry loose social consciousness from social experience. Using the language of pluralism and a full range of 'consumer choices' in a market, it actually paradoxically aims at what might be called 'depluralization,' for it articulates a vision of a classless, homogeneous society of consumers within a common, transcendent culture (Ball, 1994, pp. 6-7).

This last point about the Right's cultural project is important. We do not want to stress the economy at the expense of cultural and political dynamics and processes, especially in education—a field that is deeply implicated in cultural and political relations of power—and both of us have been at pains to stress the power of these dynamics and processes for many years. In a time when capitalist relations seem even more powerful, it is easy to be reductive. Hence, it is even more important to remember not to try to squeeze everything into being simply a mere reflection of economic relations for conceptual and political reasons.

Education does indeed have a significant degree of 'relative autonomy.' One of the dangers we face has been a tendency to ignore the space education does have to manoeuvre 'within the institutional complexes of the state, [economy], and cultural forms' (Green and Whitty, 1994, p. 22). This is especially true in those overly structural theories that ignore the role of the local, the contingent, and of individual propensities in accounting for what education does. And this is where some postmodern and poststructural theories that emphasise the local and the contingent are helpful.

The influence of such contingent circumstances can be seen, for example, in the kinds of people who tended to be recruited into school administration when centralization and bureaucratisation first arose as a project in the last century in North America. Let us give an example from the life of an early school administrator who was deeply involved in rationalizing education and bringing it 'under control.'

Some of those who were deeply committed to 'improving' schools through the use of tightened control and accountability (the state as the panopticon, in Foucault's words), were apt to employ the criterion of efficiency even to their own lives. Thus, Dexter D'Everado, a strong supporter of centralized school authority in Canada who was appointed as inspector of education for the Niagara region in 1846, was a very model of efficiency. When sitting down to eat a meal, he 'consistently placed his watch in front of him so he could monitor the time he spent chewing each mouthful of food' (Curtis, 1992, p. 3). (Whether this increased his culinary delight is not known.)

Yes, D'Everado ate his meals in a particular time and within a particular economic context. But his need to apply the norms of efficiency to even the most mundane elements of his daily life—to say nothing of schools—cannot be fully understood (if such a thing is possible) by totally reducing D'Everado back into mirror reflections of the structural realities of that context. There is a tension—if we may be permitted to use some old-fashioned words from social theory—between structure and agency here. It speaks to the necessity of trying to understand both the larger social content and the contingent, local circumstances of daily life inside and outside of schools. This is the balancing act that must be attempted. We shall attempt such a 'balancing act' by instantiating a number of our arguments within an analysis of the recent history of educational reform in England and, to some extent, elsewhere.

This will require that we extend the largely conceptual and political arguments we have made into the 'real world' of education. Thus, it is now time to examine empirically many of the issues we have raised. How might we understand recent transformations in education policy? When taken together, do they constitute a compelling case that supports major aspects of postmodern theory? We shall suggest that by unquestioningly assuming that this is the case there is a danger of establishing a new grand narrative. In a chapter of this length, we cannot deal with all aspects of post-modern theories. In what follows, we shall focus on certain key elements: the issues of the supposed break with modernity's grand narratives of progress, diversity, difference, fragmentation, multiplicity, heterogeneity, and choice.

Is recent education reform a postmodern phenomenon?

Writing about English education policy and inner cities in the mid-1980s, one of us suggested that, during the preceding decade, 'corporatist' and 'market' alternatives to traditional social democratic policies had been vying for position (Whitty, 1986). In the late 1980s, the Conservative government of Margaret Thatcher, increasingly dominated by the 'New Right', displayed a clear preference for the market alternative. While state intervention rather than the vicissitudes of a capitalist market economy came to be blamed for the industrial decline and social dislocation that characterised the urban landscapes of England and Wales, the interventionist policies of left-wing local education authorities (LEAs) were blamed for the poor educational performance of inner city schools. Just as privatization was now seen as the key to reviving the economy, so the solution to the educational problems of urban areas was seen to lie in creating a 'market' (or quasi-market) in education (Whitty, 1997).

Many of the provisions of the 1986 Education Acts and the 1988 Education Reform Act were thus intended to enhance clients' rights of 'voice', 'choice' and 'exit'. These were seen by many people on the New Right as important rights and liberties per se. But, in addition to the philosophical case for choice, it was also claimed that giving parents greater control over their children's schools and introducing more diversity into the system would make schools more responsive and thereby more effective. Referring to schooling in the capital, Kenneth Baker, the government minister responsible for the 1988 Act, argued that 'choice and diversity are the key elements to improve the quality of education for all London's children' (Baker, 1990).

In retrospect, even the earlier 1980 Education Act can now be seen to prefigure some of the later elements of education policy under the Thatcher government—namely the use of public money to support the provision of education by private providers and the attempt to make the public sector behave more like the private sector by encouraging competition and choice (Whitty and Menter, 1989). These policies of the Thatcher years posed a particular challenge to what is arguably the centrepiece of social democratic social engineering of the post-war years, the system of common comprehensive secondary schools under LEA control. In reducing the powers of LEAs to engage in the detailed planning of provision, they can also be seen as opening the way for a restructuring of the system as a whole and eventually perhaps the abolition of LEAs themselves. Alongside the apparent devolution of power to individual schools, there has also been a strengthening of the powers of central government, most noticeably in the establishment of a National Curriculum, which was a product of the thinking of neo-conservative members of the New Right rather than the market-oriented neo-liberals (Whitty, 1989).

Political fashion or postmodernity?

We want to consider whether some of the changes that have been happening in education over the past ten years or so can be regarded as an abomination of Thatcherism (and similar political tendencies in other countries) or whether they are perhaps an indication of something deeper. Although parts of the British government's Education Reform Act of 1988 could be seen as a typical New Right crusade to stimulate market forces at the expense of 'producer interests' in general, and the left educational establishment in particular, that is only one way of looking at it. In some ways, the espousal of choice and diversity in education can be seen to resonate with notions of an open, democratic society as well as with a market ideology.

Put in those terms, current policies have a potential appeal far beyond the coteries of the New Right. Part of their appeal is a declared intention to encourage the growth of different types of school, responsive to needs of particular communities and interest groups. Furthermore, we are told that diversity in types of schooling does not necessarily mean hierarchy. Thus, one former government minister (Dunn, 1988) has characterised the drift away from comprehensive education towards more specialised and differentiated types of school, not as a return to elitist approaches to educational provision, but as happening 'without any one [type of school] being regarded as inferior to the others'.

More sociologically, this apparent encouragement of a diversity of modes of provision might be seen as reflecting some of the characteristics of post-modernity. In organisational terms, current developments might then be not merely the product of the short-term ascendancy of a free-market ideology within the Conservative Party, but part of a wider retreat from modern, bureaucratised state education systems—the so-called 'one best system' in the USA, for example (Chubb and Moe, 1990; Glenn, 1987)—that are perceived as having failed to fulfil their promise and now seem inappropriate to societies of the late twentieth century. Viewed alongside changes in the way the state regulates other areas of social activity, they might be seen as new ways of resolving the core problems facing the state.

Such policies might also be seen as a response to changes in the mode of accumulation. As we mentioned earlier, the emergence of new sorts of school is sometimes characterized as the educational equivalent of what Stuart Hall describes as the rise of 'flexible specialisation in place of the old assembly-line world of mass production' (Hall and Jacques, 1989). The physical appearance of some of the new shopping mall-style City Technology Colleges, and moves towards 'niche marketing' of schools, might seem to support such a 'correspondence thesis'.

A broader view might be to see these moves towards different types of schools as a response to the complex patterns of political, economic and cultural differentiation in contemporary English society which have replaced the traditional class divisions upon which comprehensive education was predicated. Support for schools run on a variety of principles, including those of religious minorities, might also be seen as recognising a widespread collapse of a commitment to modernity. Or, put another way, a rejection of the totalising narratives of the Enlightenment Project, whether in its liberal or marxist versions, and their replacement by 'a set of cultural projects united [only] by a self-proclaimed commitment to heterogeneity, fragmentation and difference' (Boyne and Rattansi, 1990).

Support is certainly being given to the diversification of provision and of site-based control of schools from a variety of political perspectives, as well as in countries with different political regimes. Thus, although school choice policies in the USA received particular encouragement from Republican presidents Reagan and Bush, the growth in site-based management policies, magnet schools, and other schools of choice has received much broader support. A market approach to education has now entered mainstream social thinking in the USA and is by no means narrowly associated with the New Right (Chubb and Moe, 1990). Furthermore, similar policies have been pursued by Labour governments in Australia and New Zealand while, in parts of Eastern Europe, the centrally planned education systems of the Communist regimes are also being replaced with experiments in educational markets. Even Japan, where the standardization of educational provision is often seen as having contributed to the nation's modernization and its extraordinary economic success, has recently been considering policies to enhance choice and diversification, 'so as to secure such education as will be compatible with the social changes and cultural developments of our country' (Stevens, 1991, p. 148).

Many feminists have seen attractions in the shift towards the pluralist models of society associated with post-modernism and post-modernity, and there are also some parallels in the educational policies currently being pursued by ethnic minorities. In the USA, the recent reforms of the school system in Chicago are indicative of some of the dilemmas faced by such groups in relation to New Right policies. Those reforms sought to dismantle the vast bureaucracy under which the Chicago Schools District was perceived by many commentators to be failing the majority of its students, even when controlled by black politicians. The devolution and choice policies were enacted as a result of a curious alliance between New Right advocates of school choice, black groups seeking to establish community control of their local schools, together with disillusioned white liberals and some former student radicals of the 1960s. In New Zealand too advocates of community empowerment have united with exponents of consumer choice against the old bureaucratic order (Grace 1991). Such alliances appear paradoxical at first sight, but less so in the context of postmodernity, which is seen by Lyotard, one of its leading philosophers, as a pluralist, pragmatic and restless set of partially differentiated social orders. Social development is not then seen as 'the fulfilment of some grand historical narrative' but as 'a pragmatic matter of inventing new rules whose validity will reside in their effectivity rather than in their compatibility with some legitimating discourse' (Boyne and Rattansi, 1990). In that context, the notion of 'unprincipled alliances', which at one time might have prevented such a political configuration as emerged in Chicago, is less appropriate. If major attempts at social engineering have been perceived as failing, less ambitious aspirations may now be in order.

In Britain, recent softening of Labour Party policies towards choice and diversity in education might be seen as reflecting a similar shift away from grand master narratives associated with class-based politics. The emergence of comprehensive education in England was itself linked to a politics that assumed that social class was the most significant dimension of social differentiation. The party's traditional social democratic policies have certainly been perceived as unduly bureaucratic and alienating by many black parents, who it is sometimes claimed welcome the new opportunities offered by the Reform Act to be closer to their children's schools (Phillips, 1988). While not necessarily endorsing the Thatcherite dream in its entirety, some aspects of it may resonate with their aspirations. Policies which seem to emphasise heterogeneity, fragmentation and difference may thus represent more than a passing fashion amongst neo-liberal politicians. They may reflect the multiplicity of lines of social fissure that are emerging and a deeper change in modes of social solidarity.

However, some of the groups that may benefit from the devolved and pluralistic patterns of educational provision which such thinking encourages themselves espouse philosophies that are rather more totalising in their aspirations than the broadly social democratic ones which have dominated educational politics in the recent past. This is one argument that has been used against state funding of new religious schools in Britain, particularly Moslem schools with their assumed stance on the role of women (Walkling and Brannigan, 1986). This criticism, though, can itself be seen as a product of arrogant Enlightenment thinking, reflecting a prevailing stereotype of eastern culture which maintains the West's sense of its own cultural superiority (Said, 1978; Parmar, 1981; Halstead, 1986).

The issues are far from straightforward and the political implications of post-modernist tendencies and theories of post-modernity are notoriously difficult to 'read' (Giroux, 1990). Far from reflecting a real change in the nature of society, analyses that celebrate fragmentation and the atomization of decision-making at the expense of social planning and government intervention may merely be replacing one oppressive master-narrative with another, that of the market. Furthermore, the espousal of heterogeneity, pluralism and local narratives as the basis of a new social order is still seen by many sociologists as mistaking phenomenal forms for structural relations. David Harvey (1989) asks whether post-modernist cultural forms and more flexible modes of capital accumulation should be seen 'more as shifts in surface appearance rather than as signs of the emergence of some entirely new post-capitalist or even post-industrial society'. While we cannot answer this question with finality, it is clear that we do damage to reality if we see what is happening in education policy as fully postmodern.

The rhetoric and reality of 'choice' and 'diversity'

So, if the rhetoric of choice and diversity can be read in various ways, what can we make of the reality of the policies which are currently in place in Britain? Are they encouraging choice and diversity anyway? It is, of course, too early to draw any hard and fast conclusions. However, there is some evidence that enables us to give a sense of what Jennifer Ozga (1989) has termed 'the bigger picture'. It will be important to do this, since Ozga suggests that current studies of policy smuggle in a pluralist orthodoxy and detract from theoretical attempts to understand the coherence (or even incoherence) of education policy as a whole.

What about Ozga's 'bigger picture'? Looked at overall, the early analyses of the effects of the various market-oriented policies of the Thatcher government would seem to suggest that, as we hinted earlier in this chapter, far from producing a genuine pluralism and interrupting traditional modes of social reproduction, they may be providing a legitimating gloss for the perpetuation of long-standing forms of structural inequality. There is little evidence of a post-modernist 'break'. The Education Reform Act certainly seems as likely to produce greater differentiation between schools on a linear scale of quality and esteem as the positive diversity that some of its supporters hoped for. If so, the recent reforms represent a continuity with a long history in English education chronicled by Banks in 'Parity and Prestige in English Secondary Education' (Banks, 1955).

Walford and Miller (1991) claim that, while comprehensive schools attempted to overcome the historic links between diversity of provision and inequalities of class and gender, 'City Technology Colleges have played a major part in re-legitimizing inequality of provision for different pupils'. Indeed, they argue that the 'inevitable result' of the concept of CTCs, especially when coupled with Grant Maintained Schools and LMS, is 'a hierarchy of schools with the private sector at the head, the CTCs and GMSs next, and the various locally managed LEA schools following'. A senior Labour Party spokesperson on education has recently asserted that the creation of a hierarchy from elite private schools, through to CTCs and Grant Maintained Schools to a residual provision of Council schools was deliberate Conservative Party policy, a charge which is in some danger of creating a self-fulfilling prophecy.

But, whether deliberate or not, there is little evidence yet that the Education Reform Act is providing a structure that will encompass diversity and ensure equality of opportunity for all students. Rather, there is some evidence that the reforms further disadvantage those unable to compete in the market and that they do actually create a hierarchy of schools. This will have particular consequences for the predominantly working class and black populations who inhabit the inner cities. While they never gained an equitable share of educational resources under social democratic policies, the abandonment of planning in favour of the market seems unlikely to provide a solution. Indeed, there is a real possibility that an educational underclass will emerge in Britain's inner cities, much like that which is so prevalent in the USA.

On this argument, whatever the intentions of their sponsors, present policies are as likely to increase structural inequalities as challenge them, while fostering the belief that their championing of choice does provide genuinely equal opportunities for all those individuals who wish to benefit from them. For those members of disadvantaged groups who are not sponsored out of schools at the bottom of the status hierarchy, either on grounds of exceptional academic ability or alternative definitions or merit, the new arrangements are effectively just another way of reproducing deeply entrenched class and race divisions. Visions of our moving towards a post-modern education system in a post-modern society may thus be premature or a reflection of surface appearances— perhaps merely a mirage. At the very most, current reforms would seem to relate to a version of post-modernity that emphasises 'distinction' and 'hierarchy' within a fragmented social order [PM1], rather than one that positively celebrates (or even tolerates) 'difference' and 'heterogeneity' [PM2] (Lash, 1990).

National curricula

This linearity is also evident when one looks at the National Curriculum in England, the one element of recent reforms that seemed to contradict the

Thatcher government's espousal of market forces (Whitty, 1989). The National Curriculum established by the 1988 Education Reform Act specifies programmes of study and attainment targets for the three 'core' subjects, English, mathematics and science, and seven other 'foundation' subjects. While some of the extreme neo-liberals of the New Right would have liked to see the curriculum itself left to the market, the government seems to have been more persuaded on this score by the argument of neo-conservative pressure groups such as the Hillgate Group. This group argues that, even if market forces should ultimately be seen as the most desirable way of determining a school's curriculum, central government imposition of a National Curriculum on all state schools is a necessary interim strategy to undermine the vested interests of a 'liberal educational establishment' which threatens educational standards and traditional values. While there are complex alliances and motivations involved, this is the case as well in the attempt in the USA to move toward national curricula, national standards, and national testing (Apple, 1996a).

In England, the Hillgate Group is particularly concerned to counter the pressure for a multicultural curriculum that 'has been felt throughout the Western world, and most notably in France, Germany, and the United States, as well as in Britain'. It joins those 'who defend the traditional values of Western societies, and in particular who recognize that the very universalism and openness of European culture is our best justification for imparting it, even to those who come to it from other roots' (Hillgate Group, 1987). While happy to see the emergence of new and autonomous schools, including Islamic schools and such other schools as parents desire, its commitment to market forces is in the context of an insistence that all children 'be provided with the knowledge and understanding that are necessary for the full enjoyment and enhancement of British society'. 'Our' culture, being part of the universalistic culture of Europe, 'must not be sacrificed for the sake of a misguided relativism, or out of a misplaced concern for those who might not yet be aware of its strengths and weaknesses' (Hillgate Group, 1987). Behind much of this is a tension over 'the other'. Thus, racial discourse is often the absent presence behind such positions, a fact that is very visible in the USA in particular (Apple, 1996a; Apple, 1996b) and increasingly visible in Britain, France, Germany, and elsewhere.

The Hillgate pamphlet thus works both to acknowledge difference and to defuse its potential challenge to the prevailing social order. Given its influence on government policies at the time the Reform Act was being finalised, the reading of those policies with which we flirted earlier, seeing them as a reflection of the sort of post-modern society which celebrates heterogeneity and difference, becomes even more questionable. There is clearly within the discourse of the Hillgate Group a master-narrative that differentiates cultures on a hierarchical basis and which sees social progress largely in terms of assimilation into European culture.

A further aspect of the National Curriculum arrangements that is likely to arrange schools and students on a linear scale is the combination of LMS, competition amongst schools for students and the publication of assessment scores. This could well leave the most disadvantaged students concentrated in schools with low aggregate test scores and declining resources and morale.

Alternative responses

The combination of policies that characterised the Thatcher government's approach to education in Britain is well-captured in the paradoxical concept of 'conservative modernisation' (Dale, 1989), a term that also emphasizes it links with other aspects of modernity, rather than something distinctively anti-modern or post-modern. Despite the development of new forms of accumulation and changes in the state's mode of regulation, together with some limited changes in patterns of social and cultural differentiation in contemporary Britain, the continuities seem just as striking as the discontinuities. In theoretical terms, this seems to offer support for those who deny that there has been any radical rupture with modernity, but it is also consistent with a view that argues for a dialectic of continuity and discontinuity (Best and Kellner, 1991).

Thus, while there may have been no post-modernist 'break', recent conservative policies may well have been more responsive than those of others to those subtle social and cultural shifts that have been taking place in modern societies. Even though social class divisions remain an important challenge to our education system, traditional social democratic approaches to education which favour the idea of a common school and, indeed, usually some version of a common curriculum (Lawton, 1975; Whitty, 1985), will themselves have to respond to the increasing social diversity of contemporary societies. Just as current discussions on the left about citizenship are seeking ways of 'creating unity without denying specificity' (Mouffe, quoted in Giroux, 1990), so will this be a challenge for future education policy. James Donald (1989) has called for approaches which are based on 'participation and distributive justice rather than simple egalitarianism—and on cultural heterogeneity rather than a shared humanity'. Donald himself argues that this puts a question mark against the very idea of comprehensive education. While we are not convinced that is necessarily the case, it certainly requires some rethinking of the notion of comprehensive education and indicates the need for the left to rethink old orthodoxies. What it decidedly does not do, however, is require us either to fully reject 'older' ways of understanding the social world in general and education policy in particular or to fully accept 'newer' 'post' understandings and assumptions unquestioningly. Indeed, such a view expressly contradicts itself, since oddly enough it assumes a linear view of progress that is (supposedly) rejected within post-modern approaches themselves.

Conclusion

In this chapter, we have acknowledged that many of the postmodern and poststructural emphases now emerging in critical educational studies have had a number of positive effects. They have increased the number of voices that need to be made public. They have helped legitimate and/or generate a welcome return to the concrete analysis of particular ideological and discursive formations, as well as the multiple sites of their elaboration and legitimation in policy documents, social movements, and institutions such as schools (Hall, 1992, p. 537). This focus on the complexities of the concrete historical instance, without always having to search for the hidden set of determinations, in part does free us to understand the local and the contingent.

Yet, this said—and it should be—there are many dangers here too, especially involving the loss of collective memory, the loss of the gains in understanding that accompanied more structural analyses of the generation, circulation, and legitimation of educational policies within the economic, political, and cultural spheres. In many ways, there are the same silences within too many post-modern approaches that are found in one of the major figures from whom these theories have often borrowed their emphases—Michel Foucault. As Hall reminds us, it has often proven too easy to accept Foucualt's epistemological position whole and uncritically. There is a world of difference (and no pun is intended here) between emphasising the local, the contingent, and the non-correspondent and ignoring any determinacy or any structural relationship among practices. Too often, important questions surrounding the state and social formation are simply evacuated and the difficult problem of simultaneously thinking about the specificity of different practices and the forms of articulated unity they constitute are assumed out of existence as if nothing existed in structural ways (Hall, 1992, pp. 537-538). Or, as has been the case of some of the material we have examined, relatively reductive relations of 'correspondence' between the economy and education are posited, as if we have learned nothing since the days of Bowles and Gintis (See Bowles and Gintis, 1976).

Yet, our analysis of educational policies demonstrates the importance of just such 'thinking through' simultaneously. Rhetorical flights into fragmentation, diversity, 'difference', the supposed break with both 'modernity' and its grand narratives, and so on do represent certain transformations in education and the larger society. But, it is just as possible that they construct a 'story' of the world that is overstated, that misrecognises patterns of cause and effect, and in the process causes many people to forget who and what may be at stake as the conservative restoration litters the landscape of education with the effects of its aggressive policies.

Note

Parts of this chapter appear in Apple (1995) and Apple (1996). Other parts of this paper were presented by Geoff Whitty to the 'Conference on Reproduction, Social Inequality and Resistance: New Directions in the Theory of Education' at the University of Bielefeld, Germany, October 1—4, 1991. Although there have subsequently been a number of modifications to the specific policies discussed here, the major substantive and theoretical issues raised in the paper remain the same. For further discussion of these issues, see Whitty *et al.* (1993) and Whitty (1998).

CHAPTER 3

Into the Hands of Capital: the Deluge of Postmodernism and the Delusions of Resistance Postmodernism
Mike Cole and Dave Hill

Introduction

In this Chapter, we attempt an evaluation of what have been described as 'postmodernism of reaction' and 'postmodernism of resistance'.[1] We conclude that, while there are clear differences in intention and in emphasis between the 'two postmodernisms', they have too much in common to be thought of as separate discourses. It is more accurate, we suggest, to think of a continuum, with 'postmodernism of reaction' at one end and 'postmodernism of resistance' at the other. While one end of the continuum is peopled by reactionaries, engrossed in 'games of despair', the other is composed of defeatist ex-socialists, engaged in a rhetoric of left posturing.

Next, we refer to some key problems with postmodernism *per se*. Contra the postmodern rejection of the meta-narrative, a Marxist analysis, we argue, still has most purchase in explaining economic, political, social and cultural changes and developments in capitalist societies, such as, for example, the Radical Right and former social democratic restructuring of education systems. We argue that postmodernist analyses, in general, marginalise and/or neglect the determining effects of the relations of production. In particular, we suggest that postmodernism, albeit unwittingly for 'resistance postmodernists', serves to disempower the oppressed, by denying the notion of 'emancipation in a general sense'. We argue that recent major processes of restructuring social, welfare and educational provision, along with trade union legislation, are underpinned by market-led strategies, and are in line with the current requirements of capitalist states. This is either denied, ignored or underplayed in the discourse of postmodernism, or else the changes are *designated* as 'postmodern', as reflecting or being part of postmodernity.

We argue that, in rejecting the determining effects of capital, or in neutralising capitalism itself, postmodernism serves to uphold the current capitalist project. Ideologically, this project involves the privileging of individualism, consumerism and greed. Economically, at state levels, it entails a privatisation programme, incorporating the creation of a hierarchy of provision in the 'public' services. Such a hierarchy has been intensified in the education system with respect to England and Wales (Ainley 1993; Gerwitz, Ball and Bowe 1995; Hill 1997; Whitty, Power and Halpin 1998), and in the similar 'marketisation' and hierarchicalisation of schooling in Australia (Blackmore 1995) and New Zealand (Lauder *et al.* 1995).

'Postmodernism of reaction' and 'postmodernism of resistance'

Lather has contrasted what she labels 'postmodernism of reaction' to 'postmodernism of resistance'.[2] The former, which she describes as neo-Nietzschean, is concerned with the collapse of meaning, with nihilism, and with cynicism. The conception of the individual is of a fractured schizoid consumer, existing in what Lather describes as 'a cultural whirlpool of Baudrillardian simulcra' (1991 p. 160-161). This vortex is captured perfectly by Jean Baudrillard, himself.

> [Postmodernism] is a game with the vestiges of what has been destroyed ... [W]e must move in it, as though it were a kind of circular gravity ... I have the impression with postmodernism that there is an attempt to rediscover a certain pleasure in the irony of things, in the game of things. Right now one can tumble into total hopelessness— all the definitions, everything, it's all been done. What can one do? What can one become? And postmodernity is the attempt—perhaps it's desperate, I don't know—to reach a point where one can live with what is left. It is more a survival among the remnants than anything else. (Laughter). (Baudrillard 1984 in Gane 1993 p. 95)

Lather (1991) defines 'postmodernism of resistance', on the other hand, as participatory and dialogic and as encompassing pluralistic structures of authority. It is non-dualistic and anti-hierarchical and celebrates multiple sites from which the word is spoken (1991 p. 160) More recently, Lather has taken multivocality to its logical conclusion. In adopting Derrida's (1994) concept of 'ordeal of the undecidable', where 'one cannot define, finish or close', she advocates 'a praxis of not being so sure' (Lather 1998 p. 488).

For 'postmodernists of resistance', the subject is 'in-process' and capable of agency. Unlike the 'postmodernists of reaction', who stress increased normalisation and regulation, 'postmodernists of resistance', Lather claims, see difference without opposition, personal autonomy and social relatedness. Whereas the former accept the inevitability of multinational hyperspace, the latter are into ecopolitics (Lather 1991 pp. 160-161). Postmodern feminism, is somewhat immodestly described by Lather, following Kroker and Cook (1986), as 'the quantum physics of postmodernism' (ibid:160).

We would like to evaluate Lather's three claims about a separate 'postmodernism of resistance', one by one. First, she states that it is 'participatory and dialogic', encompasses 'pluralistic structures of authority', is 'anti-hierarchical' and 'celebrates multiple sites from which the word is spoken'. Our comment would be that, while the celebration of multiple voices (ibid p. 112), as a methodology, has its strengths, it also has its weaknesses, and that there is nothing inherently 'resistant' or progressive about it. We will develop this argument in the section on 'Methodology'.

Second, it is 'non-dualistic' and sees 'difference without opposition, personal autonomy and social relatedness'. It is indicative of the contradictory nature of postmodernism that Lather includes 'personal autonomy' here, since this is a concept clearly associated with the Enlightenment, an enterprise considered, by the postmodernists, to have been superceded by postmodernism (see below). As far as 'non-dualism' and 'difference without opposition' and 'social relatedness' are concerned, these are, of course, general features of postmodernism and represent, as we will argue, some of its major problems. Postmodernism is unable and unwilling to recognise a major duality in capitalist societies, that of social class (see Sanders, Hill and Hankin, and McLaren and Farahmandpur in this volume). This has, we believe, profoundly reactionary implications.

Third, the subject is 'in process' and 'capable of agency'. While 'agency' has progressive implications, the fact that the agency advocated by the 'postmodernists of resistance' relates to localised action only (e.g. Flax 1987; Yeatman 1990; Hird 1998) renders it, over all, reactionary. This argument is developed below.

We take issue with Lather's argument that postmodernism can be so neatly divide into two. We concur that the well-intentioned project of some (feminist and other) 'postmodernists of resistance' stands in stark contrast to the nihilistic and lighthearted desperation of the Baudrillardian gameplayers. However, we would argue that ultimately, the two postmodernisms lie, in fact, on one continuum. This is not to say that there are not differences in both analysis and approach. In our critique of postmodernism as a whole, we will highlight any differences as they occur. Overall, however, we believe that postmodernism does not deserve the duality afforded to it by these writers.

In the period, before his rediscovery of Marxism, when he identified with 'resistance postmodernism', Peter McLaren suggested that "resistance postmodernism' and 'critical postmodernism' ... are not alternatives to ludic postmodernism but appropriations and extensions of [the postmodern] critique [of modernity]' (1994 p. 199). Our response would be that, while recognizing the implication that McLaren accepts the notion of a continuum, we take issue with his then assertion that so-called 'postmodernists of resistance' have 'appropriated' postmodernism for an 'emancipatory project'. Indeed, in our view, McLaren's then notion of such a project may in some respects be liberating for individuals and certain selected small groups *at the local level*, but it fails to set out any visible mass strategy or programme for an emancipated future. This is in contrast to socialism, as McLaren has subsequently acknowledged (e.g. McLaren, 1998a). As Rikowski has put it, using the term 'left postmodernism' rather than 'resistance postmodernism',

> the insertion of postmodernism within educational discourses lets in some of the most unwelcome of guests—nihilism, relativism, educational marketisation, to name but a few—which makes thinking about human emancipation futile. Left postmodernism, in denying the possibility of human emancipation, merely succeeds in providing complacent cocktail-bar academic gloss ... for marketising education and deepening the rule of capital within the realm of education and training. (Rikowski 1996 p. 442)

The trouble with postmodernism

> The mass is dumb like beasts, and its silence is equal to the silence of beasts ... it says neither whether the truth is to the left or to the right, nor whether it prefers revolution or repression. It is without truth and without reason. It has been attributed with every arbitrary remark. It is without conscience and without unconscious. (Baudrillard 1983 p. 28-9)

We have dealt at length elsewhere with what we perceive to be the central problems with postmodernism (Cole and Hill 1995, 1996). Briefly, we take issue with its anti-foundationalism, its rejection of the meta-narrative, its denial of any 'totalising' system of thought like Marxism, liberalism or feminism. In short, we challenge its self-proclaimed inability to make general statements about society. This point has been made, *inter alia*, by a number of writers (c.f. Callinicos 1989; Crook 1990; Ainley 1993; Hewitt 1993; Maynard 1993; McLaren 1998a, b; in their pre-postmodern phase, Aronowitz and Giroux 1986, and Jarvis 1998). Contrary to Lyotard and Foucault, we suggest that the motor of the class struggle is still determinant and that the Enlightenment meta-narratives of Marxism and neo-Marxism, and their analysis of capital and power, best explain current and ongoing economic, political, social, educational, cultural and labour market developments, both in Britain and world-wide.

    In addition, we are in agreement with the arguments of Jurgen Habermas, with respect to the neo-Conservative implications of postmodernist 'theory'

(Habermas 1981, 1983, 1987). Postmodernism, we believe, albeit unintentionally for many postmodernists, serves the interests of capital's current hegemonic project, particularly with respect to its interrelated attempts to discredit mass ideologies, such as socialism, to disempower mass groups who are structurally oppressed, and to privilege consumption and greed over production and solidarity. An acceptance of postmodernist ideas, then, should be a cause for celebration for capital. If there are no other ways of living, and no alternative to unbridled market-led economic strategies, (give or take some minor neo-Keynesian interventions by 'Third Way' governments such as that of Tony Blair), if no alternative *fundamental* structural changes in society are possible, then the Left has indeed become an anachronism.

The 'postmodernists of resistance' would, of course, reject the implication that they are playing into the hands of capital. Butler (1998), in her justification of identitarian politics attacks the 'renewed sexual and social conservatism on the Left' which 'fault(s) new social movements for their vitality 'and whose attempts to impose unity from the outside will be rejected as a form of vanguardism' (1998 p. 38). Lather asserts that 'there is nothing in postmodernism that makes it intrinsically reactionary' (1991 p. 49). However, in its 'anti-dualism', in its rejection of the possibility of the meta-narrative, in its localism (see below) reactionary reverberations are inevitable.

There is another factor, which makes postmodernism inherently reactionary. Given postmodernists' insistence on anti-representationalism (the rejection of the view that reality is directly given, without mediation, to subjects), and their consequent reliance on 'textualism' (seeing the text as the only source of meaning), it would seem that the possibility of structural analysis and structural change is further removed from the agenda.[3]

For those at the reactionary end of the continuum, the future seems to consist of some kind of extension, albeit perhaps accelerated, of 'the present', a present, in which we are resigned to survive among the remnants. In *The Illusion of the End* Baudrillard (1994) argues that the 'present' will be continually recycled, and that the future is merely the effects of this recycling process. This, of course, implies the *eternalisation of capitalism*—with its attendant horrors, inequalities and class-based conflicts.

At the 'postmodernism of resistance' end of the continuum, the future is either an open book or a rhetorical 'future' of 'social justice', of 'emancipation' (local only) and, that catchword which is all things to all people, 'democracy'. On the first page of the Preface of *Getting Smart*, Lather declares her 'longtime interest in how to turn critical thought into emancipatory action' (1991:xv). However, after over two hundred pages of text, in which indications are made of the need for emancipatory research and praxis, in which proclamations are made of how the goals of research should be to understand the maldistribution of power and resources in society with a view to societal change, we are left wondering how all this is to come about. As other critics have pointed out (c.f. Beyer and Liston 1992; Maynard 1993), the precise nature of this maldistribution and its implications are never made clear. 'How', ask the former, 'does one identify, locate, and explain structures of oppression, much less structural contradictions' (Beyer and Liston 1992 p. 385). 'How', wonders the latter, can 'inequalities ... be ... made known through a research process which encourages us to see the social world as a text' (Maynard 1993 p. 330).

Just how close 'postmodernism of reaction' (despair and despondency) is to 'postmodernism of resistance' (rhetorics of resistance) is most clearly demonstrated in Lather's latest offering. Although she adopts Derrida's 'ordeal of the undecidable' with its obligations to openness, passage and non-mastery (1998, p. 488), she nevertheless claims to be interested in 'deconstructing the position of intellectuals in struggles for social justice towards *something more than academic heroics*' (ibid p. 490) (emphasis added). She then tells us that she is in favour of a 'post-dialectical praxis' which is about 'ontological stammering, concepts with a lower ontological weight, a praxis without guaranteed subjects or objects, oriented towards the as-yet-incompletely thinkable conditions and potentials of given arrangements' (ibid p. 495). She concludes that 'we move toward an experience of the promise that is unforeseeable from the perspective of our present conceptual frameworks' (ibid p. 497). Her academic efforts are informed by Alison Jones, who concludes 'with a call for a 'politics of disappointment', a practice of 'failure, loss, confusion, unease, limitation for dominant ethnic groups'' (ibid p. 496). Lather is claiming to be anti-colonialist in supporting Maori students in their wish to break up into 'discussion groups based on ethnic sameness' (ibid p. 496). However, since she believes that 'all oppositional knowledge is drawn into the order against which it intends to rebel' (ibid p. 493), it is difficult to see what possible progressive potential her overall project has. Just *how* is her aim of deconstructing Marxist intellectuals (ibid p. 490) in any way progressive?

Any supporter of the capitalist order who had any belief in the efficacy of academic writing would surely be delighted to hear that Patti Lather who, like so many of her postmodern contemporaries, was arguing in the 1980s that 'feminism and Marxism need each other' (Lather 1984 p. 49) and that 'the revolution is within each and every one of us and it will come about' (ibid p. 58), is now so confused that she thinks the future is an open book, with some progressive potential and in which all opposition is drawn into the dominant order! This is essentially pro-capitalist confusion. It is one of the ways that postmodernism acts as an ideological support for national and global capital. In similar vein, Myra Hird's *Theorising Student Identity as Fragmented: some implications for feminist critical pedagogy* argues that,

> Political struggle based on the universalisation of any particular difference (be that gender, social class, age and so on) will always be tenuous as (1) it relies on the effective silencing of inner diversity. (2) While this may signal the end of striving for a fixed notion of liberation, (3) it opens up a wider range of possibilities for coalition around short-term goals (Flax,1987; Yeatman, 1990). (4) Such a reformulation of social struggle offers a tangible praxis through which critical pedagogy might operate (1998 p. 526). *(The numbers 1,2,3,4 are not in the original.)*

With respect to point (1), we would suggest that women can struggle as women in localised and general struggle, workers as workers, youth as youth, without silencing other identities or other aspects of their own identity. With respect to point (2), we fail to see how a recognition of multifaceted subjectivity or of the multifaceted nature of capitalist oppression and exploitation should necessarily imply the end of striving for a generalised struggle against capitalism (see, for example, Kelly, this volume; Sanders, Hill and Hankin, this volume, Kelly, Cole and Hill, in press). With respect to (3), as stated elsewhere, we recognise (and indeed have long been active in theoretical terms and in street activism/protest) the importance of coalitional struggles around short-term goals, but would make the same point as in relation to point (2). And in connection with point (4), we have to ask why coalitional struggle around short-term goals is more tangible than generalised and long-term struggle. We would presume that critical pedagogy would need to link the short-term and the long-term, the local and the general, micro-analysis with macro-analysis, small scale action with national and global action. With respect to racism, for example, Governments do not quake and amend laws and reconsider policy in the face of localised outrage—at the police execution of black immigrants in New York, at Aboriginal deaths in custody in Australia, or at police inaction over the racist slaying of Stephen Lawrence in south-east London in 1993. But they do when the little movements join into a big/mass movement on the streets, and when the little particularistic picture is seen as part of the big picture—of racism and of societal and institutional oppression of the black working classes and of the working classes in general (see Bourne, this volume). Again, we argue that this (Hird's position) is essentially anti-solidaristic, pro-capitalist confusion. Again, we argue that it is one of the ways that postmodernism acts as an ideological support for national and global capital.

Callinicos has described postmodernism as 'the product of a socially mobile intelligentsia in a climate dominated by the retreat of the Western labour movement and the 'overconsumptionist' dynamic of capitalism in the Reagan-Thatcher era' (1989 p. 115) (see also Green, 1994 p. 74; Skeggs, 1991). Dowling (cited in Lather, 1991 p. 37) views postmodernism as 'the opiate of the intelligentsia'. 'From this perspective', Callinicos concludes, 'the term 'postmodern' has sought to articulate its political disillusionment and its aspiration to a consumption orientated lifestyle' (1989 p. 115).[4]

Current changes in education (marketisation, differentiation, pseudo consumer-choice, so-called quality control data, performance and test results, a proliferation of new routes into teaching and of new types of school) might well appear to postmodernists to be a vindication and indeed manifestation of postmodern fragmentation, consumerisation and heterogeneity, of the end of mass production, mass control and uniformity in education.

But such developments are not free-floating. Current 'reforms' in these areas can be seen as part of the ideological and repressive juridico-legal apparatuses of the state and are rigidly bounded by strengthened central control (Althusser, 1974; Hill, 1990; Hartley, 1993; Whitty, 1993; Apple, 1994; Hargreaves, 1994; Cole and Hill, 1995; Hill and Cole, 1995; Hill, 1999). Arguing in a similar vein, and addressing the issue of whether we live in post-capitalist societies, Geoff Whitty suggests that to read the espousal of heterogeneity, pluralism and local narratives as the basis of a new social order mistakes phenomenal forms for structural relations (1991 pp. 8-9). David Harvey (1989) suggests it may be more appropriate to see postmodernist cultural forms and more flexible modes of capital accumulation 'more as shifts in surface appearance rather than as signs of the emergence of some entirely new post-capitalist or even post-industrial society' (cited in Whitty 1991 pp. 8-9).[5]

It is important to recognise that (i) some post-Fordist developments in the organisation of production and consumption have taken and are taking place; (ii) the changes, while developmental, are geographically and sectorally limited and specific; (iii) such changes are not fundamentally altering workers' relations to the means of production; (iv) post-Fordist developments, where they exist, should be conflated neither with post-capitalism nor postmodernism; (v) postmodernist analysis can be seen to be an ideological and theoretical product of those restricted economic change sectors; (vi) postmodernist analysis, with its stress on segmentation, differentiation, collective disempowerment and its *telos* of individuated desire, serves well the purpose of justifying and adumbrating marketised projects of capital.

To reject the 'New Times' analysis and to deny that we live in a post-capitalist society is not of course to refute that capitalism is a dynamic and constantly adapting mode of production. Indeed, Marx, and particularly Gramsci, were acutely aware of this fact. The 'corporatist' and 'market' strategies that were vying for position between the mid 1970s and the 1980s as alternatives to traditional Social Democratic and Christian Democratic consensual 'one nation' policies both demanded, in varying degrees, that the workers pay for the crisis, as, in the 1990s, does 'the Third Way' of Clinton and Blair. While 'The Third Way' may not be hegemonic, both it, and (currently in 1999) the more neo-Keynesian 'Old Labour'/traditional Social Democratic policies and rhetorics of the majority of the European Union states are still manifestly predicated on the capitalist market imperative.

We (i) recognise contextual, historical, social and economic differences between different capitalist economies (Hill 1990 pp. 1-6), (ii) acknowledge tensions in the wars of position within and between different class fractions and strata (see Ainley 1993 for an analysis of the UK), and (iii) accept 'significant variations', e.g. low skill, low wage, UK, USA strategies and recent West German and Japanese high skill, high wage strategies (Brown and Lauder 1991). We also (iv) recognise recent (late 1990s) historical developments in Western Europe, such as the victories of interventionist traditional social democratic type governments and policies in Germany, France and Sweden. But we do consider that these are different ways out, different strategies of responding to national and international crises of capital accumulation, different ways of niching into world and regional economies, not indicators of 'New Times'. Both 'one nation' and 'two nation' strategies (Jessop 1990) demand that some subaltern groups, especially the working classes, have to be yanked into ideological conformity.[6] They require greater ideological re-structuring, greater vilification and suppression of liberal and socialist opposition, and greater state control over civil society. The major break of Thatcherism and Reaganism with the formerly hegemonic 'one nation' project, the major break with the post-war social democratic consensus continues, to a considerable extent under Blair and Clinton. On the one hand, 'New Labour's employment, economic and social policies in Britain, for example, continue to exacerbate the growth of social class inequalities, while at the same time the government's major social policy is dedicated to combating social exclusion, through the well funded and multi-agency Social Exclusion Unit. We do see this twin-pronged policy, however, as a 'carrot and stick' twin policy, accompanied, as it is, by the 'New Deal' (see Sanders, Hill and Hankin, this volume).

Clearly there are rhetorical, presentational and representational differences between Blair/Clinton and their predecessors. The stark differences between the brightly multi-coloured, multi-gendered and of different sexualities Democrat 'Congressmen' *(sic)* as compared to the besuited, squeaky clean, whey faced, white, male appearance of their Republican opponents has important symbolic political effects. This symbolic and representational difference is mirrored, to an extent, in the differences between the Labour and Conservative MPs in the House of Commons elected in May 1997. Clearly, too, there are some policy differences between the parties. In some aspects of policy, such as labour law and expenditure on some social and educational services the ratchet has been turned one notch back from unmitigated neo-liberalism. Yet this is a tepid response to the neo-liberal tightening of the ratchet by several notches over the previous twenty years which exalts consumption, denigrates social expenditure and conditions of work, and eschews solidarity. We see the promotion of individualism, consumerism and marketised 'choice' as an ideological mask for a crisis in capitalism. This mask can be implicit (c.f. Whitty, 1991) or it can be explicit, but we refute any notion that it is all part of 'the postmodern condition'. Indeed, it is one of our main contentions that postmodernism acts as an academic support system for these material and ideological developments.

The politics of postmodernism

As far as the possibilities for political action are concerned, for the 'postmodernists of reaction', there is, as we have seen, little more to do than 'survive among the remnants' (Baudrillard, 1984 in Gane, 1993 p. 95). In contrast, for the 'postmodernists of resistance', as we have also seen, despite the contradictions and the confusion, the subject is claimed to be capable of agency (Lather, 1991 p. 160; see also Aronowitz and Giroux, 1991; Giroux, 1992; McLaren, 1994). The contentious issue, however, resides in just what the project of that agency consists. For postmodern feminists, for example, what should be the task of politics? Consistent with the premises of postmodern 'theory', Judith Butler has stressed the need for an 'antifoundationalist approach to coalitional politics' which assumes neither that 'identity' is a premise nor that the shape or meaning of a coalitional assemblage can be known prior to its achievement' (1990 p. 15). See also Butler 1998). '[W]hat political possibilities', Butler asks:

> are the consequences of a radical critique of the categories of identity? What new shape of politics emerges when identity as a common ground no longer constrains the discourse on feminist politics?

And to what extent does the effort to locate a common identity as the foundation [sic] for a feminist politics preclude a radical inquiry into the political construction and regulation of identity itself? (1990 p. xi)

In order to 'denaturalize gender as such' (1990 p. 149), Butler proposes 'a strategy to denaturalize and resignify bodily categories', which she describes as 'a set of parodic practices based in a performative theory of gender acts that disrupt the categories of the body, sex, gender, and sexuality and occasion their subversive resignification and proliferation beyond the binary frame' (1990 p. xii). Her primary political aim, resulting from her (unexceptional) suggestion that 'multiple identifications can constitute a non-hierarchical configuration of shifting and overlapping identifications that call into question the primacy of any univocal gender attribution' (ibid p. 66) is 'to make gender trouble' (ibid p. 34). In more detail, her text is:

> an effort to think through the possibility of subverting and displacing those naturalized and reified notions of gender that support masculine hegemony and heterosexist power, to make gender trouble, not through strategies that figure a utopian beyond, but through the mobilisation, subversive confusion, and proliferation of precisely those constitutive categories that seek to keep gender in its place by posturing as the foundational illusions of identity. (Butler, 1990 p. 34)

However much fun this might be, we have to ask just how much difference it would make to class nature of economic and political power relationships if the 'gender parody', drag acts and widespread denaturalization of sex and gender became anti-heterosexistly coherent (Butler, 1990 p. 138).

To extend the parodic acivity to social class behaviour, we would also have to question the extent to which workers and the ruling class mimicking each other would shake the foundations of capitalism and inequality. Satirists can mock, can work with counter-hegemonic forces to destabilise. But satire does not organize. Nor does ultra-relativism, where 'anything goes'. In such a scheme of things, 'anything' can be oppressive as well as progressive.

Butler herself notes that 'parody by itself is not subversive' and suggests that there must be a way to understand what makes certain kinds of parodic repetitions effectively disruptive, truly troubling (ibid., p. 139). Again, we have to ask, how far does it get us in developing and involving large numbers of individuals in a political project to understand that '[g]ender is an identity tenuously constituted in time, instituted in an exterior space through a stylised repetition of acts' or that it is 'a constructed identity, a performative accomplishment' (ibid pp. 140-141)? In fact, transgression of (traditional) gender roles and identities is happening contemporaneously in the material realities of the labour market as more and more women return to work and 'male' work is feminised (c.f. Ainley, 1993). It is also happening contemporaneously, to a certain degree, in fashion, clothing, and sexual practice. It is not clear that the more widespread existence of transvestism, transexualism and sado-masochistic fetishism in clothing, clubbing and erotica is rocking the capitalist class at all. 'Fetishism as personal practice does not bring with it change or revolution' (Gamman and Makinen, 1994 p. 221). Nor does it as group practice protest, such as the Spanner protest (for the decriminalisation of consenting 'hard' S&M practice) and S&M Pride, or Gay Pride, mass marches and festivals. In its dominant neo-liberal form, even if less so in its neo-conservative form, capitalism can cope with, and profit from, sex drugs and rock-'n'-roll by commodifying them. The 'pink pound' and the fetish consumer market, for example, are grist to the mill of late capitalism. What it usually finds harder to deal with is solidaristic class opposition such as in industrial action (though capitalism does, at times, use industrial action for its own ends), and coalitional politics with a class perspective, as in the (successful) Anti-Poll Tax movement in the late 1980s and early 1990s in Britain.

Marxism, unlike postmodernism, addresses the issue of how the present economic and political system operates. The danger lies in the fact that postmodernism, by definition, lacks the Enlightenment project of 'emancipation in a general sense'. In addition, in its rhetoric of resistance, as opposed to a structural analysis of and prescriptions for social change, it undermines progressive social theory and plays into the hands of anti-socialist and indeed anti-feminist forces (see Kelly, this volume; see also Kelly, 1992, 1999; Kelly, Cole and Hill, in press).

Marxism encourages a future to be envisioned and worked towards. This vision can and has been extended beyond the 'brotherhood of man' concept of early socialists, to include the complex subjectivities of all (subjectivities which the postmodernists are so keen to bring centre stage). Socialism can and should be conceived of as a project where subjective identities, such as gender, 'race', ability, non-exploitative sexual preference and age, are equally valid. For postmodernists, there is only 'emancipation in a particularist sense'. Here emancipation has a 'minimum profile' (Nederveen Pieterse, 1992). This comprises, 'as regards aims, the concern with autonomy, in terms of organisation, a tendency towards network forms, and, in terms of mentality, a tendency towards self-limitation' (ibid.). It provides neither hope for, nor strategies to achieve a different social order and hence it is essentially reactionary.

In the replacement of 'emancipation in a general sense' by 'emancipation in a particularist sense', in advancing *only* localised struggle (no Marxist would ever deny the importance of local, community and workplace as well as national and international struggle—hence the omnipresence of socialists and Marxists on picket lines, protest rallies and meetings on a range of progressive issues), postmodernism ultimately plays into the hands of those whose interests lie in the maintenance of national and global systems of exploitation and oppression. As Beyer and Liston, acknowledging a debt to Svi Shapiro and Jo Anne Pagano, put it with great force and simplicity:

> the postmodern valorization of local and diffused actions, of particular projects, leads to the formation of intellectual enclaves of research and isolated and decontextualised forms of action ... Local efforts frequently require insight attainable only through the examination and critique of non-local sources of exploitation and oppression, and necessitate directions that are ascertainable through cultural and moral visions that may transcend the immediate situation. The problem with postmodernism in this respect is that it draws too sharp a distinction between the local and the more distant, the particular and the general. We would argue, on the contrary, for a more dialectical relationship between these two things: the sense that the local can illuminate the more general, and that the global can heighten our sensitivity to the more particular. (1992 p. 374)

We should point out here that some 'resistance postmodernists' attempt to have it both ways. They criticise 'reactionary' postmodernism, they are scathing of textualism, and assert a belief in a meta-narrative of social justice, with Peter McLaren, in his postmodern pre-Marxist stage, suggesting, for example, 'always totalise' (1994 pp. 206-213). McLaren claimed that he was not 'setting up a Manichean contest between the meta recits of liberation and social justice and the polyvocality and positionality of an anti-foundational approach to difference' (ibid p. 208) and that 'the invitation posed by critical pedagogy is to bend reality to the requirements of a just world, to decenter, deform, disorient, and ultimately transform modes of authority that domesticate the other' (ibid p. 218). However, just as with Butler 1998, there is no political strategy set out. There is a fundamental difference between (the then resistance postmodernist) McLaren's self-description above and our conception of his then theoretical project. To reiterate a point made earlier, whereas McLaren was then suggesting that he was appropriating postmodernism in a radical project, we believe that what he was doing, in effect, was to appropriate and thereby neutralize Marxism for postmodernism.[7]

Marxist striving towards a socialist future means more than the rhetoric of social justice and democracy so prevalent in the work of 'postmodernists of resistance'. It is about nothing less that the recognition of and the quest for a democratic socialist world, accompanied by a viable strategy for achieving that aim. The fact that historically, 'socialism' has less purchase in north America than Europe is, we consider, a reason for its North American advocates to accentuate and develop the concept, rather than to ditch it.[8] The internally incoherent attempt to link Marxism and postmodernism (e.g. Burbach *et al,* 1997) represents another indication of the contradictions within the latter.[9]

The methodology of postmodernism

We referred earlier to the postmodernist notion of anti-representationalism and the consequent reliance on 'textualism'. Textualism, as used here, derives from the work of Jacques Derrida, who once wrote, 'there is no outside text' (Spivak, 1976 p. 158). Whereas modernists assumed a tight and identifiable relationship between what was being said ('the signified') and how it was being said ('the signifier'), poststructuralism sees these as 'continually breaking apart and re-attaching in new combinations' (Harvey, 1989 p. 49). The task, therefore, is to 'deconstruct the text'. Since 'there is no outside text', cultural life is viewed as a series of texts intersecting with other texts, producing yet more texts (ibid.). The cultural producer merely creates raw materials, which can be recombined by consumers in any way they wish. The effect is to break (deconstruct) the power of the author to impose meanings or to offer a continuous narrative and to call into question all fixed systems of representation (ibid p. 51).

While there is nothing new in this (it was done by modernist authors like James Joyce and by the surrealists), there are apparent progressive implications here, in calling into question apparently fixed and definitive texts. Moreover, as Ollman (1971) observes, Marx himself deployed his concepts relationally, so that concepts like, value', 'labour' and 'capital' are 'continually breaking apart and reattaching in new combinations' in an open-ended struggle to come to terms with the totalising processes of capitalism (cited in Harvey, 1989 p. 51). However, perceiving no reality beyond the text is essentially reactionary. This is perhaps best illustrated by a story about Derrida, analysed by Callinicos. Derrida once contributed a piece to a catalogue of an exhibition of anti-apartheid art, which was, in turn, criticized by two American literary theorists for its lack of historical specificity (it was, according to Callinicos, full of banalities, like '[h]asn't apartheid always been the archival record of the unnameable' (Callinicos, 1989 p. 78). This 'silence' was justified by Derrida on the grounds that a 'discourse would compel us to reckon with the present state of force and law. It would draw up contracts, dialecticize itself, let itself be reappropriated' (cited in Callinicos, ibid.). According to this view, resistance to apartheid must remain inarticulate, must not seek the formulation of a political programme and strategy, since any such attempt would simply involve reincorporation into 'the present state of force and law' (Callinicos, 1989 p. 78). As Callinicos concludes, Derrida is unable to rationally ground any political commitments, 'because he denies himself the means either to analyse those existing social arrangements which he rejects or to justify this rejection by outlining some more desirable state of affairs' (ibid p. 79). The reactionary implications of such a position are, once again, obvious.

Many postmodern feminists, while largely reliant on discourse/textual analysis, do not resort to this Derridean 'negative ontology' (Ferry and Renaut, cited in Callinicos, 1989 p. 78). One worthy, though not new, feature of poststructuralist feminist analysis is the shift away from the disadvantage focus. As Alison Jones explains, in the context of educational analysis, '[a]n interest in the unevenness of power means that, while in the past feminist analyses of classrooms have tended uniformly to position girls as having oppressive and negative classroom experience, studies might focus on the ways in which the girls are variously positioned in the classroom' (1993 pp. 160-1) (see also Walkerdine, 1990). While such an approach is to be welcomed, it is reminiscent of the approach taken by the Marxist feminist AnnMarie Wolpe (c.f. Wolpe, 1988).[10] In the final chapter of her book, *Getting Smart*, Lather attempts to demonstrate the praxis which she describes as being 'at the heart of 'getting smart' (1991 p. 11). It involves a project on 'Student Resistance to Liberatory Curriculum'. Lather asks a series of important questions, not just for feminists but for all engaged in research.

These have been neatly summed up by Mary Maynard and include: 1. whether it is possible to develop research techniques which do not involve the researcher in control and surveillance; 2. what does it mean to do empirical research in an unjust world?; 3. how do we explain the lives of others without violating their reality?; 4. how can it be made possible for the people for whom theory is supposed to be emancipatory to take part in its construction and validation?; 5. can this be done without violating the happiness of those, who, retrospectively, might have preferred to remain ignorant and unfree'? (Maynard, 1993 p. 329). However, as Maynard points out, not only are these questions, in the main, already part of existing feminist work but the result of Lather's endeavours tells us little about student resistance or pedagogy). For our part, while recognising the importance and validity of the five questions, we fail to see what is pre-eminently 'postmodern' about them. Maynard is critical of Lather's heralding of a new postpositivist era in social research, partly because

Lather gives the impression that postmodernism is the only voice to be heard which is critical of positivism (Maynard, 1993 p. 329). More importantly, she is critical because, as many feminists are beginning to realise, quantitative research does have an important role to play (ibid p. 330).

Finally given Lather's postmodernist preference for 'multi-voiced, multi-centred discourse' (1991 p. 112), and her adoption of Derrida's 'ordeal of the undecidable', (Lather, 1998 p. 488), a valid question that must be asked is, 'assuming that these voices will at least sometimes conflict ... [must we] confront the status and validity of these multiple views—or simply assume they are all equally true (or false), equally revealing (or opaque)' (Beyer and Liston, 1992 p. 385). Beyer and Liston's conclusion is that postmodern theory, at least of this type, does not provide an answer (ibid.). In addition, an emphasis on making sure that the voices of 'the other' become heard has made some postmodernists even suspicious of or hostile to 'community', which is seen as 'necessarily oppressive, patriarchal and limiting' (ibid p. 380). Writers such as Elizabeth Ellsworth have expressed the fear that 'multiple voices' will be lost or silenced in communities and have therefore suggested that the most that might be hoped for is a gathering of voices within increasingly small and homogenous groups (cited in ibid.). Arguing against this position, Beyer and Liston suggest, with considerable efficacy and clarity (although, to the oppressions of patriarchy, racism and social class, we would add sexuality and disability):

> [W]e agree that personal and social conditions need to be continually created, recreated, and reinforced that will encourage, respect, and value expressions of difference. Yet if the valorization of otherness precludes the search for some common good that can engender solidarity even while it recognizes and respects that difference, we will be left with a cacophony of voices that disallow political and social action that is morally compelling. If a concern for otherness precludes community in any form, how can political action be undertaken, aimed at establishing a common good that disarms patriarchy, racism and social class oppression? What difference can difference then make in the public space? (1992 pp. 380-1)

We reject the arguments of those academics who have espoused postmodernism as a new emancipatory politics. Contrary to the claims and hopes of its advocates, we believe that 'resistance postmodernism' is essentially flawed. While we fully support and encourage the need to organize around and struggle for various equalities, we believe that there is a common enemy and that ultimately there is a need to contest, *in a united way,* the horrors of global capitalism. Postmodernism negates or deflects that ultimate struggle.

Notes

1. This chapter is a development of some of the arguments set out in Cole and Hill, 1996. For a further development, relating to the 1998 debate in *Education Theory*, see Kelly, Cole and Hill, forthcoming. See note 18, Chapter 6 for a more succinct exposition and Cole and Hill 1999.

2. Others have used different formulations. For an analysis, see Jarvis, 1998. He cites, inter alia, Rosenau's categorisation of 'affirmative' and 'skeptical' postmodernism (1992); Rorty's 'deconstructionist' and 'bourgeois' postmodernism (1980); Foster's 'neo-conservative' and 'poststructuralist' varieties Foster (ed.), 1985).

    Jarvis identifies 'three broad, and by no means inclusive, categories of postmodern theory' (1998 p. 108). These are 'technological or productionist', 'reflecting the themes of techno-scientific change and their reflexive social, political and economic effects'; 'critical', 'reflecting the growth of new theoretical mediums and new ways of doing theory, particularly those concerned with assessing critically foundational propositions and foundational knowledge', and 'subversive-deconstructive', 'reflecting the themes of negation and resistance' (idem).

3. See, for example, Sarup (1983 pp. 101-102, 153, 157-159) and Jessop (1990 pp. 288-301) for a critique of the textualism of Laclau and Mouffe. Jarvis 1998 is concise on this, as is McLaren's critique of 'ludic postmodernism' (1994). See also Hatcher and Troyna (1994) and Evans and Penney (1994) for a critique of Foucauldian and Derridean aspects within Ball (1994) and within Bowe, Ball with Gold (1992). We criticise recent work by Stephen Ball, for example Ball (1990, 1994) together with Bowe and Ball with Gold (1992, 1996). It underestimates the role and power of the state, and overestimates Foucauldian notions of the dispersion of power, in particular, the power of Radical Right discourse, and for overestimating the relative autonomy of (education) state apparatuses. Such work, in its over-concentration on text and discourse, and on the local and contingent, renders the state too 'invisible' and power too 'dispersed', thereby failing to acknowledge sufficiently the material power of the ruling coalition of capital. This work we have identified as 'quasi-postmodernist' (Hill and Cole 1995 p. 221). Capitalism *is* everywhere hence capital as social force and power is dispersed. This gives a material basis for Foucauldian and postmodernist positions on power. However, capital is also concentrated—especially in its money form—in the hands of the capitalist class. Concentration of industrial capital (mergers, take-overs, quasi-monopolies etc.) is accompanied by concentration of personal wealth and income. It is this concentration of power and of capital that postmodernists refuse to acknowledge adequately, indeed, frequently petulantly reject.

4. Seldom, we would suggest, has this coagulation been more redolently expressed than in the discourse of 'New Times' (Hall and Jacques, 1989). Leading 'New

Times' theorists Stuart Hall and Martin Jacques claim that New Times is neither a new orthodoxy nor a finished piece of work. Instead, they define it as 'work in progress' (1989 p. 13). The project began with a seminar in May 1988, organised by the journal, *Marxism Today*'s editorial board. Throughout the early 1990s, *Marxism Today* was a leading intellectual force in Britain in the 'New Times' movement. It ceased publication at approximately the same time as the Communist Party of Great Britain dissolved itself into the pressure group *Democratic Left*. This followed the dissolution of the Soviet Union, and was paralleled by the dissolution of many formerly Eurocommunist 'New Times' type Communist Parties throughout the world, though not of Trotskyite, Leninist, Marxist-Leninist parties and sects.

The New Times argument is that the world has changed, both quantitatively and qualitatively, and that the advanced capitalist countries are 'increasingly characterised by diversity, differentiation and fragmentation' (Hall and Jacques 1989:11). 'New Times' has a number of recurring themes: the decline of mass production and of the traditional industrial, the rise of myriad political and social struggles and individualism, style and consumption. This postmodern prioritisation of market/consumption/lifestyle over production is derived from Max Weber and is commonplace analysis in many sociological accounts of social class. Arguing against too much stress on consumption, Michael Rustin has suggested, correctly in our view, that the Marxist tradition has been right all along in its emphasis on creative work (paid or unpaid) as the central form of human fulfilment and on the importance of the work group, neither of which can be replaced by consumption (1989 p. 314). This is certainly true in our own experience, and we expect also true in the experiences of the 'New Times' writers, who, we suspect derived much satisfaction from their creative endeavours. We have dealt at length elsewhere with our own critique of New Times (Cole and Hill, 1995; see also Cole, 1992). We would accept wholeheartedly the position of A. Sivanandan who has summed up cryptically what New Times means for him:

a shift in focus from economic determinism, from changing the world to changing the word, from class in and for itself to the individual in and for himself or herself. Use value has ceded to exchange value, need to choice, community to identity, anti-imperialism to international humanism. And the self that new timers make so much play about [has] become a small, selfish inward-looking self that finds pride in life-style, exuberance in consumption and commitment in pleasure—and then elevates them all into a politics of this and that, positioning itself this way and that way (with every position a politics and every politics a position) into a 'miscellany of movements and organisations' stretching from hobbies and pleasure to services (1990 p. 23).

Our argument, resisting 'New Times' and following Marx, is that capitalism can only be adequately theorised if 'the economic' and social class are centrally placed. The 'work in progress' continued through the early 1990s. In 1992, Hall posed the question of whether we are entering a 'new constellation of political, economic, social and cultural life' and the 'New Times' that we confront (Hall,

Held and McLennan 1992 p. 4). Andy Green has suggested that the fact that postmodernism serves as the structuring paradigm of several readers for the Open University course *Understanding Modern Societies* indicates how central it has become to theoretical debates in the U.K (Green, 1994 p. 3). It is hugely ironic that in a 1998 one-off issue of *Marxism Today* Hall, one of the major midwives of 'New Times', and of 'New Labour' as a Party fit to represent and lead us on the journey into the 'New Times' of postmodernity, is now returning to a more class-based analysis redolent of his early work such as *Policing the Crisis* (1978). Here, the teacher is lamenting how well his nostrums and prescriptions and lessons were learned.

5.   Harvey, however, is somewhat inconsistent; his endorsement of the transition to post-Fordist capitalism (1989, pp. 121-197) indicates more than a mere 'surface change'.

6.   The move away from the rhetoric that we are all part of 'one nation', to a rhetoric which accepts a notion of an undeserving malignant and anti-social 'underclass' which threatens the 'rest of us' (the 'two nation' project) is functional to the economic interests of the ruling class at this particular crisis in capital accumulation, since it justifies the replacement of universal benefits with targeted benefits and further justifies a reduction or withdrawal of these benefits from 'the undeserving'. This project entails the scapegoating and vilification of these 'enemies within', unlike the 'one nation' project, which implies that 'we are all in it together'.

7.   This is recognised by McLaren in a number of subsequent writings (see, for example, his contributions to this volume; see also McLaren 1998a, b).

8.   We would wish to point out that we are restricting our critique to the academic writing, and not the practical activity, of those who describe themselves as 'postmodernists of resistance' (or similar). These are not arguments against the person. We laud the involvement in Radical Left politics, inside and outside the academy. We also realize the importance of localised understandings and struggles. Our point remains, however, that, to be politically valid, an analysis must link 'the small picture' to 'the big picture' of general and generalized analysis and struggles. We maintain that, essentially, postmodernism cannot do this.

9.   For a critique of Burbach *et al.* see Cole (1998, p. 31). For a discussion of different varieties of 'postmodern Marxism', written from a 'postmodern Marxist' perspective, see Burbach (1998).

10.   For recent analyses of gender and education, informed by Marxism, see for example Martin (1999) and Hirom *et al.* (1999).

CHAPTER 4

Education, Capital and the Transhuman
Glenn Rikowski

There is ... no need to search for alien intelligent life since it is
already deep within us. (Keith Ansell-Pearson, *Viroid Life: On
Machines, Technics and Evolution*, 1997b, p. 182)

Capital is presented as if it were an extra-human thing and labour a
human thing, rather than labour as an extra-human thing and capital as
what humans are. ... [For] ... In a society dominated by money, *I am
money*. I am an embodied manifestation of money in all its contradictory
manifestations. (Neary & Taylor, *Money and the Human Condition*,
1998, p. 130 and 128, original emphasis)

Prelude

The development of capitalism coincides with the capitalisation of humanity.
Humans increasingly become something Other than human; a new life-form,
a 'new species' (Marx, 1844b). This is because capital is a progressive
movement towards totality, and its development on this basis 'consists precisely
in subordinating all elements of society to itself' for 'this is historically how it
becomes a totality' (Marx, 1858). This includes the 'human'; with the deepening
of capitalist social relations, and hence capital as a social force, we evolve
into a new life-form: human-capital. As capital globalises, integrates and flows
with increasing speeds and strength into its constantly expanding universe,
then what was our 'humanity' becomes increasingly primordial and distant.
There is no 'essence' of the human to 'recover', and 'going back to where we
once belonged' is impossible and unsustainable; our 'needs' have been
redefined and integrated into the expansion of capital throughout the social
universe (Marx, 1858).

As the capitalisation of humanity deepens and strengthens we become a
life-form which increasingly incorporates the *contradictions* of capital. Capital
assumes a number of *forms*—value, money, commodity, state and other forms.
The capitalisation of humanity implies that, as capital, these forms take on
real existence within us and within our everyday lives as human-capital.
Furthermore, as this process gathers pace, there is increasingly no 'individual'
or 'society' duality, no 'outside' or 'inside' and no 'beyond' the realm of capital:
capital progressively and exponentially becomes *all that there is*.

Our form of life changes too. We become a life-form invaded by an 'alien' force which is variegated, riven and contradictory in its motions, effects and outcomes. And our mode of existence is expressed increasingly through capital as a set of *living contradictions*. Our lives—our whole mode of existence— therefore, increasingly spin(s) out of control through successive generations as the force of capital within us gains strength; we progressively come to live, drink, sleep and exist through the contradictions of ourselves as capitalised life-form. In this historical process, capital starts out as the 'horror within', the 'alien force'; but as it gathers hold *it is the human element* that is marginalised. Erasure of the 'human' exists as possibility in this historical development as each new generation is faced with ever stronger processes (expressed in institutional and organisational forms) of capitalisation.

It follows then, that with the development of capital towards totality, the *becoming* of capital (Marx, 1858, p. 729), human-capital comes to take on an increasingly *real existence* as new life-form. Thus, as we increasingly become less 'human' and take on the existence of capital, then we are also increasingly subjected to the *contradictions* of capital, living our lives through it as a series of contradictions. Our lives really do have less *coherence*, less 'meaning', as we are torn between competing drives and subject to conflicting forces—within and beyond our reconfigured personhoods—on a progressive scale. In this way, however, capital *uncovers* and *reveals* itself as social force within our lives. The stronger capital becomes within us, and as capitalist social relations (and capital as social force flowing through these relations) expand towards totality—then the *speed of life* (Luke, 1998) increases. In the process, our lives become more fractured, battered and pressurised, even though the productive forces are ever more capable of wealth production.

The range of contradictions within human-capital as life-form, expressed through and manifested within 'everyday life', are further compounded and extended upon the basis of *labour against capital* (Neary, 1997). As labourers (potential, actual, future) we are forced, by our relation to capital, to become antagonistic towards it and its personal representatives (capitalists and functionaries of capital). Our needs derived from labour are oppositional to our constitution as capital. We labour against capital (as well as within it), and are consequently divided *within* ourselves and between ourselves, on this basis. Furthermore, our needs, desires and aspirations *as labour* continually clash with the drives of capital as social force, even though these are *constituted* by the capital relation. Hence, as labour, we are divided *within* and against ourselves as *capital* (Holloway, 1995; Neary, 1997). The class struggle, therefore, is not just 'out there'—on picket lines, demonstrations and other forms of confrontation—but is everywhere, including *within* human-capital as life-form constituted *by* capital.

Main street postmodernists have grasped all this, though they play out this drama at the level of 'discourse', language and the indeterminacy of 'meaning'. The 'de-centred self' of postmodernist folklore mirrors our lives and personhoods fractured by capital, whilst we are simultaneously subject to, and *centred by*, capital. The key point, however, is that the increasing and deepening colonisation of the 'human' by capital is becoming more susceptible to analysis as its 'obviousness' is exposed *by its own developing intensity.* Hence, the less 'human' we become, then, paradoxically, the greater is the potential for starting to grasp our real predicament. Our capacity for *awareness* of our situation as capitalised life-form *increases* as our 'humanity' is left behind. The process of capitalisation of humanity includes our 'consciousness' too; our sentient powers of thought, reflection, deliberation and capacity for 'reflexivity' (much beloved by some postmodern and liberal Left thinkers) are also incorporated within capital.

It appears, then, that we 'become the machine' (Neary and Taylor, 1998); we progressively become subordinated by, and incorporated within, capital in *all* respects. It further appears that capital, as developing totality, as enveloping force, constructs the social universe in its own image. And this includes us as *individuals*, as nodes within the totality of social forces and relations. As Marx notes: 'The individual *is the social being*' (1844b, p. 99, original emphasis); there is no 'society' in abstraction from 'individuals'.

However, as a 'new species' our consciousness does indeed become subordinated, *but is always open* and never *entirely determined.* This is because our fragmented existences and contradictory lives force us to think through, to live and to work through, the contradictions, tensions, dilemmas and *conflicts* generated by capital as a conglomeration of contradictory drives and forces. As capitalised life-forms we cannot avoid this: *capital forces us to think and live its contradictions.* When we think these contradictions, as and through ourselves as capital, it is only then that *capital reflects itself as consciousness of itself* in the forms that it has invaded and incorporated the human. It is through this process that capital exposes and uncovers itself within us *as it thinks itself through us.* At this moment, it reveals its weaknesses. Hence, another paradox is that more we think *as capital* the more clearly we can view 'its' (which are simultaneously 'our' own) problems and pathologies, and our capacity to think as capital *increases historically* as we progressively *become capital.* Marx was able to think from the 'standpoint of capital', and to articulate its contradictions and unfolding, only because he *was capital*, capital thinking itself. Today, we can think as capital more easily than Marx could in his day—

as our incorporation and subordination by capital has deepened through its historical development since Marx's death.

As our thought, action and practices are driven on by the need to seek 'solutions' to the lived tensions arising from ourselves as capitalised life-forms, there comes a point, for Marx, when these pressures build up to such an extent, and the effort to think through (non-existent) solutions becomes so great that the *dissolution* of these tensions and contradictions asserts itself as the only real solution. For Marx, possibilities for this response to lives lived increasingly through and as capital expand with the historical development of capitalism. The historical drive towards communist thought, practice, organisation and *praxis* is *immanent* within the unfolding of capital itself, and takes on increasing significance as human possession by capital deepens. The becoming of capital opens up possibilities for us to *think communism* and to put communist thought into action. Communism is grounded historically in 'its thinking consciousness, the *comprehended* and *known* process of its *becoming*' (Marx, *Economic and Philosophical Manuscripts*, 1844b, p. 97—original emphases). The greatest paradox perhaps, is that: to the extent that we *are* capital, we are capable of *thinking* communism—and dissolving capital through *praxis* and thence to give ourselves—as post-human, and *post-capitalist* life-forms—an alternative, and *open*, future.

Introduction

Marx's *Capital* can be viewed as an articulation of the *horror* of capital, as social life made horrific by capital. We labour for, we exist as, and we *are*—capital (Neary and Taylor, 1998, p. 130). Through our own labour, we create an 'animated monster' (Marx in Callard, 1998, p. 396), a social force which then comes to dominate us (Postone, 1996).

This article aims to expand awareness of our contemporary situation *vis-à-vis* capital through expressing the capitalisation of humanity, ourselves as capital, 'human capital' as the flip-side of labour-power. Secondly, it shows where education and training—through the social production of labour-power—enter into processes of the capitalisation of humanity. Thirdly, the article shows how theories of the post/trans-human typically become encumbered with some old problems—such as technological determinism, teleology and romanticism—in the absence of any explanatory and dynamic framework, which the article will start to develop.

The key difference between the analysis presented here and postmodern post/trans-human positions is that the former argues that the 'transhuman' is an effect of the development of capital (not something which has only just arrived, or will arrive in the future). The latter tend to take technology (forcibly abstracted from social relations) as the germ of the transhuman.

Beginning with the third aim, the first section provides a brief outline of some of the problems associated with postmodernised versions of contemporary and futurised human-technology relations. The following five sections make the difficult arguments involved in exploring and explaining how we become, and in what sense, we *are* capital. These arguments rest upon an examination of labour-power: that abominable commodity on which the whole capitalist system rests. Elsewhere I have indicated the importance of labour-power as the starting point for rebuilding and re-energising Marxist educational theory (Rikowski, 1995, 1996, 1997). These sections of the article can be viewed as some opening shots in the *repositioning* of Marxist educational theory onto the ground of a labour-power theory which articulates the social production of labour-power in capitalism. The Conclusion pulls the various strands of the article together and points towards the significance of critical pedagogy as one of prerequisites for emancipation from the social domination of capital.

The post/trans-human

Postmodernism is an excessive intellectual phenomenon. As Cole, Hill and Rikowski (1997) illustrate, in its de(con)structive frenzy—with the brakes off—postmodern theory runs into one or more of the dead-ends of relativism, nihilism, solipsism and despair. It then occasionally splatters out into false hopes, nostalgia, Romanticism or (typically vague) visions of 'new politics' (as in Blake, 1996). Pointing all this out (as in Cole, Hill and Rikowski, 1997) yields predictable indignation (as in Blake, 1997). Postmodern excess leads to de-centred selves, shattered meta-narratives and the capacity for judgement frozen (through trepidation brought on by the abnegation of 'truth' and 'knowledge' engendered by a corrosive scepticism)—with terrible consequences for stirring up any worthwhile 'politics'. One way of attempting to 'justify' this excess is by arguing that it is a symptom of repression (Ormer, Miller and Ellsworth, 1996); excessiveness—in social and educational theory, or any other sphere of social life—is that 'which exceeds the *norms* proposed as *proper* and *natural* by those with social control' (ibid.). Hence, 'excessiveness' is:

> ... meaning out of control, meaning that exceeds the norms of ideological control or the requirements of any specific text. Excess is overflowing semiosis, the excessive sign performs the work of the dominant ideology, but then exceeds and overspills it, leaving excess meaning that escapes ideological control and is free to be used to resist

or evade it ... Norms that are exceeded lose their invisibility, lose their status as natural common sense and are brought out into the open. (Fiske, 1991, p. 114—in Ormer, Miller and Ellsworth, 1996, p. 72)

But when meaning is really 'out of control' the spinners of 'discourse' seek to detach it from specific aspects of social reality which are never lost absolutely; meaning appears to 'escape', but rather enters a trajectory on which it *never escapes beyond* (the universe of capital) and morphs into idealist form.[1]

David Harvey (1998) has recently pinpointed an effect of postmodernist excess which is the opposite to that charted by Ormer, Miller and Ellsworth. He argues that the loss of confidence in 'previously established categories' (p. 401) brought about by postmodernist and poststructuralist theory has resulted in the re-location of theory onto the terrain of the body. With all referents 'destabilized':

> ... there still remains one referent apart from all the other destabilized referents, whose presence cannot be denied, and that is the body referent, our very own lived body. (Lowe, 1995, in Harvey, 1998, p. 401)

The problem with this, argues Harvey, is that the body—'as the measure of all things'—has also been destabilise through the writings of the post-human theorists. Theorists such as Pepperell and Max More argue that post-human persons of the future will '... overcome the biological, neurological, and psychological constraints evolved into humans' (More in Pepperell, 1997, p. 175). Post-humans are posited as beings of 'unprecedented physical, intellectual, and psychological ability, self-programming and self-defining, potentially immortal, unlimited individuals' (ibid.). Thus, not only is 'the body' in question but the 'human' is too. The development of post-human life forms can be viewed as the *practical deconstruction* of the 'human' body, which parallels the text-mediated deconstruction of postmodern theory. In the post-human future, the cyborg (fused and hybrid human-machine entity) stalks planet Earth. The 'transhuman' is active engagement with such a future, for:

> We are transhuman to the extent that we *seek* to become post-human and take action to prepare for a posthuman future. This involves learning about and making use of new technologies that can increase our capacities and life expectancy, questioning common assumptions, and transforming ourselves ready for the future ...' (More in Pepperell, 1997, pp. 174-175, my emphasis)

The 'transhuman', for More, then, is a 'politics of the post-human'; humans actively striving to *become* post-humans. It is a politics of 'rising above outmoded human beliefs and behaviours' (More in Pepperell, 1997, p. 175).

In his *Viroid Life*, however, Keith Ansell-Pearson (1997a) attempts to establish the 'transhuman condition' as supercession of the 'human'. Here, the 'transhuman' is viewed similarly to Max More's post-human condition; as a result, as constituting an entity (situated within a techno-social habitat) which is decidedly beyond the 'human'. For Ansell-Pearson, the 'transhuman condition' can be understood as the 'human as a site of contamination by alien forces' (1997a, p. 1). Virtual reality machines, genetic and biochemical engineering, performance-enhancing drugs and advanced human-computer/ machine interaction and symbiosis constitute the collective 'alien within', for Ansell-Pearson. He dramatises his prognosis for a transhuman future by talking in terms of 'alien abduction' by the collective powers of the techno-biochemical invasive forces. Whilst signalling that he does not wish to reduce the 'transhuman' to crass empirical developments which herald a 'biological' or 'technological' condition for humanity (1997a, pp. 1-2), he also makes the point that the 'transhuman' should not be conceived as a 'paranoid and phobic anthropocentrism that is bent on imperialistically and entropically colonizing the entire known and unknown universe, for the sake of immortal life' (1997a, p. 2). Yet in stating that *Viroid Life* is about the 'future of the human' and that he wishes to avoid writing teleologically regarding human development, Ansell-Pearson sets himself a tall order. In the event, he tends to lapse into teleology and forms of technological determinism and these criticisms of his heroic efforts to *say* something about the 'future of the human' are expounded elsewhere.[2] Ansell-Pearson (1997a, b) locates some of the dangers and pitfalls lurking within post/trans-human discourses, and it is to these we now turn.

There are a number of weaknesses, critical aporias and manic vistas embedded within post/trans-human discourses. First, the concept of '*post-human*' appears to be premised upon some naturalistic conception of the 'human' which implies an unwarranted essentialism. Of course, different conceptions of the 'human subject' have been proposed down the centuries (as charted by Morris, 1991) and ideas of human nature have changed substantially throughout history, from Plato to Wittgenstein and beyond (Trigg, 1988), but the post-human points towards a fundamental surpassing of the 'human'. As 'humans' are technologised, invaded, taken over, shaped and moulded by biochemical manipulation, computer-tech implants and human-computer interaction then they *become something else*—post-human. However, unless the 'human' has been fixed beforehand—perhaps resting on some biological or genetic bottom-line—then the post-human theorists are never

ever in a position to say whether the *post*—has really arrived, that the 'human' is history. Hence, an assessment of the actuality of surpassing logically rests upon essentialising the 'human'.

A second danger within some discourses on the post/trans-human notes Ansell-Pearson (1997a), is that they can induce a kind of Romanticism; revulsion in the face of our Fate as cyborgs, 'humans without organs' or some sci-fi fusion of brain, flesh and hyper-technology can engender a yearning to 'reclaim our humanity' and our mastery over all the new technologies *as humans*. The problem here, argues Ansell-Pearson, is that as 'the human' evolves through technologisation of persons then we increasingly lose our capacity to realise the myth of a Golden Age of Humanity. Backward-looking authoritarian political structures could be organised in order to spawn a phase of state—and extra-state global Luddism. But this involves putting a limit to what we can become, as well as calling forth repression on a monumental scale and sowing seeds that may evolve into a Fascism fired by an attempt to freeze history (Ansell-Pearson, 1997a). The major weakness of the Romantic position is that, as the concept of 'the human' is so contested and open (as, argues Ansell-Pearson, is the future of the human), then there can be no sure resting place for the species.

The third problem results from attempting to solve the previous two. Say, as in *The Lost World* (Crichton, 1995) (sequel to *Jurassic Park*, Crichton, 1991), that *something survives* in the evolution of the 'human'; that 'the human' is literally the chain of development from *Homo sapiens* to what it eventually becomes, and onwards. The 'human' as an eternalised form of transhumanity, in whatever form the future 'humans'—as represented by this evolutionary chain—survive. On this basis, though, we are amoebae (as amoebae became human), or even the primordial slime from whence they emerged (Ansell-Pearson, 1997a, b). Worse, this perspective enlists an anthropomorphism where human-species immortality is guaranteed at the cost of sacrificing the universe to this development. This only makes sense, argues Ansell-Pearson (1997a), if 'the human' is placed at the centre of the universe (one more time) by fiat, whereas 'it is necessary to free the logic of life from anthropocentric naivety and blindness' (ibid., p. 115).

Fourthly, and finally, many of the cyber-eulogies to human-machine fusion rest on technological determinist foundations. Paul Virilio (1995), for example, views the 'transhuman' as a form of post-Darwinism. In an age, and for a future, of human-machine integration, symbiosis and fusion it is artificial (not natural) selection that will determine survival of types. Although there is some latitude for shaping a future based on this starting point, nevertheless, this perspective rests upon a technological determinism allied to an eternalisation of the rule of capital (Ansell-Pearson, 1997a). Technology and bio-chemical inventions, innovations and products invade human bodies for consumption (or consumption aids), or for enhancing the productivity of labour. These technological developments, abstracted from capitalist social relations and the structuring elements of capitalist society (value, commodity, labour-power, abstract labour, capital: Postone, 1996), form the backdrop to the most horrific of vistas and science fiction nightmares. The machine preys upon humanity, which heralds the end of (human) history, accompanied by new Luddite calls to 'control the machine'. Post/trans-human theorists who terrorise today's humanity with prognoses of genetically designed bodies, microchips in the brain and the rest typically lack an explanatory dynamic which underpins such developments and projections. If free-floating technology was a reality, if it really had a 'life of it own', then it would not be the powerful enemy it appears for those fearful of the future for 'the human'. Its externality to humans heralds our ability to halt its entry into our bodies, which at least opens up the possibilities for terminating its menace. But technology is an expression of capitalist social relations, and these cannot just be sent to the breaker's yard; they require fundamental forms of social destruction.

Following from the previous point, the real challenge is not to pinpoint weaknesses within post/trans-human positions, but to show how it is *capital* that is the 'alien within'. We are extra-human as we are capital (Neary and Taylor, 1998). This is the deep possession (with no outward signs) which is our reality. In starting to express this reality, the argument turns towards that most abominable of commodities: labour-power.

Labour-power: fuel for the 'living fire'

> Labour is the living, form-giving fire; it is the transitoriness of things, their temporality, as their formation by living time. (Marx, *Grundrisse*, 1858, p. 361)

It well known that Marx begins his analysis of capital and critique of political economy by considering the commodity. Capitalist wealth 'presents itself as an immense accumulation of commodities' which *in toto* comprise a single commodity (Marx, 1859, p. 27; Marx, 1867a, p. 43). For Marx, the commodity was the 'economic cell-form' (Marx, 1867b, p. 19) of capitalist society. It incorporated the basic structuring elements of this social formation: value, use-value and exchange-value posited on the basis of abstract labour as measured by labour time (Postone, 1996, pp. 127-128). The commodity was a perfect starting point for analysis as it was the condensed 'general form of the product' in capitalist society (ibid., p. 148), the 'most elementary form of bourgeois wealth' (Marx, 1863, p. 173) and hence the 'formation and premiss of capitalist production' (Marx, 1866, p. 1004). Commodities were also 'the *first result* of the immediate process of capitalist production, its product' (Marx, 1866, p. 974—my emphasis).

What is less well known is that Marx held that there were 'two great classes' of commodities: labour-power and 'commodities as distinct from labour-power itself' (Marx, 1863, p. 167) or 'commodities themselves' (ibid., p. 171). Whilst the 'two great classes' of commodities had certain similarities they also differed in two key respects.

First, the similarities. For Marx, in relation to 'commodities themselves' (i.e. excluding labour-power) productive labour is labour exchanged against capital, labour which 'produces commodities, material products, whose production has cost a definite quantity of labour or labour-time' (Marx, 1863, p. 172). Two points are required for understanding here, notes Marx. The first is that it is not the case that these commodities had to be literally 'material' products, such as bricks or sugar. For:

> When we speak of the commodity as a materialisation of labour— in the sense of its exchange-value—this is only an imaginary, that is to say, a purely *social mode* of existence of the commodity *which has nothing to do with its corporeal reality*; it is conceived as a definite quantity of social labour or of money. (Marx, 1863, p. 171—my emphases)

Marx chides Adam Smith for holding that productive labour only referred to 'hard' products; those products occupying physical space for a duration and detectable by the senses (ibid. p. 172). Yet, argued Marx, the production of value (and surplus-value) did not depend on this base empiricism, and, in turn, whether the labour engaged was un/productive. What was important was that unpaid labour time resulted in (and took the form of) surplus-value, and this could include examples where the product was synonymous with the labour performed (as in the case of drama performances) or in those cases where there were no physical changes in the product themselves (as in the transportation of products) (ibid., pp. 171-172).

The second point is that having fixed productive labour in terms of the 'general class of commodities' Marx goes on to argue that it also refers to 'such labour as produces commodities or directly produces, trains, develops, maintains or reproduces labour-power itself' (1863, p. 172).[3] The social production of labour-power is also a form of productive labour for Marx.[4] In summary, labour-power is a commodity 'neither more nor less than sugar' (Marx, 1847, p. 152).

Secondly, the differences between 'general commodities' and labour-power. The first difference flows from Marx's definition of 'general commodities':

The commodity is, first of all, an external object, a thing which through its qualities satisfies human needs of whatever kind. (Marx, 1858, p. 125) ... [and] ... A *commodity*—as distinguished from labour-power itself—is a material thing confronting man, a thing of a certain utility, in which a definite quantity of labour is fixed or materialised. (Marx, 1863, p. 164—Marx's emphasis)

Labour-power, however, does 'not exist apart from him [the labourer] at all' (Marx, 1858, p. 267); it is not an *external object* (to the person). This observation inclines Marx to make the distinction between 'general commodities' and labour-power, and he notes the 'uniqueness' of labour-power in this respect (1863, p. 45). The second crucial difference between the class of 'general commodities' and labour-power is that the latter—incorporated within the person of the labourer—is an aspect of a conscious, sentient and living being. Labour-power is incorporated within personhood (unlike commodities such as bricks) and is under the sway of a potentially hostile will internal to itself (unlike sugar). Thus, internality and consciousness differentiate labour-power from 'general commodities'. These two key differences determine the need for a separate, but complementary (i.e. still based on the value-form of labour), analysis of labour-power to go along with Marx's analysis of the 'general commodity' in *Capital*. Marx did not provide such an analysis. Labour-power largely figures in Marx's work when he explores the value of labour-power in relation to the production of value and surplus-value on the ground of 'general commodities'. Indeed, in the second volume of *Capital* Marx explained that in the first two volumes he had assumed that labour-power is 'always on hand' (1878, p. 577). Hence, there was no need to provide an account of how labour-power was socially produced through education and training. This was reasonable since, at the time Marx was writing, what I will later outline as the 'social production of labour-power in capitalism', did not exist in a clear form. The rise of mass state education unfolded this form of production, education as production.[5]

It is important to acknowledge some key features of this weird, living commodity: labour-power. First, to expand upon a point made earlier, the 'basis for the development of capitalist production' is that:

... *labour-power*, as the commodity belonging to the workers, confronts the conditions of labour as commodities maintained in the form of capital and existing independently of the workers. (Marx, 1863, p. 45—original emphases)

Although labour-power is bought (by the capitalist) and sold (by the worker) beyond the process of production 'it yet forms the absolute foundation of capitalist production and it is an integral moment within it.' (Marx, 1866, p. 1005), for 'money cannot become capital [in the exchange movement M-C-M'] unless it is exchanged for labour-power' (ibid., p. 1005-1006). Labour-power is that commodity' 'whose *use-value* possesses the peculiar property of being a *source of value*' (Marx, 1865a, p. 164—original emphases), and being a source of 'more value than it has itself' (ibid., p. 188): surplus-value.

Secondly, although labour-power is a commodity (Marx, 1858, p. 674; 1863, p. 51; 1878, p. 121), it only exists as a commodity within the labour market, or, more accurately, the market in labour-power (McNally, 1993). Both 'general commodities' and labour-power exist as commodities 'only on the market' (Marx, 1858, p. 534). At the level of the market, labour-power exists 'only in potentiality' (Marx, 1858, p. 267), as a 'capacity'—the 'capacity to labour' (Marx, 1858, p. 282;).[6] Marx notes that one of the chief failings of classical political economy was that it confused the sale of labour-power with its purchase and 'absorption in the labour process' (1866, p. 1009). As will become clear, this point is not only crucial for an understanding of labour-power but also for grasping the transformation of labour-power into capital and *vice versa*. In selling herself, the worker sells her abilities and talents (Marx, 1878, p. 285) as the basis of a capacity for value-creation. The use-value entailed in the sale of labour-power 'exists only as an ability, a capacity of his [the worker's] bodily existence' (Marx, 1858, p282) and the worker sells a 'temporary disposition over his labouring capacity" (ibid., p. 293).

Thirdly, just because the labourer sells his labouring capacity as a commodity in exchange for a wage this does not make him a capitalist, argues Marx (1878, p. 121, p. 285 and p. 515). This is the case for a number of reasons. Labour-power 'is a *commodity* in the hands of the workers and *not capital*' (Marx, 1878, pp. 456-457) and only 'becomes capital'—is transformed into, and realised as capital—'when in the hands of the capitalist, to whom it falls its temporary use.' (Marx, 1878, p121). This is because to become capital, labour-power has first to be transformed into labour in the labour process, and the resulting value produced must exceed that as represented in the wage; that is, emerge as surplus-value. Surplus-value is the lifeblood of capital. It is the basis of subsequent production cycles and of profit. These considerations point towards a process of labour-power *becoming* capital, through labour in the labour process resulting in surplus-value. Thus, although labourers sell their labour-powers as commodities there is no guarantee that their labour will result in surplus-value, and hence labour-power is bought by representatives of capital as a *variable* commodity; workers will work more or less hard, effectively or productively. The capitalist does not pay for labour but 'only for labour capacity' (Marx, 1858, p. 593). The basis of capital is that workers are so organised, disciplined, skilled and so on in order to labour sufficiently for capitalists so as to make their labour productive; that is, as labour which produces surplus-value. Hence, when capitalists shell out on labour-power through wages the money represents *variable capital*, so:

> During the labour process, the capitalist has the variable capital in his hands as *self-activating*, value-creating labour-power, but not as value of a given magnitude. (Marx, 1878, p. 523)

And the magnitude of real import is reached when surplus-value arises from the transformation of labour-power into labour and into 'general commodities' which incorporate value and finally surplus-value. At the end of the process surplus-value is appropriated by representatives of capital, and this is another reason why it is erroneous to view workers as capitalists just because they sell labour-power as their commodity. They sell their commodity (labour-power) for wages (which represents the value necessary to maintain and reproduce them as workers), but they *create* capital in the form of surplus-value (in the labour process), value over-and-above that represented in the wage.

Fourthly, once workers sell their labour-powers and enter the capitalist labour process these labour-powers are transformed from commodities with the *potential* for value-creation into a real, active *force*. Labour-power is transformed from a capacity into a force which really 'exists in [the worker's] vitality' (Marx, 1858, p. 323; 1865b, p. 56). Labour-power as 'value-creating force' (ibid., p. 674), and as active 'force-expenditure' (ibid., p. 464) within the labour process, attains social reality and is realised as *social* force; as collectivity of labour-powers integrated through division of labour. Throughout his mature corpus, Marx reiterates that, as social force, labour-power 'exists only as a power' (1863, p. 393) within the labour process. He explains at a number of points that it is crucial to grasp the difference between the sale and purchase of labour-power (as commodity, potentiality and capacity for labour) and its actual consumption within the labour process (as value-creating power, and as social force for value-production).[7] Its consumption (as human energy and force) as use-value for capital within the labour process is simultaneously (through the application of this force, this power, within the immediate process of production) a process of value-creation, flowing into (through surplus-value) the formation of capital. However, what follows from this is that labour-power preserves 'its property of producing value only so long as it is employed and materialised in the labour process' (Marx, 1865a, p. 381). It 'comes alive' as active value-creating force only when consumed by capital in the labour process. This is an aspect of the 'tragedy of labour' in capitalism, as the active and creative powers incorporated as labour-power within sentient human beings are expressed as labour in a form—the value-form—which breathes life into a force which comes to dominate the labourers: capital (Postone, 1996).

The notion of labour-power as social force which exists within individuals as the life-force, or vitality, of individual labourers, underpins Marx's conception of labour-power as:

> ... the aggregate of those mental and physical capabilities existing in a human being, which he exercises whenever he produces a use-value of any description. (1867a, p. 164)

Hence, the life-force of individuals as labour-power is expressed through, and as, those 'mental and physical capabilities' activated by the labourer when producing use-values, which, within the capitalist labour process, is also value. The capitalist labour process is also a valorisation process.

Labour-power, as noted previously, 'becomes a reality only when it has been solicited by capital, is set in motion' (Marx, 1858, p. 267). That is, it exists only through its transformation into labour within the labour process. However, there is also a process of inversion, where capital—as social force created by the transformation of labour-power into value-creating labour—is incorporated within the labourer through labour-power development within the labour-process. Thus, although labour-power is 'fuel for the living fire' (labour), it can also be viewed as a particular *form* of fuel for a historically specific form of labour; the value-form of labour—which, in turn, is grounded upon capital as emergent form and result. Showing this also opens a window on the processes through which we become extra-human, humans capitalised. The next section approaches this result.

Labour-power into labour: transformation, sacrifice and loss

On the perspective of the previous section, labour-power is transformed into labour within the labour process when the labourer enters this domain, this lair of capital. Labour-power is activated by the labourer organising her mental and physical capabilities (by acts of will) into a coherent force which sets her labour in motion, in conjunction with instruments of labour or machines and raw materials (where applicable), to produce commodities which incorporate value and surplus-value. Labour is the 'temporary manifestation' of labour-power (Marx, 1863, p. 171), and can be viewed as the 'activity of labour-power' (Marx, 1866, p. 1016), labour-power expressed 'in action' (ibid., p.

1043). Labour-power flits in and out of existence as it is activated by the will of the labourer within the labour process. It 'becomes a reality only through its exercise' and 'it sets itself in motion only by working.' (Marx, 1867a, p. 188). On the market, it is mere capacity, potential. Value-production rests on the transformation of labour-power into labour, and the capitalist pays for labour-power as owned by the worker when it has 'taken effect .. [and] ... materialised itself in a product' (ibid.). The transformation of labour-power into labour is simultaneously an active process of self-transformation on the part of the worker and an act of production (of commodities which incorporate value). Hence, labour-power:

> ... is *self-activating capacity*, a labour-power *that expresses itself* purposively by converting the means of production into the material objects of its activity, *transforming* them from their original form into a new form of the product. (Marx, 1866, p. 980—original emphases)

The self-activating nature of labour-power indicates that is under the sway of a potentially hostile will within the person of the labourer. This is a huge problem for capital; its existence depends on workers *activating* their labour-powers. The will-determined activity of the labourer expressed as labour-power *'objectifies'* itself in the course of production and so becomes *value'* (Marx, 1866, p. 1016—original emphases), and surplus-value as capital in its emergent form.

Marx views this process as an instance of loss and sacrifice on the part of the labourer. Living labour appears as alien, argues Marx, in relation to labour-power 'whose labour it is, whose own life expression it is', as it has been 'surrendered to capital' (1858, p. 462).[8] In his early work, especially the *Economic and Philosophical Manuscripts* (1844b), Marx indicated that he viewed labour as a 'sacrifice' *pace* Adam Smith and elaborates this view in the *Grundrisse* too (1858, p. 614). In the *Manuscripts*, Marx saw work within capitalism as self-denial, as ruination of mind and body; labour as 'self-sacrifice, as mortification' (1844b, p. 71). On this basis, labour in capitalism is:

> ... activity as suffering, strength as weakness, begetting as emasculating, the worker's own physical and mental energy, his personal life ... as an activity which is turned against him, independent of him and not belonging to him. (Marx, 1844b, p. 71)

In this process, man (not labour-power—as Marx had not divined the significance of this concept at the time of writing the *Manuscripts*) is produced as a commodity, as a dehumanised being (Marx, 1844b, p. 82). Furthermore, the worker's activity is under the sway of *'inhuman* power' (Marx, 1844b, p.

118—original emphasis). In this process of dehumanisation, the worker's life-force, her activity, is not spontaneous; this constitutes 'loss of self' (ibid., p. 71, and 1844a, p. 266). Political economy, noted Marx in the *Manuscripts*, was a 'true moral science' of 'self-renunciation' (1844b, p. 112).

This view of labour as 'loss' and as 'sacrifice' in the *Manuscripts* is developed by Marx in a more sophisticated way, and in relation to labour-power, in the *Grundrisse*. There, Marx views 'all powers of labour' as being 'transposed into powers of capital' (p. 701). Later on (in the *Resultate*), Marx argues that the vampiric capitalist 'devours the labour-power of the worker' or 'appropriates his living being as the life-blood of capitalism.' (1866, p. 1008). The worker 'expends [his abilities], uses them up in the act of production' (Marx, 1857, p. 90).

On the analysis here, labour-power becomes a real active force within the capitalist labour process. It is transformed into labour as its constituent items—mental and physical capabilities—are organised through the will of the labourer. Labour-power as force is transferred into labour and thence into value, surplus-value and capital. This entails a loss of human energy deriving from the utilisation of physical and mental capabilities as labour-power. For Marx, this energy and power is made good through the labourer exchanging the wage for the 'bundle of necessities' (1867a) which are consumed by herself and her family, thus socially reproducing herself as labourer—and hence labour-power—and providing necessities and conditions for labourers of the future through rearing children. Workers are drained during labour in the labour process. Their labour-powers are replenished and re-energised as potential force through consumption.

Finally, there is a theory of dehumanisation at work here—especially in the *Economic and Philosophical Manuscripts*. This emptying-out and loss of self which is occasioned by the alienation of the active powers of workers which confront them as powers of capital, points towards 'the human' free from these social conditions and demonic forces. There is a certain Romanticism or philosophical anthropology which has the 'essential human being' as its basis. Recovery of the 'human essence' resolves itself into the destruction of alienating labour which is underscored by capitalist social relations. Therefore, this entails the annihilation of capitalist social relations, and hence capital. In this view, capital is a relation, and an *externality*. Social relations and external forces can be destroyed without destroying our 'selves'. But if we are capital then the destruction of capital implies terminating the 'monster within', self-destruction and transformation. We must become someone else, destroy our (capitalised) 'selves' as we destroy capital. The working-class, as partially capitalised humanity, must dissolve itself, as well as capital and the social relations (of worker to capitalist) its labour engenders. The argument that follows expands these perspectives.

Capital as social force

The conventional way to view the relationship between capital and labour is either as an externality or as ideological relation. In the latter case, *The German Ideology* (Marx and Engels, 1846) summarises the situation, with its notion of 'the ruling ideas' being the ideas of the ruling class, which come to permeate workers' consciousness' in various ways.[9] Here, we are more concerned with the former perspective as the argument will be that capital is not just a (external) social relation but is also a social force internal to labour as labour-power, yielding an internality (to personhood) of capital as social relation too. Furthermore, the perspective on capital determines the expressed relation between capital and labour. Marx stressed this a number of times in his insistence that capital *is* a social relation, as opposed to commodities as 'things' or means of production (Marx in Postone, 1996, p. 351). Some of these issues can be unravelled through considering aspects of the work of Moishe Postone, in particular his *Time, Labor and Social Domination* (1996).

First, Postone notes that the conventional way of viewing the relationship between capital and labour is to see its as a *class relation*: an antagonistic relation between those who own the means of production (the capitalist class) and those who have no means of production themselves and are therefore forced to sell themselves as labour-power (the working-class). As owners of the means of production the former are driven to maximise surplus-value in the form of profit, whilst working-class interests are served through driving up wages, enhancing working conditions and driving down working hours to gain more 'free' time as leisure. These antipathetic drives form the basis of class conflict. Working-class emancipation, on this view, entails appropriating the means of production from the capitalist class, abolishing private property and establishing a society based on meeting human needs. Postone's *Time, Labor and Social Domination* can be viewed as a running critique of this approach to socialist grand strategy. His key point is that the abolition of the capitalist class does not entail abolition of capital as the value-form of production. He also argues that capital cannot be understood as:

> ... the social relation between the capitalist and working classes, structured by private ownership of the means of production and mediated by the market. (1996, p. 349)

It is not necessary to go into his critique of the class conflict view of the capital-labour relation here.[10] Rather, we now move on to Postone's positive account of capital as a social relation, which is of more use for understanding capital as social force.

Following Marx, Postone emphasises that capital is not a 'thing' (material objects as products) but a social relation,[11] for:

> Capital is not a thing, any more than money is a thing. In capital, as in money, certain specific social relations of production between people appear as relations of things to people, or else certain social relations appear as natural properties of things in society. (Marx, 1866, p. 1005)

To view capital as a 'thing' is the basis of the commodity fetishism explored by Marx in the first volume of *Capital*. For Marx, the result of the process of production is 'above all, the reproduction and new production of the relation of capital and labour, of capitalist and worker' (1858, p. 458), and:

> This social relation, production relation, appears in fact as an even more important result of the process than its material manifestation [products as commodities: GR]. (ibid.)

In this process, individual capitalists are personifications of capital. As personifications of capital the 'relation of every capitalist to his own workers is the relation as such of capital and labour' (Marx, 1858, p. 420).

For Postone too:

> ... the category of capital refers to a peculiar sort of social relation, to a dynamic, totalistic, and contradictory social form that is constituted by labor in its duality as an activity mediating people's relations with each other and with nature. (1996, p. 349)

Marx's *Capital* is an unfolding of capital as a constantly moving entity brought to 'life' through 'socially general powers' (ibid.—which includes science and knowledge, as well as labour), according to Postone. However:

> ... these productive powers serve to reinforce the abstract compulsions exerted on the producers; they heighten the degree of exertion and intensity of exertion required, as well as the fragmentation of labor. (Postone, 1996, p. 350)

Postone notes that capital (like the commodity) has a double nature: an abstract dimension (as self-valorising value, in the movement M-C-M') and a concrete dimension (labour as productive activity). Capital is the 'alienated form' of both these dimensions of social labour in capitalist society, and confronts individuals as 'an alien, totalistic Other' (Postone, 1996, p. 351). In sum: capital can be viewed as 'an alienated structure of labour-mediated relations of production' which 'promotes the development of socially general forces of production while incorporating them as its attributes' (ibid.). For Postone, capital as social relation takes on a real existence as the Subject of history within capitalism; its existence is constituted by labour, and its various metamorphoses and transformations—into the value, money and state forms— are effected and mediated by labour. The 'tragedy of labour' is that this mediation, which produces an 'enormous increase in the productive powers of the use value of labor' (Postone, 1996, p. 350), is the conduit for the establishment of capital as an independent power, as social force and as social relation, which oppresses individuals throughout the social formation (not just within the labour process); all forms of human activity are subordinated to the value-form of social production.

What is interesting about this account is that there seems to be an externality to the relation between capital and labour. Labour *confronts* capital as Other. Capital as social force compels the individuals to labour through its form of mediation, which rests on labour-power having to transform itself into labour in order to reap the wage reward. Of course, powers of the state, law and other institutions (such as schools) also have their effects on forcing labour to assume the value-form of wealth creation, but Postone insists that this harsh compulsion is inscribed within the core elements of capital itself as an unfolding, moving (but ego-less) entity constituted by labour. Aspects of the use-value dimension of labour 'also function structurally to reinforce and reconstitute this framework' for they 'function as attributes of capital' (Postone, 1996, p. 354), a point which will not be pursued here.

In this account, capital—as constituted and mediated by labour—appears as a vast, global oppressive social force which, although *we* bring it to 'life' are nevertheless enthralled by. There is no escape; capital, in its various forms is everywhere, as social force pressing us into the service of its many-faceted forms of 'life' and reincarnations (value, money, commodity, state, law and so on). What is more, it appears to be an *external* social force to individuals in this account, oppressing them from without their personhoods as a *structure* of social relations, with similarities to standard sociological accounts of 'social structures' as limits to human 'agency'. There is something of this in Marx too. On numerous occasions he refers to capital, the 'objective, self-sufficient indifference' (Marx, 1858, p. 452), as constituting the conditions within which workers labour and these conditions confront them as alien property. These conditions take on a 'personality' towards labour (ibid., p. 512), they assume the form of 'objective powers, even of overpowering objects—of things independent of the relations among individuals themselves' (ibid., p. 652). In the *Resultate*, Marx notes that in the capitalist labour process labour is objectified 'in opposition to living labour-power' (1866, p. 1016). The conditions of production, and its results (commodities) seem to be 'endowed with a will and a soul of their own' (ibid. p. 1004).

For both Postone and Marx, on this account, capital is an oppressive Other, independent of labour, a force which dominates labour by pressing it to expend its force or power (labour-power) in the service of its own self-expansion. But the externality involved here, capital as an oppressive social relation 'out there', beyond the personhood of the labourer, is only half the picture. Things are much worse; capital is also within personhood. Hence, capital as social relation is *internal* to personhood, not as a 'thing', but as a social force. This other perspective on capital can be found in Marx (and to some extent in Postone), but the relation is invariably veiled through viewing capital as externality first and foremost.

In *Capital*—or at least the first two volumes—Marx's unfolds capital as a social relation constituted by labour on the basis of *equal exchange*. For Marx, the labourer is not simply tricked in production through attaining a wage below its value; the wage is equal to the value of the labourer's labour-power. However, the argument here is that, within the labour process, there is also an exchange of social *force*. In the previous section, it was argued that labour-power is a social force which is transformed, through self-organising acts of will on the part of labourers, into labour and thence into all the various forms of capital as self-expanding value. In this process of emptying out, loss and sacrifice, there is also a reciprocal process of self-constitution by capital as negative social force. An exchange of social force occurs where the expenditure of labour-power is paralleled by an influx of an 'alien' force which becomes incorporated within individuals: capital as social force, through the social relation of labour to capital. Hence, on this perspective, the social relation of capital to labour is *internal* (as well as external) to labour; capital is an invasive social force as the capital relation is shot through labourers as persons. 'Human capital' is not just a bourgeois abstraction which can be safely ridiculed; it expresses the process of humans being capitalised, the capitalisation of humanity. According to John Holloway (1995), such a position is central to Marxism, for Marxism 'distinguishes itself from other varieties of radical theory' in its claim to 'dissolve all externality' (p. 159). For Holloway, it is precisely because 'capital is *not* external to labour, that we can understand the vulnerability of capitalist domination' and, in turn, grasp the '*fragility* of oppression' (ibid., original emphases). But I would wish to press Holloway's point further, to drive him towards the most radical of conclusions: that capital is also incorporated within *labour-power* too, and as labour-power is 'inseparable from the worker' and exists as the 'bodiliness of the worker', and is an aspect of her 'living vitality' (Marx, 1858), then capital exists as social force within the person.

We can go some way towards providing substance to this claim by reconsidering labour-power. For Marx, although labour-power is a transhistorical concept (Marx, 1844b, 1858) it assumes a specific form in capitalism, and hence becomes *historical*. This is based on the fact that labour is 'free' within capitalism in a double sense: first in terms of the labourer having control over her own body, and hence being free to sell her labour-power on the best possible terms and where the capitalist buys labour-power as commodity for a duration which is established as free exchange between worker and capitalist (labour-power for the wage), so labourers have control over their persons; and, secondly, free in the negative sense of not owning means of production which would allow labourers to reproduce their own labour-powers, and hence having to obtain the means of consumption through commodity exchange (Postone, 1996, p. 270).[12] When the labourer sells her labour-power to the capitalist, as witnessed earlier, within the labour process she is actively engaged in transforming her force, energy, living vitality into labour through self-organising of her skills, knowledges, strength and all the other attributes necessary for effective labour. However, this force expenditure is accompanied by an inflow of capital as social force *into labour-power as it sets itself in motion*.

In the capitalist labour process, labour-power becomes part of capital, it is *capitalised*, becomes human capital. As Marx notes:

> ... the worker functions here as a special natural form of this capital, as distinct from the elements of capital that exist in the natural form of means of production. (1878, pp. 455-456)

Furthermore, labourers *develop themselves* as labour-power within the labour process, but as labour-power of a specific kind: human capital, as the form that labour-power takes in capitalism. Marx notes the twofold process going on when labourers labour within the capitalist labour process:

> ... the individual not only develops his abilities in production but also expends them, uses them up in the act of production. (1857, p. 90)
> ... [And hence] ... Universal prostitution appears as a necessary phase in the development of the social character of personal talents, capacities, abilities, activities ... (1858, p. 163)

There is force-expenditure (of human labour-power), but also development of this labour-power on the basis of capital, labour-power capitalised—and as labour-power is inseparable from the person, then we have *personhood capitalised, humans capitalised, human capital.* Capital becomes a living social force within the human and internal and internalised social relation within individuals—*and this is the basis of the transhuman; it is this which makes us 'extra-human'.* Capital is not just 'out there'; we are it, it is us.

Invasive force: deep possession of labourers by capital

> I'm having the most perfect hallucination;
>
> Green and blue goblins are crawling all over me—
> Like a deck of cards. ...
> ... (...) ... I don't feel I'll ever be the same again.
> Please help me ...
> Please help me ...
>
> (Ash Ra Tempel, 1996)

Capital is a *social force*, as well as a social relation through which it is expressed and manifested *as* social force. Unlike demon possession, as portrayed in *The Exorcist*, there are 'no outward signs'. Or, rather, no such signs that are immediately verificatory. Unlike the levitation, speaking in ancient languages and facial dis/contortions of the demon-possessed victim in *The Exorcist*, there is nothing to immediately witness on the surface.

The natural force which can be viewed an analogous to capital as social force is gravity. Like gravity, it cannot be immediately sensed, but exists with accompanying real effects. The effects of such *deep possession* of humans by capital as social force can be observed—as can the effects of gravity as natural force—but only on *presupposition* of the pertinent force.

Marx hints at several points that we are capital, humanity capitalised, and that this is a form of deep possession of the human by capital as social force. In *The German Ideology*, for example, he and Engels argue that:

> As individuals express their life, so they are. What they are, therefore, coincides with their production, both *what* they produce and *how* they produce. Hence what individuals are depends on the material conditions of their production. (1846, p. 37—original emphases)

And when the material conditions of their production are forms of capital, then it follows those individuals *are capital*; they are socially produced as individuals on the basis of capital. In the immediate process of production 'the worker produces himself as labour capacity' (Marx, 1858, p. 458), and labour-power is incorporated within the person—as noted earlier.

Capital, however, is a *negative* social force. Marx notes that labour-power produces capital as its negation through producing the product as alien (1858,

p. 458), but fails to grasp that—connected to the social production of labour-power—capital also becomes a social force within the human. It is a deep invasive force; humans are deeply possessed by capital as negative force. But why capital is a *negative* social force requires explanation.

The fact that is a *alien* force cannot be the whole answer, though the thought that we are possessed by something Other—as in horror and science fiction films—is not immediately appealing. No, capital's negativity arises from the fact that it is, first of all, a *limiting social force*. It drives us as internal compulsive force, reinforcing itself as external compulsive social relation configured as a set of social structures, to *submit to the value-form of labour*. What is required to explicate this is a *critical psychology of labour in capitalism*, a psychology that is yet to be written, but to which the work of Lucien Seve (1975) gives first expression.[13]

As well as being a limiting social force within the human, capital is also a containing social force. Labour-power is the most explosive commodity within capitalism, not just because the whole capitalist systems rests upon it—as witnessed earlier—but because it has a capacity to *go beyond capital, the latent power to expand its force beyond the control of capital through being utilised in non—and anti-capitalist forms of social production*. Labour-power has the potential to become a social force for the abolition of capitalism through being the power behind (really) post-capitalist productive forms. Hence, capital as force internal to labour-power, and the person, contains and restrains labour-power as creative and dynamic force, whilst limiting its expression as force for value-creation labour. Limiting, constraining-restraining within labour-power, and hence within the vitality and consciousness of the person; in these ways, capital is a *negative* social force.

Marx ascribes to capital the quality of determining 'the specific gravity of every being which is materialised within it' (1857, p. 107). In arguing thus, he views all sentient beings, not just humans, as life-forms constituted by capital; for capital is the 'all-dominating economic power of bourgeois society' (ibid.). However, in the *Manuscripts*, Marx had argued for a different position to that being expressed in this article; he pointed towards estrangement as the 'inaccessible possession' of another, though he acknowledges there that 'everything is itself something different from itself' and that the worker's activity was under the sway of 'inhuman power' (1844b, p. 118). Even in the *Grundrisse*, Marx acknowledges that living labour can penetrate 'dead labour' (means of production) with 'an animating soul', but nevertheless ends up losing 'its own soul to it' (1858, p. 461). There are only hints that capital comes to possess individuals as a negative force, which limits and restrains the human soul in turn.[14] The analysis of this article has taken Marx's fleeting insights on the capitalisation of the human to a deeper and more radical level of analysis.

On the analysis expounded, the transhuman is a specific form of humanity; humanity within capitalism and capital within humanity. The transhuman, on this account, is not something only just beginning or an effect of new technologies and biochemical engineering whose searing development is located in the future. Rather, the transhuman is a relatively old phenomenon, as old as capitalism itself.

The 'logic' of capitalised humanity at work within the labour process

As we are capitalised as humans within the labour process, where an exchange of forces (human labour-power with capital) takes place, then we are also subject to a vicious unfolding of the dynamic of the labour process as partially explicated by Marx in *Capital*. The capitalist labour process is the key social space where the *practical* development of labour-power on the basis of capital takes place. The development of the capitalist labour process can, therefore, also be viewed as a deepening and complexification of the transhuman in the form of human capital. In unfolding the 'logic' of this development we are not 'predicting' the future, but pointing towards what certain elements of the future could become *if* capitalism is not terminated. Explication of this unfolding of the labour process as it relates to labour and labour-power in this section is necessarily fragmentary; it is a first shot, and will be developed in future work. It is based on the fact that Marx did not unfold *all logical possibilities* for surplus-value production within the labour process.

The capitalist labour process is the immediate process of production, the social site where value is first created through labourers transforming their labour-powers into labour which forms commodities incorporating value, thence surplus-value and capital (which then spirals off into its various forms within a huge cycle of reproduction). In *Capital*, Marx outlined two main forms of surplus-value production; absolute and relative. Absolute surplus-value production is where the labourers are made to work longer, through extending the working day. In this (inefficient) way, surplus-value is increased.

With relative surplus-value production, the form 'most adequate' to mature capitalist production (Marx, 1866), and the form which finally fixes capitalist production as the dominant form of production in society, machinery is utilised on an increasing scale. The effect of this is that the labour-time represented by the value of the wage is reduced, leaving an increased proportion of labour-time devoted to surplus-value production.

However, Marx was not fully aware of the different forms of relative surplus-value. First, he was aware of the effect that *work intensity* could have on value production, though in *Capital* he was ambivalent about where this figured in relation to absolute/relative forms. The position here is that work intensity—allied to forms of management control which attained complexity after the rise of 'scientific' management in the early twentieth century—has functioned as a means to raise the productivity of workers through minimising labour-time constituting the wage. Hence, it can be viewed as another form of relative surplus-value production.

A further form of relative surplus-value production is given by the possibility that *labour-power itself* can be worked upon—through education and training. This is the topic of the next section, so only the basic point will be outlined here. This is that, as capital comes to take over the whole of society, then both old institutions are re-cast in its image and new ones established to enhance value-production. Forms of the social production of labour-power have been established in almost all contemporary notions. These social forms are characterised by their relation to the enhancement of the *quality of labour-power* in a number of respects, so that the transformation of labour-power into labour is maximised, and hence relative surplus-value is increased as workers work with greater commitment and effectiveness.

However, there is a fourth form of relative surplus-value production. This involves *fusion* of all the other forms. This could express itself in fusion of humans and machines: the cyborg as labourer. This is no longer science fiction. Brain implants have recently been developed which 'allow a computer to be operated by thought' (*The Guardian*, 1998). It is early days, but this is one of the first signs.

The point of this sketch is that this narrative of the 'logic' of development underpinning the capitalist labour process provides a social dynamic, as opposed to a technological determinism, regarding why we could end up as cyborg workers. It provides an explanation based *on the development of capitalist production*. Of course, capitalist consumption provides a further dynamic for calling forth the human-machine, but this is not dealt with here. The strength of the account is that it enables an explanation of a cyborg future, whilst denying that this is *identical to the transhuman*. On this view, the post/trans-human theorists see only effects, not (pre)conditions. They also have no explanatory framework or dynamic for their prognostications. Let's raise the game once more; at last, in the next section, education and training enter in.

Forcing process: education and the social production of labour-power

The previous section pointed towards how the capitalist labour process encapsulates a 'logic' of development which unfolds the transhuman within, and as, capital. It also indicated that the capitalisation of humanity continues within the sphere of consumption (though the dynamic pushing forward this development of capitalist transhumanity was not addressed). This indicates that there are processes through which we are capitalised *beyond* the labour process. This section focuses on an element within another set of such processes implicated in the capitalisation of humanity, many of which exist beyond the labour process.

In developed capitalism, as noted in the previous section, *labour-power* increasingly comes to be the focus of forms and processes of *social production*, reproduction and maintenance. Labour-power theory can be viewed as the attempt to understand the social dynamics, empirical manifestation and histories of these forms and processes pertaining to labour-power development. A subset of these processes explored in this section is the *social production of labour-power* in capitalism; this is where education and training make their greatest impact in the capitalisation of humans in contemporary society.

As a starting point for approaching an understanding of the nature and significance of the social production of labour-power in capitalism it is necessary to revisit the section on *Labour-power: fuel for the 'living fire'*. There, it was argued that Marx held that 'two great classes of commodities' existed; the 'general class' and labour-power. The latter was a 'unique' commodity in some respects—and this uniqueness was elaborated in the same *'Labour-power'* section. What follows from this is that, although Marx examined the production of the first class of commodities, he did not explore the social production of labour-power in any depth. Lebowitz (1992) makes a similar point. Marx did, however, distinguish these two interrelated forms of social production at a number of key points, though he sometimes confused or conflated them as forms of commodity production that had aspects in common—for, as we saw earlier, 'general commodities' and labour-power had indeed some shared aspects.[15]

The social production of labour-power is the conglomeration of the social processes involved in producing the 'unique' or 'thinking' commodity. Although there are some general and elementary forms of the social production of labour-power,[16] the fragmented forms in which labour-power is socially produced in capitalism, with its institutional splits in contemporary capitalist societies makes for great difficulties—theoretically and in terms of empirical work. Listing institutional forms involved in labour-power production we have: schooling; on/off-the-job training; further and higher education; character and attitude training; the development of abilities in the labour process—as *some* of the elements. Empirical and historical research and analysis is necessary to ascertain the productive forms for particular categories of labour. The last in the list—developing labour-power in production—links up the production of 'general commodities' and labour-power production; at this nodal point, labour-power and 'general commodities' are produced simultaneously through acts of labour in the labour process.

The task here, however, is not to explore the social production of labour-power in any depth, but to explicate its role in the capitalisation of humanity. There are three key points here.

First, to reiterate, labouring in the labour process is an element within the process of socially producing labour-power. The attributes of labour-power (attitudes, skills, knowledges, physical strength and dexterity, apposite personality traits and aspects) are socially produced in different ways and to varying extents, depending upon the type of industry, occupation, level of expression of labour-power, work discipline regimes and so on—*within the labour process*. As argued earlier, the development of labour-power in the labour process—as exchange of social force—simultaneously involves the capitalisation of the human, as labour-power (developed on the basis of capital) becomes *capitalised*.

Secondly, a far stronger claim could be made. This is that we do not just exist as virtual labour-power/capitalised humanity when outside the labour process, but *we are capital wherever we may be*. The processes of consumption (re-energising, re-vitalising and refreshing labour-power), and all the social processes making for the reproduction, social production and maintenance of labour-power *also* constitute labour-power (and hence the person as capital). To show this would require a colossal exploration and vast explication; the hint must be sufficient here. However, an example can be used to illustrate the more general point; the social production of labour-power, and this takes us to the third point.

The social production of labour-power can be viewed as just one set of social processes involved in the *capitalisation of the human beyond the labour process* (though, as witnessed above, part of the process is *internal* to the labour process). Considering education and training—as key elements within most contemporary forms of labour-power production—as implicated in socially producing labour-power, what is going on is that attributes of the person are being developed, enhanced and formed which then figure as labour-power, the life-force which gives 'life' to capital as social force, within the labour process. There are two aspects to this. Firstly, there is the development of labour-power *potential*, the capacity to labour effectively within the labour process. Secondly, there is the development of the willingness of workers to utilise their labouring power, to expend themselves within the labour process as value-creating force. This is manifested in all the studies which pinpoint work attitudes as the most sought after and significant attribute of workers in recruitment studies[17], and the exhortations of employers that schools must produce 'well motivated' young people, with sound attitudes to work and recruits who are 'work-ready' and embody 'employability'—though these points would need to be driven home through focused empirical and historical studies. What all this amounts to is a process of *capitalisation* of youth and adults; of developing persons as labour-power (and hence human capital), *beyond* the labour process.

There is, of course, an issue of *intentionality* here. The social actors (teachers, trainers and so on) might (and fortunately many do) have alternative perspectives, and work from a different basis and outlook. They might not *intentionally* set about producing labour-power, or, if they are aware that this is a practice within which they are implicated then they might try to subvert or ameliorate it. Students themselves might not view 'learning' as capitalist social form, or, when they do, might resist it as such. However, these points miss the mark on two counts.

First, although empirical forms of the social production of labour-power are amorphous and relatively 'weak' in terms of intentionality—they are poorly defined as productive forms—nevertheless, education and policy in the United Kingdom has, since the mid-1970s, set to *harden* the intentionality and enhance the policy framework which develops persons as human capital (labour-power). Education and training policies of the New Labour Government are based as firmly on human capital formation as were the 1979-1997 Conservative administrations (Hatcher, 1998, pp. 486-490). Furthermore, it might be possible to point to a long-term historical trend towards incorporating education and training as forms of labour-power enhancement within an ideology and process of human capital formation as the capitalisation of humanity. Such an outlook builds upon what Marx says in the *Grundrisse*, as, in capitalism:

> development to its totality consists precisely in subordinating all elements of society to itself, or in creating out of it organs which it still lacks. This is historically how it becomes a totality. (Marx, 1858, p. 278)

Marx points towards the tendency of capital to conquer all other modes of production in all respects, and to 'bring them under the rule of capital' (ibid., pp. 729-730). In this process, the law of value and 'its abstract forms of alienated capitalist power: money, the law and the state' are just as important as exploitation of labour in the labour process (Neary, 1997, p. 22). Marx also notes that: 'Competition is the mode generally in which capital secures the victory of its mode of production' (ibid. p. 730), and the increasing competition, fragmentation and marketisation of education (quintessentially, *further* education in the UK) can be viewed as a mode of *subordinating educational and training institutions to the rule of capital through energising them as sites of labour-power enhancement*, through both competitive pressures and encompassing policy constraints (state activity also as a form of capital). Marx notes, caustically, that the 'severe discipline of capital, acting on succeeding generations, has developed general industriousness as the general property of the new species' (1858, p. 325). Hence, in modern industrial conditions, where all significant institutions have morphed into capital, then it can be expected that the social production of labour-power, as a definite organisation of the formation and enhancement of labour-power, becomes *increasingly stronger*. On this 'logic', the state-form of capital comes increasingly to express education and training policy as *labour-power* policy, or human capital policy—which is the same thing. The intentionality of the process is tightened at the level of the capitalist state. Globalisation and competitiveness, as ideologies and real process, strengthen the social *definition* of a process of labour-power production still further. The strengthening of the *social* intentionality requires historical description and analysis, not to be pursued here.

Secondly, a narrow focus on the intentionality of individuals engaged within the social production of labour-power misses the mark in another respect. In the recruitment of labour-power, and within the labour process, representatives of capital are concerned with *using* and utilising labour-power. In terms of the skills, knowledges, attitudes, aspects of personality and the rest which constitute items, or attributes of labour-power (which are reified by employers, and in educational research which takes the constituents of labour-power as 'things'), the question is their utilisation. Thus, it is logically possible—and likely— that teachers and students may develop all kinds of attributes within educational and training institutions on the basis of motivations, goals and visions *irrespective* of the labour-power 'needs' of capital. Yet these can still figure as labour-power attributes.

In the social production of labour-power, we are humanised (civilised) as capital and capitalised as humans. Transhumanisation in its capitalist form 'catches 'em young', from birth, and goes on beyond death (death *made money* through the funeral process, and perhaps survival as virtual humans). In concrete terms, it involves *forcing* self-formation through a specific social form; to *become* for capital (alienation), and to engage in fixing 'being' as capitalised life-form. This invasive process affects all aspects of consciousness and body. It simultaneously shatters and unifies the soul on the basis of a social force which flows into the 'human' through the capital relation.

The effectivity of processes of labour-power production are limited on the basis of a contradiction: that the social production of labour-power in capitalism is premised upon the objectification of subjectivity. Practical attempts to 'fix' labour-power attributes within personhood, which, *in toto*, would constitute the formation of our 'being' as capital, are limited on the following considerations:

- first, the contradictory drives incorporated within ourselves as capital;
- second, the fact that these drives are infinite—there are no limits to them as drives, but their expression is limited by the *clash* of contradictory drives;
- third, the process of labour-power production has no 'logical' end point (unto death), as the *quality* of labour-power can always be enhanced, and it can also deteriorate the further it gets away from practical expression within the labour process (a factor which studies of the unemployed reflect)—and therefore labour-power is never *finally* 'produced'.
- fourth, the contradictions resulting from ourselves, our existence, as *labour against capital* (as opposed to labour *within* and *as* capital);
- fifth, our attempts to 'solve' these contradictions opens possibilities for dissolving them through subversion;
- and finally, our capacity for reflexivity, to attain awareness of the existence and practical application of processes of the production of ourselves as labour-power, raises the issue of a politics of human resistance to these processes.

The social production of labour-power has, up to the present, been a relatively 'weak' form of production (though its 'strength' is growing). Its 'weakness' rests: partly on the contradictory nature of the process; partly on historical liberal Left or religious values within some sections of educational *élites*, states and Governments which have effects for educational policy and organisation running *counter* to viewing education and training as human capital development. Furthermore, the alternative perspectives of teachers and students also have effects. Finally, the compounding of all the factors listed above, their inter-relations and political expressions is also pertinent.

Hence, there are limits to the process of capital invading (abducting) the 'human'. If there were not, humans would be automatons, and the social domination of the whole human and human-related (nature as human resource) universe would dance to the hyper-determination by capital and its forms (money, value and so on) (Rikowski, 1990b). The importance of human consciousness is the potential for awareness of the creeping possession it yields. Our ability to think can unravel the dread.

But this is a problem for capital: education and training have the potential for opening, developing and increasing an *awareness* of ourselves as labour-power, as human-capital, humans *capitalised*. Hence, social control (through National Curricula, 'new managerialism') of the process is crucial. This great educational fear—education as subversion, education as uncovering *what we have become*—is chronic and endemic within the social universe of capital. The second fear relates to the fact that, as competition—which entrenches the rule of capital—flourishes, then *wage* competition increases economic and social inequalities. For these two fears, our booster therapy must be a *critical pedagogy* which makes representatives of capital even more afraid, very afraid, through uncovering their *worst* fear through educational programmes which 'think the—really—unthinkable'. Fortunately, the horror works both ways.

Conclusion: education, capital and the transhuman

In this chapter, the 'transhuman' has been presented as the capitalisation of humanity. Rather than viewing the transhuman in a *transhistorical* manner, or as some just-about-to-be or futurised technologisation of the human (the reign of the cyborg), the argument here is that we are *already* extra-human as *capital*. The 'transhuman' has existed since the rise of capitalism; it is nothing new. The cybernauts have attempted to think a future where the 'machine' dominates the human, but without being able to provide an explanation of this development. In unfolding the 'logic' of the labour process as valorisation process, it is clear that some of the futures suggested by the cybernauts (science-centred post-human theorists) and transhumanists are incorporated within this unfolding. The key to understanding the form of transhumanisation explored (historical, specific to capitalism) here is that labour-power *becomes* capital in the process of its social production, becomes human capital. This is attained through an exchange of social force; labour-power for capital and *vice versa* as each constitutes the other—simultaneously—within the labour process. As labour-power is inseparable from the labourer, it cannot be 'isolated'; as it is a power or force flowing throughout personhood, then, by default, *humans are capitalised too*. We *are* capital. But the capitalisation of the 'human' also exists beyond the labour process. The social production of labour-power is one of the processes involved. As education and training are elements within most forms of the social production of labour-power they are implicated in the process of the transformation of humans into human capital, the capitalisation of the 'human'.

However, processes of the capitalisation of humanity are never complete, as labour-power, although incorporated within personhood, is also under the sway of a potentially hostile (for capital) will. Individual and collective consciousness *exceeds* the processes of capitalisation. Furthermore, through alerting individuals to what they have become, through enhancing *awareness* (Marx, 1858) of their situation as constituted by capital, a double-loop fuelled by anger yields *possibilities* for the formation of collective strategies, modes of subversion and *politics of human resistance* aimed at smashing the social relations through which capital as social force invades the 'human'.

Capitalist education is a contradictory phenomenon. On the one hand it is enmeshed in the capitalisation of 'humans'. On the other hand it can function as a basis for exposure and awareness of this state of being. How this might be done—the actual pedagogics of the thing—are best explained elsewhere. But the importance of a viable *critical pedagogy* which has this exposure of the 'horror' as a pedagogic aim is crucial. As Peter McLaren and Ramin Farahmandpur (1999) have indicated, there is an urgent need to rescue critical pedagogy from a neo-Kantian Left liberalism where it becomes just another classroom technique. Critical pedagogy needs to 'place liberation on the agenda of history again', to make it useful for the task of 'devising a transition beyond capitalism' (ibid.). Through a series of recent publications and conference papers, Peter McLaren has embarked on a process of *reclaiming* critical pedagogy from liberalism for the urgent task of increasing our *awareness* of our social condition (Marx) as a first step towards changing it *vis-à-vis* capital and the social injustices thrown up by its world domination (see especially— McLaren, 1995, 1997, 1998; McLaren *et al*, 1998; McLaren and Faranhmandpur, in this volume.). As McLaren *et al.* (1998) note, awareness or consciousness of our plight is 'not enough to guarantee personal or collective praxis' (p. 36). A commitment to social justice is necessary for providing the spark within individuals and collectivities if awareness is to be transformed into action. We need to educate for this too. I would wish to add that an appreciation of capital as the 'horror within' provides an additional argument for leaving capitalism as a form of social life in the rear-view mirror of history. So, let us scare ourselves: read *Capital*—with no need to wait until capitalism's midnight!

Acknowledgements

Ruth Rikowski read the first draft and made a number of criticisms, which led to some re-thinking and re-writing. Mike Neary's criticisms of the first draft, and our conversations over the last three years, played a significant part in both developing and sharpening up some of the ideas and their expression. Mike's urgings to 'go the extra mile' and develop some of the ideas further than I had originally intended has had significant impact on the form and content of the article. But the responsibility for the final outcome is mine.

Notes

1.   There is no 'escape'; no matter what the velocity, and even given infinite generation and proliferation of meaning, the hottest of hot air can be sucked to ground. Idealism is the attempt to attain the unattainable, to seek to cast adrift from the real universe of capital through ideas as excess meaning, as shown by Marx and Engels early on in *The German Ideology* (1846).

2.   A critique of Ansell-Pearson will emerge in Neary and Rikowski (1999). This paper will also deepen and develop some of the arguments of this article.

3.   This time Marx is a little more charitable to Adam Smith. He noted that although Smith excluded the social production of labour-power through education and training from his category of productive labour 'arbitrarily', he had done this 'with a certain correct instinct' believing that if he included it then it would have opened the 'flood gates for false pretensions to the title of productive labour' (Marx, 1863, p. 172).

4.   Contemporary Marxist theorists have invariably ignored the crucial differences between 'general commodities' and labour-power. Postone (1996) for example, in his reinterpretation of Marx's theory, is typical in ignoring these differences. Lebowitz (1992), on the other hand, noted that Marx's *Capital* was an incomplete enterprise which called for a further analysis of wage-labour—something which Marx saw the need for but did not get round to writing. However, Lebowitz's analysis does not start from the key social form which structures wage-labour, labour-power as commodity, but jumps straight in to an analysis of wage-labour. His analysis starts from too concrete a level. Marx, after all, did not start his analysis in *Capital* with capital, but set out from the commodity. He realised that the value-form of labour grounded the development, or becoming, of capital and this could be best explicated through unfolding the contents of the commodity as the 'economic cell-form' of the whole capitalist system.

5.   Education could most obviously coincide with the general form of productive labour in the case of private schools. Such profit-making schools aim to produce value over-and-above the value as represented in teachers wages, the product being 'educated youth' (Marx, 1863). In this case, there is no difference in the form of productive labour as between 'general commodities' and labour-power, and hence no special and separate analysis of the latter is called for on this basis. Where state education becomes dominant—a situation Marx did not face in the 1850s and 1860s when writing his various drafts of *Capital*—the fact that education

for profit does not pertain alters nothing if the state is taken as a form of capital, the state-form of capital. This point clearly requires expansion, a task be to undertaken elsewhere.

6.   Also Marx: 1858, p. 672; 1865a, p. 167; 1866, p. 1066.

7.   For example, see Marx: 1866, p. 1009 and pp. 1017-1019; 1867a, pp. 164-166. Only on the market is a commodity a commodity (Marx, 1858, p. 534)—and this applies to labour-power too.

8.   See also Marx (1858, p. 462), he notes that 'Labour capacity relates to its labour as to an alien.'

9.   Giving force to such notions as 'false consciousness', the Althusserian stress on ideology and Gramscian hegemony. These 'cultural' Marxist positions at least have the merit of posing 'capital within the human' as a real possibility—though typically at the level of 'ideas', thus melding easily into Left sociological and liberal Left political perspectives; where the task is to unmask the effects of the media, schools and so on, as a step in banishing capitalist hegemony for a re-distributive social justice.

10.   For more on Postone's critique of the conventional view of the social relations of production and his wider critique of 'traditional Marxism' see: *Time, Labor and Social Domination*, chapters 1-2. See also Neary: 'The law of value is undermined by itself, in the very act of production. While it is true that this opposition [within value itself] expresses itself in the form of working class organisation, it is not its organisation that has provided the dynamic for the antagonism in the first place.' (1998b, p. 31). Marx noted that:

> Of course, socialists sometimes say we need capital, but not the capitalist. Then capital appears as a pure thing, not as a relation of production, which, reflected in itself, is precisely the capitalist ... [For] ... capital is indeed separable from an individual capitalist, but not from *the* capitalist, who, as such confronts *the* worker. (1858, p. 303—original emphases)

On Postone's (1996) and Neary's (1998) accounts—following Marx in the *Grundrisse*—the basic antagonism within capitalism is not between capitalist and worker, but is internal to, and immanent within, the unfolding of capital expressed as the value-form of labour, as the 'value-expansion' process (Neary, 1998, p. 31). Class struggle is an effect or result of this basic antagonism.

11.   As Marx noted in *Theories of Surplus Value—2*:

> Instead of *labour*, Ricardo should have discussed labour-*power*. But had he done so, *capital* would also have been revealed as the material conditions of labour, confronting the labourer as power that had acquired an independent existence and capital would at once have been revealed as a *definite social relationship*. (1863, p. 400—original emphases)

He also criticised Adam Smith in the *Grundrisse* for holding the view that capital is objectified labour (1858, pp. 257-258), which also results in it being viewed as a 'thing'.

12.   In *Excerpts from James Mill*, Marx points towards: ... the determination of the labourer by social needs alien to him and which act upon him with compulsive force. He must submit to this force from egoistic need, from necessity ... his actual labours serve only as means to this end. He thus activates his life to acquire the means of *life* (1844a, p. 269—original emphases). The labourer is driven by his separation from the means of production

to undertake labour. Again, the 'compulsive force' driving the labourer seems to be entirely external in nature.

13.   Michael Neary (1997) and Graham Taylor (Neary and Taylor, 1998) have gone furthest along this route, building upon the pioneering work of Seve (1975).

14.   Hints such as: viewing capital as the 'thing' that 'subjectifies itself in the person'— alluding to possession of individuals by capital (1857, p. 89); and where the worker's human qualities 'only exist insofar as they exist for capital *alien* to him' (1844b, p. 5)—but even here the 'alien' appears as purely external; political economy being an expression of an anti-human perspective (1844b, p. 90); and, that the worker is estranged from himself in capitalism (1844b).

15.   Marx most clearly refers to labour-power undergoing a process of social production in the third volume of *Theories of Surplus Value*, when he notes:

> What does the labour required for its [labour-power's] production consist of? Apart from the labour involved in developing a person's labour-power, his *education,* his apprenticeship—and this hardly arises in relation to unskilled labour—its reproduction costs no more labour apart from that involved in the reproduction of the means of subsistence which the labourer consumes. (Marx, 1863, p. 148—original emphasis)

Two points here: First, education—as a key element in the social production of labour-power—is now a multi-billion dollar enterprise in contemporary leading capitalist nations. Thus, it is no longer the case (as it was in Marx's day) that relatively little labour enters into the development of a person's labour-power. Secondly, Marx is here viewing labour-power as a set of 'skills' and knowledge-related attributes. Elsewhere (Rikowski, 1990a) I have argued for a wider conception of labour-power, taking in attitudes, personality traits and all those personal attributes incorporated within labour-power in acts of production. Other instances of Marx referring to the social production of labour-power can be found in: 1847, p. 158; 1858, p. 527, p. 575; 1863, p. 167; 1865a, p. 292; 1865b, p. 56; 1866, p. 1066, p. 1032, p. 1066; 1867a, p. 168. As Marx noted in the first volume of *Theories of Surplus Value*, 'education produces labour-power' (1863, p. 210).

16.   In unpublished work I have explored the 'amoebic', elementary and complex forms of labour-power production as part of a method for understanding and explaining the fragmentary nature of the social production of labour-power, i.e. the myriad of empirical institutional forms and processes involved in this heterogeneous productive form. The relation between the abstract (but nevertheless real) and general forms, and their concrete, empirical manifestations, constitutes the basis of an empirical and historical *research programme*. Given the bias against 'Marxist research' in contemporary research funding priorities, it is doubtful whether such a programme could be undertaken in my lifetime.

17.   Rikowski (1992) summarises these studyies. A recent example of a study which places work attitudes and personality traits making for 'employability' at the top of employers shopping lists of desirable labour-power attributes is Meagher's (1998) work on Tyneside, England.

CHAPTER 5

Youth, Training and the Politics of 'Cool'
Michael Neary

'Culture... is a mere training to act as the machine', Karl Marx and Friedrich Engels, *The Communist Manifesto*, 1848.

In the second half of the twentieth century youth emerged as a distinctive and dramatic form of human sociability. At first reinvented as a precious resource for the reconstructed post-War labour markets youth quickly degenerated into delinquency, an offence against the moral conscience of the modern world and a threat to the social order. The critical reappraisal of social life that youth expressed in this period was reflected in a radical sociology inspired by the subversive ideas that appeared to rescue a discredited orthodox Marxism from its economism and dialectic materialism by extending its critical capacity to include, among other things, race, gender and the powerful discursive practices of continental philosophy[1]. Paramount among these new energies was the recognition of culture as a site for the reappraisal of a radical critique of everyday life.

In Britain this cultural preoccupation within radical sociology was given greater emphasis by the setting up of the Birmingham Centre for Contemporary Cultural Studies (BCCCS), with a clear focus on youth. For these researchers, youth was *the* metaphor for social change (Hall and Jefferson, 1975). This analysis located the resistances of youth in the material experience of working class cultures. Its importance was that it identified these oppositions as symbolic deconstructions of middle class values and norms that made up the dominant ideology. This metaphorical symbolism gave youthful antagonisms a radical edge that had previously been denied in the sociology of youth. Its appeal lay in the fact that it took the explanations for youthful resistances beyond the dysfunctions of a functional society and formulated it in terms of a political threat to a political order—i.e. as part of a political crisis. However, the very success attributed to these sub-cultural strategies—by which young people were able to redefine themselves within, rather than against, massive social upheavals—undermined the radicality that the theory purported to represent. By solving their dilemmas through strategies of sub-cultural resistance, young people were transforming their own condition to exist within the cultural, economic and political logics of capital. Human resistance was reduced to the status of ritual opposition within which any radicality was more imaginary than real.

However, despite this disability, the 1980s spawned a rash of sub-cultural and cultural studies of young people as the political crisis deepened and the 'problem of youth' refused to go away—indeed, intensified after the 1981 urban riots. While the new work was critical of early cultural studies or the theoretical assumptions that underpinned it, the criticism was contained within the framework of a cultural paradigm (Hebdige, 1979, 1988; Cole and Skelton, 1980; Frith, 1983; Cohen, 1997; Finn, 1987; Clarke, 1991; Hollands, 1990; Willis, 1990a,b; McRobbie, 1994). The effect was to consolidate the position of the work as a radical alternative and to ritualise cultural studies rituals as the basis for alternative study and a theory of human resistance.

In recent years the uncritical presuppositions of cultural studies, energised by the work of Baudrillard and Bourdieu, have asserted themselves as the distinctiveness of youth as a radical form of sociability has dissolved.[2] Whatever critical capacity sub-cultural studies claimed to represent has been replaced by work that mirrors the affirmative nature of club, drug and cyber cultures (Willis, 1990a; Redhead, 1993; McRobbie, 1994), presents an uncritical celebration of counter cultures (Gilroy, 1993; McKay, 1996) or frames the youth question as a problem of integrating excluded young people into social democratic models of citizenship (Cohen, 1997; Wyn and While, 1997). The result is that any attempt to suggest a theory of human resistance through a radical sociology of youth has been abandoned.

In what follows I will suggest a theory of human resistance through critical exposition of the concept of youth.[3] I will explain this through a logical and historical account inspired by advances in Marxist science. This approach is derived from the subterranean Marxisms that were re-established in the 1970s through the Conference of Socialist Economists which subjected the closed categories of orthodox and traditional Marxisms to the subversions found within the work of Marx himself. This approach has coalesced around the term 'Open Marxism' (Bonefeld *et al.,* 1992, 1995). Central to this critique is the awareness of the real and actually existing subjectivity of capital; the centrality of human practice: work, in the constitution of the social world and the immanence of the relation between capital and labour within which labour exists as a form of capital, wage-labour, in and against capital.

My intention is not to attempt to go beyond Marx; but, rather, to use Marx's method in hitherto unexplored areas and to drive Marx towards his own radical conclusions (Sohn-Rethel, 1978). By developing areas for critical enquiry outside of the limits of political economy, but based within Marx's theory of the law of value, I hope to open up new areas for critical Marxist research while at the same time undermining the claims of radical sociologists. In doing this I accept, of course, the empirical reality of the new critical categories on which this research agenda for a radical sociology is based, e.g. gender, race, generation and culture; but I want to argue that the critical capacity of these categories is disabled by the unexplained presuppositions on which they are based. By concentrating on the process out of which these categories are derived I hope to resist these presuppositions and provide a real theory of human resistance.

A theory of human resistance

The theoretical significance of Marxism for a study of human resistance is that class struggle is the history of all hitherto existing societies. However, the content of class struggle for Marx is not just the struggle between capitalists and workers; but, rather that class struggle is derived out of the inner contradiction within the capital relation:

> Capitalist society does not just develop through class struggle. Rather class struggle is a constitute moment of the capital relation because of labour within the concept of capital. (Bonefeld, 1995, p. 202)

For Marx:

> The worker is the subjective manifestation of the fact that capital is man completely lost to himself, just as capital is the objective manifestation of the fact that labour is man lost to himself. But the worker has the misfortune to be a living capital, and hence a capital with needs, which forfeits its interest and hence its existence ... The worker produces capital and capital produces him, which means that he produces himself; man as a worker, as a commodity is the product of this entire cycle ... The worker exists as a worker only when he exists for himself as capital, and he exists as capital only when capital exists for him. The existence of capital is his existence, his life, for it determines the content of his life in a manner indifferent to him. (Marx, *Economic and Philosophical Manuscripts of 1844*, in: 'Early Writings', 1992, p. 10—my emphasis added.)

This focus on the derivation of class struggle forces us to consider the abstract condition of human life. This explanation for the existence of human life as abstract labour is not metaphysical, even though it may appear so (Marx, *Capital 1*, p. 163). It is the result of the specific way in which unpaid surplus labour is pumped out of direct producers determining the relationship between capital and labour and labour to itself. An understanding of this process reveals the innermost secret, the basis for the way in which modern human life is constituted (Marx, *Capital 3*, p. 799).

Marx developed the philosophical categories of his earlier work through an explanation of the processes within which human life is constituted. Working directly from the most simple determination in modern society: the commodity form, Marx unpacked the contradictory value relations through which the commodity form was determined, as use-value and exchange-value, to reveal the social form of labour in capitalist society.

Labour takes the form of and is socially realised through the commodity. The commodity is a contradictory social form owing to the way it expresses the contradiction between use value and exchange-value. In this condition concrete (useful) labour is mediated by and becomes socially realised through its opposite: abstract labour. The substance of abstract labour is not labour embodied in the commodity; but, rather, the labour time socially necessary to produce the commodity. Socially necessary labour time is the labour-time required to produce any use value under the conditions of production normal for a given society and with the average degree of skill and intensity of labour prevalent in society. What exclusively determines the magnitude of the value of an article is therefore the amount of labour socially necessary, or the labour-time socially necessary for its production (Marx, *Capital 1*, p. 129). Socially necessary labour-time is not simply a chronological measurement of time but the imposition of a particular form of existence on labour: abstract labour.

Values then are not established by reference to the intrinsic or concrete qualities of the direct producer, but by reference to the total labour expended in the generalised commodity producing system understood as labour in general, or abstract labour. Human labour exists only to the extent that it is recognised as a component part of this homogeneous and global substance. This recognition has nothing to do with the 'corporeal reality' of human labour (Marx, *Theories of Surplus Value (Part 1)*: p. 167), but is a purely social mode of existence. In this mode, each human life exists as a moment of the expanding social universe. A unique configuration of time and space within the process by which time and space are reconstituted. As existence is only possible through the formal recognition of the commodity itself in the process of exchange the commodity comes to dominate the labour that produced it. This attribution of exchange-value takes place without participants being aware of what is actually being recognised (Marx, *Capital 1*, p. 166). It is assumed, because of the way in which revenues are accrued to the owners of particular commodities, that value is an intrinsic quality of the commodity itself, rather than a substance derived from a particular social relation (Clarke, 1991, p. 126). This is the basis of commodity fetishism:

The mysterious character of the commodity-form consists therefore simply in the fact that the commodity reflects the social characteristics of men's own labour as objective characteristics of the products of labour themselves, as the socio-natural properties of these things. Hence it also reflects the social relation of the producers to the sum total of labour as a social relation between objects, a relation which exists apart from and outside the producers. Through this substitution, the products of labour become commodities, sensuous things which are at the same time supra-sensible or social. (Marx, *Capital 1*, pp. 164-165)

The significance of this is that in the moment when abstract labour is materialised, in the recognised form of a commodity, human life is disembodied or dematerialised, and 'All that is solid melts into air...' (Marx and Engels, *The Communist Manifesto*). Its recognition as abstract labour is confirmed by its recognition as a form of value: money in the human form as wage-labour. The content of this arrangement is obscured by the fact that abstract labour, although immaterial, needs to exist in a material form: as a real abstraction. In the same moment that human life is dematerialised, immaterial life is confirmed or commodified as labour and forced to exist in a virtual form:

> ...our use-value may interest men, but it does not belong to us as objects. What does belong to us as objects however is our value. Our own intercourse as commodities proves it. We relate to each other merely as exchange values. (Marx, *Capital 1*, pp. 176-177)

The dramatic conclusion to be drawn from this analysis is that capital is an impersonal form of social domination generated by labour itself which, in the form of abstract labour, mediates its own existence. Abstract labour is not a mental generalisation of various sorts of concrete labour but the real expression of something real (Postone, 1993, p. 146). It becomes the identity of value in motion as it expands through itself. Labour in capital is not mediated by social relations, rather it constitutes the mediation and is a form of the mediation. The domination of labour is self-domination (ibid., pp. 172-173). As a real abstraction humanity exists as forms of self-expanding value. This suggests that the real subject of social life is not labour, but capital:

> Its [value] is constantly changing from one into another without becoming lost in this movement: it thus transforms itself into an automatic subject ...In truth, however, value is here the subject of a process in which, while constantly assuming the form in turn of money and commodities, it changes its own magnitude ... and thus valorises itself ... For the movement in the course of which it adds surplus value

is its own movement, its valorisation is therefore self valorisation ... [Value] suddenly presents itself as a self-moving substance which passes through a process of its own, and for which the commodity and money are both mere forms. (Marx, *Capital 1*, pp. 255-256)

But the subjectivity of capital is peculiar: the subject is an unknowing, unconscious, subject without an ego, historically determinate and blind (Postone, 1993, p. 77); and whose existence demands the denial of its self generating, or self-valorising negative capacity, i.e. *itself*.

From this account capital cannot produce itself. Value is not produced by Capital (Holloway, 1995). Capital is the expanded form of abstract labour. Abstract labour is the presupposition of capital but it is also the immediate result of the capitalist process of production (Marx, *Capital 1*, p. 949). Capital and labour then do not simply oppose each other as discrete factors of production, 'capital exists only in and through labour' (Bonefeld, 1995, p. 189) What this means is that the capital relation contains the substance for a revolutionary critique and the possibility for social transformation.

In the form of abstract labour, human life exists as the constitutive power of social labour in the form of being denied.[4] This is a peculiar and perverse arrangement within which the real process of the social world is inverted forming the basis for:

> ... the unrealism of the real world... Human life as proxy... The autonomous movement of the non-living... The concrete inversion of life... In a world that really is topsy turvy the true is a moment of the false... A negation of life which has become visible'. (Debord, 1977)

This relation is, therefore, deeply and irreconcilably antagonistic. Human life exists in a form that is oppositional not only to the institutions within which, and through which, it is constantly recomposed: money and the state (Clarke, 1988), but in and against *itself*. The consequence of this condition is that there is no aspect of essential human life to which it can rely to rescue itself as an 'alien being' (Bonefeld, 1995, p. 199).

The positive and transforming nature of the relationship is that, as a being that is alien to itself, abstract labour contains the possibility of its own negation, to be not-capital, to dissolve itself and the relation within which it exists and to recompose the relation without negating the constitutive power of labour as the creative force of the social world (Holloway, 1995, p. 172). This formulation does not suggest an essential humanism as an alternative to capital, but provides the basis for an existential reality not yet constituted within which human life is the project rather than a resource (Bonefeld, 1995).

In the next section I will illustrate this theory of human resistance through an historical account of the production of a specific form of human sociability: youth, through a particular form of regulation: training. I will concentrate on an important piece of legislation: the Employment and Training Act 1948, ignored by the sociology of youth, to reveal how the modern category of youth was constructed. According to my account the post war youth phenomena is not the result of changes in patterns of consumption and communication; but, rather, is derived from intensification and restructuring of the processes of production and, within these processes, the recomposition of youth as the imposition of work through the commodity-form: abstract labour.

Youth training

The modern condition of 'youth' was invented in 1948 as a part of Employment and Training Act 1948 (ETA). The Act was intended to support the drive for productivity that formed the basis for British economic recovery and political importance in the reconstructed post-War world.

The class relations of the post-War period were formalised within this productivity drive as capital sought to reconstruct the conditions for sustained accumulation within an efficient and stable national regime (Clarke, 1988, pp. 244-286). Productivity, however, is not simply a technical problem to be overcome based on the mutual recognition of natural advantage between workers and employers, regulated through market rationalities; but is, as Marx showed through his exposition of the law of value, an antagonistic and contradictory process derived from the fact that in modern society social reproduction is subordinate to the production, accumulation and appropriation of surplus value: a process which depends on the co-operation of the producers it subordinates. The social relations of capital are therefore the social relations of struggle between capital and the subordinate class: labour.

The concrete expression of productivity appeared at this time as increasing state intervention at the international level through currency adjustments, GATT, IMF and Marshall Aid; nationally through social insurance and administration, rising wages, credit, full employment and a system of industrial relations model led around new 'Americanised' methods of mass production which developed new models of work intensification and a new form of mass worker (Negri, 1988). In Britain this period marks the culmination of a process within which the working class is finally subsumed within the relations of capitalist production (Kay and Mott, 1982). The place for young people in this new fully integrated form of regulation was prepared by the Employment and Training Act 1948.

The 1948 Act: a revolution in social progress

The Employment and Training Act (ETA) of 1948 lacked the spectacular provisions associated with the socialisation of consumption and the intoxicating wish-fulfilment of the policy of full employment. The ETA 1948 was a significant moment in the history of vocational education and training in the UK, representing the first co-ordinated response by the state to the disequilibrium, as it was portrayed, in the labour market and, as such, it did not lack passionate advocates. Lord Hewerson, the First Lord of the Admiralty, was in no doubt about the importance of the Act: 'From the days of Kier Hardie', he said, 'men of vision have had this ideal before them [forming part of] a revolution in social progress' (Notes from a speech in Ministry of Labour papers at the National Record Office (NRO), *Employment and Training Bill*, 8/1507, June 1948).

Charles Tennyson, president of the British Association of Commercial and Industrial Education (BACIE), addressing its national conference in July 1948, articulated these sentiments:

> The conditions confronting the country are so new, and so little original thought has been given in the past to the subject [training] that it is practically a new subject.

Therefore, it was felt that young people should be connected more intimately to the capitalist labour process. The device through which this could be achieved was 'national training schemes which would be made compulsory in law in all industry', within the context of manpower planning and full employment (TUC Report, 1947).

The purpose of the Act was to consolidate existing labour legislation in a way that recognised the final subsumption of labour within the capital relation and provide an effective labour market across all sectors, skills and age ranges. The first part of the Act dealt with general matters to facilitate this process. The second part of the act, deemed 'more interesting' by *The Economist* (3 April) was designed, 'to create a more effective organisation for giving young people advice and assistance in choosing their careers' and to end the confusion between what 'some regard as an education service and others more closely aligned to the world of employments' (NRO Ministry of Labour papers, 8/1508). It was hoped that this clarification would allow for better labour market planning, to make for higher quality and common standards and to address the chronic labour shortage of young people: 'rare and precious creatures' (The *Economist*, 3rd April 1948), the seriousness of which demanded 'a revolution in thought about the training of the young' (*The Economist*, 29th November 1946). All this would be achieved by centralising schemes for young people under a Central Juvenile Employment Executive, staffed by the Minister of Labour and the Minister of Education and advised by a National Juvenile Employment Council, consisting of teachers, employers, Trade Unionists, Local Authority representatives and five independent persons (NRO Ministry of Labour papers, 8/1508).

The scheme was marketed as a structure to ease the transition from school to work for all 'boys and girls', a vital component for 'their future development and happiness' and a 'sympathetic and practical guide' to those 'boys and girls' who had ideas for work but 'are too shy to talk about them' or for whom 'their teachers were not experienced to deal with'. Provision was to be made, 'where appropriate, for a grant to be given to young people with a special aptitude for a particular occupation, but with no local outlet, so as to be able to leave home and be placed with an employer in another area as an apprentice or learner' (Issacs, NRO, Ministry of Labour papers, Notes on First Reading of the Employment and Training Bill, 1948)

The area of most dispute centred on the question of compulsion. Such was the shortage of young people that it was originally felt that attachment to the scheme should be mandatory: parents and children should be required to attend at Employment Exchanges in order that they might receive advice and be made aware of the opportunities available. It was, however, eventually decided that persuasion as to the benefits of the scheme would be more appropriate (TUC Report, 1948, p. 224). The drafters of the Employment and Training Act, therefore, paid a good deal of attention to 'propaganda', i.e. as to how the world of capitalist work could be made attractive to the young working class. Much of that discussion centred around what to call the new employment scheme for the young working class and, more particularly, what to call the young working class.[5] This is a fascinating and critical moment in the creation of modern youth and yet it has been completely ignored by the sociology of youth.

The debate focused on what to call young workers. This problem was discussed at length by Members of Parliament (MPs) in debates on the floor of the House and in Committee. The problem was that, as Issacs, the Minister of Labour (Isaacs), pointed out there is no English word that properly describes those between the ages of 15 and 18. Other MPs (Dumpleton, Langford-Holt, Lindsay,) argued that the former title of 'juvenile' was too offensive, suggesting delinquency, and likely to dissuade young people from approaching the new employment service However, as Issacs made clear, there were real practical difficulties in replacing 'juvenile' as it was carved on the headings outside employment exchanges. Suggestions for a new title included the serious and the not so serious. Maitland's suggestion 'careerist advisee' was rejected for its 'bourgeois, middle-class snobbishness'; the term 'young people' suggested by Dumpleton, a self-proclaimed expert on such matters, was refused as being 'patronising and priggish'; and 'adultry', recommended by Orr-Ewing, was not taken seriously. In the end the title 'youth', suggested by Lindsay was agreed on despite the fact that Dumpleton felt it to be 'too abstract and refer to young people en mass' (Dumpleton, MP). And so the Juvenile Employment Service became the Youth Employment Service.

Youth: a real abstraction

At first reading this might seem like a trivial amendment, but I want to suggest that it reflects a significant recomposition that occurred in the world of work through the recomposition of youthful labour. This discussion among MPs is, in fact, a spectacular example of the way in which the real process by which labour is recomposed as abstract labour is reflected by its definition as a *real abstraction*. The term youth is chosen precisely because of its abstract and depersonalised character and its ability to convey the characteristic of immaterial life. The category 'youth' was a recognition of the new condition of massified and intensified labour as it was to apply to the young working class.

It is precisely because 'youth' was an abstract term and did not apply to any young body in particular that it was felt to be so appropriate. The status of 'youth' does not refer to any person in particular nor is it based on the particular attributes of any young person, but is a status attributed to the young working class based entirely on their capacity to become the commodity labour power: to exist as abstract labour. As such it marks the culmination of a process by which the young working class were fully and really subsumed within the capital relation as commodity labour power. The recognition of this new status by MPs is not a conscious decision but is the outcome of a process that occurs 'behind the backs' of the politicians. While recognition occurs in the minds of the legislators it is not the product of the mind but is derived from the real status of young people in the production of the social relations of capitalist society.[6]

By recognising modern youth as a real abstraction it is possible to reformulate the way in which youth can be understood in this period, while at the same time undermining and overcoming the sociology of youth. As a real abstraction youth is understood not simply as an empirical reality that is defined by its consumptive characteristics; but, rather, as a productive energy within the social relations of capitalist society. The condition of youth is not defined by physical attributes but is a status attributed to youth as a result of its position within the productive relations of capital. In this form it is possible to explain the conformity of modern youth: as abstract labour youth exists as a form of capital, and its antagonism: as a form of abstract labour youth exists in the form of being denied, a form that is antagonistic not only to the institutions within which it is maintained but also to itself. Youth is a being that is alien to itself. The theory of human resistance derived from this condition is that as a being that is alien to itself, youth as a form of abstract labour contains the possibility of its own negation, to be not-capital, to dissolve itself and the relation within which it exists and to recompose the relation without negating the constitutive power of labour as the creative force of the social world.

Training culture: against human resistance

Utilising this methodology it is possible to invert the critical devices of cultural studies of youth to provide a much richer and fuller account of the development of post-War youth, its conformity, its radicality and its eventual demise. Through an examination of the dynamic principle contained within the production of the commodity-form it is possible to argue that young people were not accommodating themselves to the social upheavals caused by massive economic and political upheavals; but, rather, as a result of the productive negativity of abstract labour, capital and its institutions are forced to recompose themselves into institutional forms that exist to contain the power of labour.

By recognising the significance of this struggle, rather than accepting the cultural logics of the capitalist machine, it is possible to reassess the institutional forms of the state. Confronted by the resistance of the working class it was capital that was forced to find solutions to the uncompromising character of the form of sociability that they had produced. From this line of argument it is possible to reconsider the training legislation of the period. Rather than understanding post-War training regimes, e.g. Industrial Training Boards, as a rational response to the 'white hot' capacities of the new technologies, or as instruments to resolve labour market inefficiencies, e.g. Employment and Training Act, 1972, or even more critically as functional agents of social control, e.g. the Manpower Services Commission, this analysis allows us to understand that:

> ... every innovation, new body, tribunal or commission originates either directly or at one removed from working class resistance to the formal conditions of its life. Just as machinery is the product of labour which then confronts its producer as an alien force, so [training] administration is the appropriation of the revolutionary will by the state, and its transformation into a counter-revolutionary force'. (Kay and Mott, 1982, p. 96)

The training regimes of the period are a dramatic demonstration of an attempt by capital to recompose young labour into an appropriate form. These solutions are not imaginary, but neither are they convincing. This lack of conviction leads to further recomposition and intensification of struggle and resistance.

Human resistance and the politics of 'cool'

This account also allows us to theorise resistance beyond the orthodox account of working class struggle: to conceive of a theory of human resistance that does not derive its radicality from its attachment to a dramatic category of human sociability, nor gain its radical credibility through attempts to affirm these categories. Instead, the critical purpose of this theory is to reveal the dynamic principle out of which those critical categories are derived so as to dissolve the categorical way in which human life is constructed. From this account young people are not simply struggling in and against the alienated institutional power of capital in the form of money and the state, they are also struggling in and against the institutional form of human sociability through which their own existence is determined. Youth is struggling in and against itself. The distinct forms of sociability that young people adopted in this period are not accommodating solutions to the problem of enormous social, political and economic restructuring; but are, rather, the outcome of a very developed form of labour (abstract labour) within which all identity has been destroyed. The dramatic and distinctive styles that young people produce are not based on attachments to working class history (e.g. skinheads) or the aspirations for a higher class status (e.g. mods); but are, in fact, derived from the *destruction of class categories*, the lack of any defining particularity of work and the need for abstract labour to take on a specific human identity. The defining characteristic of this arrangement is indifference, or 'cool'.

Although this most youthful condition appears as a mental event or attitude, it is not a product of the mind. Cool indifference corresponds to the world of abstract labour, where individuals can with ease transfer from one labour to another, or one style to another and where the specific kind of labour, or style, is a matter of chance or indifference to its demonstrators. But 'cool' is not simply a matter of fashion: as an expression of abstract labour 'cool' also contains the possibility of its own negation, to exist as 'not youth'. In this significant way, indifference carries within it the logic of human indiscipline and resistance. 'Cool' is not only the actuality of a revolt into style (Hebdige, 1979), but also carries within it the possibility of a revolt into *revolt*.

In the current moment, the form of youthful labour created in 1948 and the life and culture that was associated with it is being destroyed. Young workers have been redesigned not as a trained and integral parts of a dynamic productive process, but as cheap labour (Rikowski and Neary, 1997). In this condition the irresponsibility and indifference that characterised the post-War generation is denied and young people are forced to exist as responsible citizens. For the moment the politics of resistance are elsewhere, but from Marx's theory of human resistance and from the modern history of human struggle we know it cannot be contained.

Notes

1.   This approach was inspired by, among other things, proponents of Western Marxism (e.g. Gramsci, Poulantzas), writers from the Frankfurt school (e.g. Adorno), British Marxist history (e.g. E. P. Thompson) and various types of French structuralism and post structuralism (Levi-Strauss, Foucault).

2.   It has become commonplace to mourn the loss of youth culture. This approach is more prevalent in journalistic accounts than in radical sociological perspectives, which seem intent on keeping the category alive. See *The Modern Review*, March 1998, on the transition of adolescence into adultescence.

3.   I have chosen this category for the radicality it seemed to offer to sociology. I do not mean to privilege youth above any other critical concept. Indeed, the basis of my argument is that my critical approach towards the sociology of youth is generalisable to all other critical categories of radical sociology.

4.   Gunn (in Bonefeld *el al*, 1992). The same point is developed by Kay and Mott in *Political Order and the Law of Labour* (1982):

Administration is working-class power *post festum*; working class political victories captured and formalised at their moment of triumph ... The development of administration and the advance of technology both appear in the same light, as rationalisations which unfold themselves, each moment forward seeming to arise from a logical development of the previous one, but in both cases the appearance is false. In capitalist society technology has always developed in response to specific conditions as a means of overcoming working class opposition to existing methods of production, and in this sense, of being precipitated by working class struggles, new techniques can be seen as their obituary (p. 96).

5.   These extracts are taken from Hansard, Employment and Training Bill, 16th April 1948, pp. 1379-1386, and in Committee, 4 May 1948, Employment and Training Bill, Hansard 1948, Vol III, pp. 486-49. For a full account of this debate see Neary (1997).

6.   For a theoretical exposition of the relationship between consciousness and human action see Sohn-Rethel (1978).

7.   The most dramatic form of youth being not youth was demonstrated by Punk. This extraordinary phenomena appeared in the moment when the world for which youth had been created in 1948 collapsed and the process of the recomposition of youth began. Punk was a refusal by young people to accept their new condition.

CHAPTER 6

Education Theory and the Return to Class Analysis
Mike Sanders, Dave Hill and Ted Hankin

Introduction: a class divided society

The overall economic context in which educational, social, economic and political inequalities are reproduced is a class-based capitalist mode of production. In this chapter we challenge the analyses and pronouncements that: 'class is dead'; 'we live in a classless society'; 'class identity and affiliation are archaic formulae'; 'relations of production have been superseded in political, educational and social importance by relations of consumption'; 'we live in a postmodern and post-Fordist society and economy'; 'there is no class struggle;' and the notion that political and educational practices and theories of class struggle are totalitarian, oppressive of other social groups, and doomed to failure.

Postmodern academics at one level and a range of politicians and political theorists at another, have attempted to consign Marxist analysis and socialist egalitarian educational and political programmes to the dustbin of history. In addition to postmodernist academics, political groups seeking to inter Marxism include both Radical Right Thatcherites/Reaganites and their neo-liberal/neo-conservative successors, and 'Third Way' politicians such as Clinton, Blair and Schroeder.[1] However, the perspective put forward in this chapter is that a Marxist analysis and understanding of *social class* is crucially significant for an understanding of contemporary capitalism, and for grasping the restructuring of education that has occurred through the nineteen-eighties and nineties in many of the advanced capitalist industrial states. It is also argued that an understanding of social class is essential for developing and constructing economic, political and education systems based on social justice and egalitarianism.

Social class: what are the facts?

Despite proclamations from politicians and pundits that we now inhabit a classless society, or that 'we are all middle class now' (White, 1999) the simple truth is, that for the last two decades class divisions and class-based forms of inequality have increased. For example, Michael Barratt Brown and Ken Coates (1996) in *The Blair Revolution: Deliverance for Whom?* provide data on income distribution and capital ownership in the UK showing that in the last twenty years the top fifth of income earners in Britain have seen their incomes increase by 40% in real terms, while the bottom fifth have actually become poorer. As a result the top fifth of households were taking 51% of all original income in 1994 compared with 43% in 1979.[2]

At the same time that salaries and wages have risen at the top end of the scale, there has been an accompanying shift from such labour income to property income. In 1995 while wages and salaries rose by 4% before tax, income from dividends and interest is estimated to have grown by 38% in money terms before tax. In the years 1992-95 there was a redistribution of around £24 billion each year from British wages and salaries to gross profits.

Britain is thus a far more unequal society than 20 years ago. One quarter of adults in the UK in 1998 have no savings whatsoever, and are in debt, living poorly, running out of money for food and fares before the next pay-day or the next welfare cheque. In this context, postmodernism's celebration of consumerism, consumption and 'lifestyle choices' seems a hollow, if not an obscene mockery. What, we might ask, does postmodernism have to say about poverty and inequality? The answer is very little. Indeed, it is difficult to see how postmodernism can address these issues. After all, where Marxism sees structural inequality, postmodernism sees 'social difference'. Similarly, when Marxism argues that poverty is an offence against the notion of a just social order it betrays (at least to postmodern opponents) its nostalgic, if not reactionary, commitment to those meta-narratives of the Englightenment which postmodernism rejects.

The pressure group 'Justice', has, in its 1997 Report, pointed out that in Britain:

- One in three children lives in poverty
- The divide between highest–paid and lowest–paid workers is the greatest since 1886
- Almost four in 10 adults earn less than Council of Europe 'decency threshold'
- Women are still paid 20 per cent less than men
- Benefits for lone parents fall short of their needs by up to £23 a week
- Sixty–five per cent of disabled people live below the poverty line
- Up to 300,000 young people experience homelessness each year
- As many as 1.4 million homes are unfit and 2.3 million need renovation
- More than 250,000 people a year suffer racial harassment
- Numbers of children excluded from school have increased 300 percent since 1992   (Brindle, 1997).

Adonis and Pollard's *A Class Act, The Myth of Britain's Classless Society* (1997), also shows how Britain is still a deeply divided society, characterised by class distinctions. In particular, Adonis and Pollard focus on the system of secondary education, which is rigidly separated into a flourishing, lavishly funded private sector, as compared to demoralised, under-financed public sector. They point out that those who benefit from private education are almost invariably from privileged backgrounds: the fact that they attend the best schools in the country merely entrenches their privileges and enhances their prospects still further (Adonis and Pollard, 1997).

Postmodernism and social class

Given the decisive role played by class as a structuring factor in people's lives, the question which arises is this—why have so many ostensibly, and often self-proclaimed, 'radical' critics and theorists enlisted under the banner of postmodernism and abandoned class as a category of analysis? For there can be no doubt that class *has* been abandoned by many critics who would describe themselves as committed to a progressive politics, for example as 'resistance postmodernists'.[3]

In the following paragraphs we identify the cultural-historical factors which underpin the abandonment of class by sections of the radical intelligentsia. These are grouped under two main headings which for convenience we might term *extrinsic* problems with class analysis and *intrinsic* problems of class analysis. This distinction is necessary because it is important to disentangle those wider cultural and historical factors informing the retreat from class from the internal problems of inadequate theorisation within class based analyses which have allowed the retreat from class to cover itself with a veneer of intellectual sophistication. It is also vital that class-based analyses address their own theoretical weaknesses as these have contributed to class's loss of purchase within the academy.

Extrinsic problems with class analysis

We begin with the briefest of sketches of changing intellectual trends within the Western academy. During the sixties and seventies Marxism became fashionable in academia, although in the latter decade it was increasingly contested by a variety of post-structuralisms which, cumulatively, contributed to the formation of postmodernism. The timing, extent and success of this challenge to Marxism varied across disciplines but, generally speaking, by the mid-eighties postmodernism had installed itself as the fashionable, and thereafter dominant, intellectual trend. In order to understand the reasons for postmodernism's dominance within the academy we must situate that rise within the wider historical and social context which produced it. As Aijaz

Ahmad (1992) observes in, *In Theory: Classes, Nations, Literatures*, a Marxist analysis of theory must engage with the following questions:

> the issue of the institutional sites from which that theory emanates; the actual class practices and concrete social locations, in systems of power and powerlessness, of the agents who produce it; the circuits through which it circulates and the class fractions who endow it with whatever power it gains; hence the objective determination of the theory itself by these material co-ordinates of its production, regardless of the individual agent's personal stance towards these locations and co-ordinates ... The characteristic feature of contemporary literary radicalism is that it rarely addresses the question of its own determination by the conditions of its production and the class location of its agents. (Ahmad, 1992 p. 5-6)

Ahmad argues that post-structuralism is conditioned by the contradictory experiences of, on the one hand the anti-imperialist struggles, student radicalism and labour militancy of the late-1960s/early-1970s, and on the other hand their containment by the mid-1970s and the subsequent capitalist counter-offensive of the 1980s. The class background of many of the students who participated in this 'revolutionary wave' meant that most lacked any previous connection with the organised labour movement and even fewer developed a lasting commitment to it. Almost by definition, Ahmad suggests, those students who completed their PhDs and became academics were those who were least involved in the political movements.

> It was, in other words, mostly the *survivors* of the 'movement' who later became so successful in the profession. Radicalism had been, for most of them, a state of mind, brought about by an intellectual identification with the revolutionary wave that had gripped so much of the world when they were truly young; of the day-to-day drudgeries of, say, a political party or a trade union they had been (and were to remain) largely innocent. (Ahmad, 1992 p. 66)

Many critics of postmodernism, ourselves included, have insisted that it is the product of a very particular historical conjuncture. Callinicos (1989), for example, has described postmodernism as 'the product of a socially mobile intelligentsia in a climate dominated by the retreat of the Western labour movement and the 'overconsumptionist' dynamic of capitalism in the Reagan-Thatcher era' (1989, p. 115). Callinicos also suggests that postmodernism allows that same intelligentsia 'to articulate its political disillusionment and its aspiration to a consumption orientated lifestyle' (1989, p.115). While the attractions of a consumerist lifestyle are obvious, the claim of 'political disillusionment' requires closer attention. On one level postmodernist political disillusion would appear to replicate a well-established cultural pattern whereby young radicals become old conservatives. Yet unlike earlier examples (for example, Wordsworth and Coleridge, or many 'Marxist' intellectuals of the 1930s), conversion to postmodernism is usually accompanied by declarations of an *increased*, rather than abandoned, radicalism. These claims have generally been accepted by the rising generation of academic 'resistance postmodernists' who proudly insist on the ultra-radicalism of their postmodernist affiliations and denounce the conservatism of Marxism with its 'reactionary' attachment to a range of discredited, 'totalitarian' meta-narratives.[4]

Amongst the attractions of postmodernism is the way in which it harmonised with the career needs of a rising generation of professional intellectuals. Postmodernism, with its rejection of 'foundationalist' modes of thought, provided the theoretical underpinning for an assault on the established, academic order. In this respect, postmodernism was able to posit itself as standing in the same relation to Marxism, as (academic) Marxism had to 'Liberal Humanism'. Moreover, postmodernism had the added attraction of promising something entirely new, and in this respect it fully deserves its characterisation (by Frederic Jameson) as 'the cultural logic of late capitalism' (Jameson 1984, 1992). For in representing itself as 'new', it was simultaneously laying claim to the epithet—which always accompanies newness in contemporary advertising—'improved'. There is an interesting homology here between commodity production and theoretical production. Just as under late capitalism any change to a product leads to its being advertised as 'new and improved' (even when, as in the case of a certain soap-powder, this improvement actually entailed the more rapid degradation and destruction of your clothing), so in the realm of academia the new theoretical paradigm pronounced itself to be 'new and improved' (with similarly corrosive and destructive results as regards the 'fabric' of progressive action as the aforementioned soap-powder).

Postmodernism, however, offered a rather different account of its relationship to late capitalism. It had emerged (so it claimed) precisely because the old paradigms were no longer capable of explaining the new social and cultural order which, postmodernism claimed, had recently arisen. There is a sense in which postmodernism can be seen as the latest in a long line of theories which have proclaimed the transformation of capitalism into something qualitatively different, the latest incarnation of the type of revisionist and class-collaborationist politics associated with the social democracy of the Edward Bernstein. In conformity to this tradition, postmodernism also has 'the obvious ideological mission of demonstrating, to their own relief, that the new social formation in question no longer obeys the laws of classical capitalism, namely, the primacy of industrial production and the omnipresence of class struggle (Jameson, 1992, p. 3). As such, postmodernism is likely to founder on the same rocks which have shattered all of its ancestors—economic crisis, rising class antagonism, inter-imperialist rivalry.

No doubt, postmodernists would reject the charge of class-collaboration. After all, a key part of their analysis denies that there are such things as social classes. It is this part of the theoretical project of postmodernism—its jettisoning of class analysis as something which is no longer relevant in the postmodern world—that we want to examine in greater depth. We want to begin with what is perhaps the most frequent 'common-sense' rejection of class which is that is an anachronistic category which is no longer relevant in the context of a (postmodern) society which has become 'classless'—as, for example, claimed by the former Conservative British Prime Minister, John Major.

The basic thesis of classlessness comes (appropriately enough considering postmodernism's emphasis on the importance of consumer choice) in a wide range of models with varying degrees of theoretical sophistication and varying accounts of how this state of affairs was produced. For the most part these theorists agree that class has only disappeared relatively recently from the historical stage (i.e. in the post-war period and for many not until the political changes of the 1980s). They also argue that the disappearance of class has resulted from cultural changes occurring as a result of the transition from a 'Fordist' to a 'post-Fordist' economy. Champions of this position point to the destruction variously of 'traditional' class signifiers (the decline of flat caps and whippets), class institutions (such as Trades Unions, the Co-op, the Workers Educational Association), class locations (such as the mining village, the steel town, factory area), and therefore of class consciousness (evidenced by four successive Conservative electoral victories between 1979 and 1997 and by 'New Labour's 'classless' appeal in its 1997 general election victory). The social and cultural order organised around class has been replaced, they assert, by a 'new order' based on individual rights, mobility, choice (consumer and life-style in particular), and freedom.

It needs to be acknowledged, however, that the 'autonomous consumer' account of recent cultural changes has convinced many people and that its appeal is based on its *apparent* accuracy—it does appear to offer a convincing explanation of recent history. Our contention, however, is that this account is only *superficially* accurate; homelessness and unemployment for example have rapidly expanded; and even then it is predicated on an ideological surrender to neo-liberalism. In other words, the acceptance of this account of recent changes depends on a prior acceptance of its ideological assumptions.

A willingness to be convinced by postmodernism is influenced to a considerable extent by class position and/or affiliation. This assertion will no doubt provoke outrage from those postmodernists who are happy to demonstrate the ways in which the theoretical preferences of particular individuals are always—already determined by wider networks of power but are far less willing to accept that their own position (by their own logic) is generated by and serves 'power' beyond themselves .[5]

In response to the above account of the disappearance of class we would like to draw attention to the way in which it depends on an account of class which is not so much a theory as a caricature. Consider, for example, John Urry's summary of the conventional Marxist account of class:

> Marxism has traditionally held that social classes are generated by the economic base of societies, in particular by their dominant form of exploitation; that such classes have a relatively unambiguous 'interest', either to preserve or to destroy existing social relations; that there is a once-and-for-all establishment of classes-for-themselves which are nationally (or even internationally) unified and which have a clear class interest; that such classes generate forms of politics and culture which, except at the point of revolutionary transformation, cannot reflect back upon the class structure; and that the only social forces of real significance within capitalism are the bourgeoisie and the proletariat, meaning that other social classes and forces do not possess significant transformative powers. (Urry, 1995, p. 169)

Outside the Marxist tradition, it is clear that many critics of class analysis (such as Jan Pakulski, referred to below) confound (whether deliberately or accidentally) class consciousness with the fact of class—and tend to deduce the non-existence of the latter from the 'absence' of the former.[6]

As noted earlier, the collapse of many traditional signifiers of 'working-classness' has led many to pronounce the demise of class. Our first response to this is to observe with Beverley Skeggs:

> To abandon class as a theoretical tool does not mean that it does not exist anymore; only that some theorists do not value it. It does not mean ... [working-class people] experience inequality any differently; rather, it would make it more difficult for them to identify and challenge the basis of the inequality which they experience. *Class inequality exists beyond its theoretical representation.* (Skeggs, 1997, p. 6, our emphasis added.)

To this we might add that the structural effects of class persist, and are in fact more pernicious in their operation and effects, precisely because of the difficulties of finding adequate cultural (as well as theoretical) representations of 'working-classness'. To extend the military metaphor of the 'class war', we might say that whilst the class war still rages[7] the working class in general has been culturally—and more importantly, politically-demobilised and only the capitalist class knows itself to be in uniform. It always does. In this context the denial of the relevance of a class analysis by postmodernism has contributed to the ideological disarming of the working-class movement.

Class struggle from above and below

The arguments concerning the disappearance of class *might appear* to possess a certain purchase when the focus is placed exclusively on the 'working class', these arguments are far less persuasive if we turn our attention to the question of the existence of a capitalist class. Is there, we wonder, anyone amongst the postmodernists who would dispute the existence of a relatively small group of people owning tremendous amounts of material wealth, wielding immense power, sharing similar cultural backgrounds and aspirations often reinforced by close family and other personal ties, who are adept at defending and promoting their interests?

In *Divided Societies* (1991) Ralph Miliband makes an analytical distinction between 'class struggle from below' (waged by the working class) and 'class struggle from above' (whose 'crucial protagonists are usually those who own or control the main means of domination in capitalist society') (Miliband, 1991:56, 117). This distinction seems particularly appropriate when considering the history of the last twenty-five years or so. In Britain, we could describe the period between 1970 and 1985 as one of intense class struggle from below (as well as from above) marked by a series of major industrial actions: the miners', dockers', and construction workers' strikes of the early 1970s, the Grunwick photo development workers strike of the late 1970s, the so-called 'Winter of Discontent' which preceded the defeat of the Callaghan Labour government in 1979, the 'Great Miners' Strike of 1984-85 and the Wapping printworkers' strike against the Murdoch Press which marked the end of this sequence.[8]

In contrast, the period during and after the Great Miners' Strike can be described as one of class struggle from above waged against a disorientated, divided, and let us not forget an effectively criminalised working-class movement.[9] With the changed balance of forces between the classes, consequent on the defeat of the miners, a whole series of anti-Trade Union laws, and a series of fines and sequestrations against Trade Union assets were passed by the Thatcher government. Mass picketing had been criminalised prior to the

Miners' strike—with the number of pickets limited to six—although during the miners' strike this was not enforced. Widespread and violent policing against strike action took place during the strike, epitomised by the horseback police baton wielding and occupation of the coal-mining village of Orgreave. Following the Thatcher government's victory over the miners, sympathetic strikes were banned, cooling-off periods and compulsory postal ballots prior to strike action were enforced, widescale union derecognition occurred.[10]

One of the crucial differences between these two forms of class struggle is the relative invisibility of many aspects of the class struggle from above (such as, for example, anti-union legislation, changes to the taxation system, privatisation, quango-isation). The post-1985 intensification of (invisible) class struggle from above combined with the decline of visible resistance from below has led many commentators to announce, both complacently and erroneously, the end of class society. Jan Pakulski provides a model example: 'The key assumption of class analysis—that all important social conflicts have a class basis and class character because class represents the key social dimension of modern (capitalist) society—does not withstand critical scrutiny' (Pakulski, 1995 p. 75). We are suggesting that most of the 'evidence' demonstrating the disappearance of class is in fact highly trumpeted and orchestrated evidence of the disappearance of traditional working-class consciousness and working-class action *as traditionally conceived*. It is simply incorrect to suggest that there is no 'human resistance', whether individual or collective, to capitalism, to the intensification of work demanded of workers by capital, both nationally and internationally.

Moreover, it could be argued that the decline in 'traditional' forms of working class action, such as strikes, have been exaggerated as a result of a 'changed' media agenda. In short, there has, at the current juncture, been a decline in working class protest such as strikes in the 1990s. Over the last five years, each year, one after the other, has seen the lowest number of days lost through strikes since records began in the 1890s. Accompanying this decline there has been a wider decline in media coverage of such action. The media, as one of the most important ideological state apparatuses[11] clearly play a censorship role here which tends to reinforce positions such as that of Pakulski. For example, through the mid-1990s there have been a constant series of, *illegal*, strikes by London Underground ('Tube') workers which have hit the news headlines, because of their obvious impact on millions of Londoners. But there have also been others, such as the series of illegal stoppages by Royal Mail employees which have either been under-reported or never reported at all, presumably because they have *not* led to any sanctions against these workers and reporting them may give other groups of workers ideas? Again, at this current juncture, the strikes that have occurred in the late 1990s—such as the Magnet workers, the Liverpool dockworkers and the Hillingdon Hospital workers—have been defensive, usually against redundancies or attacks on working conditions.

From the perspective of the socialist left it is not enough simply to demonstrate the shoddy conceptualisations of much postmodernist orthodoxy. To demonstrate the flaws in many postmodern arguments should be of little comfort whilst the working class in Britain has continued to experience political defeat after political defeat by the conservative state and the capitalist class, whether under the Conservative governments of 1979-1997 or under the 'New Labour' government which was elected on May Day 1997.

Intrinsic problems with class analysis

In the earlier sections we have outlined the historical, cultural and ideological forces conditioning postmodernism's rise to a position of theoretical orthodoxy within the academy, and we have criticised the ways in which postmodernism has theorised class. In this section we will focus on what we have termed the 'intrinsic problems with class analysis'. Our reason for doing this is, as we noted earlier, that the inadequate theorisation of class within Marxism constitutes a fundamental intellectual weakness which it is vital that Marxism addresses. What we wish to do in this section is recover that sense of social class as simultaneously a category of analysis *and* a theoretical and political problem which is always in process and never finally resolved. *What we need to recover is a sense of the complexity of social class as a multi-dimensional category of analysis which seeks to negotiate the relationships between class as a category of: economic analysis, cultural analysis, individual identification, and political mobilisation.* This, we feel, is one of the most important theoretical legacies left by Marx and one which has exercised many subsequent Marxist theoreticians. It is through a brief summary of this tradition that we hope to demonstrate the problematic yet sophisticated theorisation of class within Marxism and suggest ways in which a non-reductive understanding of class must play an important role in any project of liberation.

The relationship between economic and social class

Marx provided an 'objective' definition of class. He argued that an individual's class-position is determined by their relationship to the means of production and exists independently of their subjective evaluation of their own class position. A condensed definition is that,

> Classes are large groups of people differing from each other by the place they occupy in a historically determined system of social

production, by their relation (in most cases fixed and formulated by law) to the means of production, by their role in the social organisation of labour, by the dimensions of the share of the social wealth of which they dispose and their mode of acquiring it. (Lenin 1965 p. 421)

This notion of 'objective class position' has always been subject to two major objections. Either it is condemned as 'reductive' precisely because it refuses to consider the question of how social actors understand and make sense of class (at which point the Weberian tradition with its notion of 'status' is usually mobilised); or, and this has been the more recent phenomenon, under the influence of various perspectivist schools of thought (which usually derive from Nietzsche) the possibility of their being any such thing as an 'objective' definition of class is denied or even ridiculed as being, at best, a positivist illusion or at worst, an example of oppressive, totalising Enlightenment rationalism.[12]

It seems to us that we cannot afford to jettison the notion of objective class position because it allows us to identify and understand a number of inter-related, significant social truths. Firstly, it enables us to identify and account for the massive inequalities in material wealth which exists in Britain. Class allows us to see such inequalities not as the chance result of some cosmic lottery game, 'the luck of the draw', but as the determinate result of existing property relations. Beyond this, class (in combination with the labour-theory of value) allows us to understand why the economic relationship between the owners and non-owners is necessarily antagonistic. 'Supermarkets Inc.' profits arise out of the difference between the value (wages) which they pay their workers and the value which those workers produce as a result of their labour. This is not a 'win-win' game: more for 'Supermarkets Inc.' means less for their workforce, and vice-versa. It also explains the daily struggle (familiar to all workers) to control the working-day which is usually fought over such things as start/finish times, length of breaks, frequency of toilet-breaks. Attempts by line managers to 'persuade' their subordinates to start work five minutes early or finish five minutes late are not just arbitrary displays of local authority, they are intended to increase surplus value and ultimately profit. They point to the permanent presence of class struggle waged at the point of production. The technical term for this is 'class exploitation'. Such a concept has no place in the vocabulary of leading postmodernist philosophers such as Lyotard and Baudrillard, and appears to be of little consequence to others such as Foucault. Various 'Resistance Postmodernists' such as Henry Giroux and Peter McLaren in their postmodern phases—(respectively, arguably, 1992 to the present; 1992 till 1997)—would accept the concept, though, in their postmodern phases, would dispute its salience *vis-à-vis* other forms of exploitation.

The same pattern is repeated in the political sphere. Governments do not take neutral decisions based on the 'national interest':

> Politics is about the allocation of scarce resources in society. It is about who gets what and who doesn't, who wins and who loses, who is empowered and who is disempowered, who gets the gravy and who has to make it. It is also about how this system is organised, legitimated and resisted. And it is about how ideological state apparatuses (*such as the education system* and the mass media) and the repressive state apparatuses (such as the police, the law, the army) seek to ensure the continuation and enforcement of the current system. (Hill, 1999a)

Every decision and policy made in the realms of taxation and expenditure, in particular, has the effect of moving material resources from one class to another. When the government reduces corporation tax it redistributes wealth in favour of the owners. Similarly, when it increases VAT it redistributes wealth away from the non-owners. Privatisation and the burgeoning of 'quangos' divert state finances from public into private hands, thereby returning us to the world of 'Old Corruption' as practised in the late-eighteenth and early-nineteenth centuries, whereby the state served as a conduit through which revenue raised by taxing the working population was diverted into the pockets of those closely connected with the political *élites* at both national and local level (Saville, 1994 pp. 41-50).

The analysis outlined above—economic exploitation compounded by political expropriation—can be (and historically has been) used by the socialist left to try and persuade all wage-labourers that they have a common interest in seeking the end of capitalism. Postmodernists have objected to this project on the grounds that it denies or suppresses the facts of 'social difference'. David Harvey succinctly summarises this critique:

> Concentration on class alone is seen to hide, marginalise, disempower, repress and perhaps even oppress all kinds of 'others' precisely because it cannot and does not acknowledge explicitly the existence of heterogeneities and differences based on, for example, race, gender, age, ability, culture, locality, ethnicity, religion, community, consumer preferences, group affiliation, and the like. (Harvey, 1993, p. 101)

And there can be no doubt that at times in the history of the socialist project the white, male, heterosexual worker was represented as the exclusive (or at least the most significant) model of the interpellated wage-labourer, and that criticism of this project on these grounds is both well-founded and has needed to be acknowledged and acted upon by the left. However, many institutions within the labour movement particularly the trade unions have responded and are continuing to respond, with varying degrees of effectiveness, to this challenge through the creation of equal opportunities committees, advisories and officers. Lynne Segal has noted that in those countries with stronger trade union and social-democratic traditions than exist in the USA 'there is far less pay-differential and occupational segregation (both vertical and horizontal) between women and men, and far greater expansion of welfare services' (Segal, 1991 pp. 81-91). Even more pertinently Segal contends that at a time when the advances of some women are overshadowed by the increasing poverty of others 'it seems perverse to pose women's specific interests *against* rather than *alongside* more traditional socialist goals' (Segal, 1991, p. 90-91).

In the light of this it is interesting to note the renewed interest in class analysis within British Feminism see, for example, Beverly Skeggs', *Formations of Class and Gender*, (1997), and the first of a proposed new series on 'Women and Social Class', *Class Matters*, (1997) edited by Pat Mahony and Christine Zmroczek. Of course, for socialist feminists such as Jane Kelly (1992, 1999) this class analysis never went away! (See Jane Kelly's chapter in this volume). Socialists such as Segal and Kelly call for a reaffirmation of the value of 'traditional socialist goals' is one which we fully support. In particular, we would suggest that classical Marxism's emphasis on the ethical necessity of greater social equality, its conception of individual liberty as something which can only be realised collectively, and its quest for an alternative basis for social relations to that offered by the 'cash nexus'— encapsulated in two memorable maxims, 'from each according to their ability to each according to their need' and 'the free development of each is the condition for the free development of all'—provide an outline of a transformative social programme which is politically more radical and ethically far superior to that offered by postmodernism.

At its best the socialist project is not about denying the fact of social difference but about the need to construct *solidarity*, which is, we would argue, as important to the socialist project as 'choice' is to the neo-liberal one. Historically, the socialist movement has worked to establish solidarity as both a normative value ('an injury to one is an injury to all'), and a practical pre-requisite for successful struggle (based on an achieved understanding that it is through collective self-organisation and alliance formation that relatively disempowered social groups have improved their conditions).

We argue that implicit in the notion of 'solidarity' is respect for difference. As David Harvey observes, 'to discover the basis of similarity (rather than to presume sameness) is to uncover the basis for alliance formation between seemingly disparate groups' (Harvey, 1993:114). This is exactly what happened in the 1984-5 British Miner's Strike which was supported by a disparate array of gay and lesbian, Irish republican, environmental, black and women's groups. It is also, to an extent, what happened during the years of (left-wing) Labour Party control of the Greater London Council and the Inner London Education Authority, until their abolition by the Conservative government in the late 1980s. Both were supported by an array—a coalition—of socialist, working class and trade union, minority ethnic group, womens' movement and gay and lesbian movement groups.[13] And it is what happened in Labour groups (of Councillors) virtually wherever the Left within the party held local control.

Harvey continues by arguing that in contemporary society those similarities which are capable of grounding alliances (and thereby engendering solidarity) are generated by the prevailing economic conditions (and, therefore, the objective class positions) which 'we' share.

In defending the notion of objective class position we do not claim it as anything other than the *starting-point* for a Marxist class analysis. It is important that analysis is not arrested at this level, the point after all is not merely to describe the world but to change it. And at the risk of simplification we might say *'economic class describes the world, social classes (conscious of their exploitation and of the possibility of ending it) transform it.'* In moving from a concept of 'economic class' to that of 'social class' we are trying to define a category capable of dealing with the specificities of class as it exists and operates at a particular historical moment and within a determinate social formation. This involves those questions of class consciousness and subjective identification as well as the interaction of gender, race, sexuality, religious and spatial (nation, region, locality) factors in the construction of what we might term a concrete class identity. Again at this point we would like to emphasise that we remain firmly within the 'problematic' of classical Marxism. In Volume Three of *Capital*, Marx offers us a tantalising glimpse of the more complete theorisation of class on which he was engaged:

> What constitutes a class?—and the reply to this follows naturally from the reply to another question, namely: What makes wage-labourers, capitalists and landlords constitute the three great social classes? At first glance—the identity of revenues and sources of revenue. There are three great social groups whose members, the individuals forming them, live on wages, profit and ground-rent

respectively, on the realisation of their labour power, their capital, and their landed property. However, from this standpoint, physicians and officials, e.g. would also constitute two classes, for they belong to two distinct social groups, the members of each of these groups receiving their revenue from one and the same source. The same would also be true of the infinite fragmentation of interest and rank into which the division of social labour splits labourers as well as capitalists and landlords—the latter, e.g. into owners of vineyards, farm owners, owners of forests, mine owners and owners of fisheries. (Marx, 1894, in Tucker, 1978 pp. 441/2)

Class as internally differentiated

This statement of Marx has a number of important implications for our theorisation of class. In the first place, it conceives of classes as internally differentiated entities. Class, for Marx, is not simply monolithic nor static. Under capitalist economic laws of motion the working class in particular is constantly decomposed and reconstituted due to changes in the forces of production: forces of which the working class are themselves a part.[14]

Furthermore, Marx had taken great pains to stress that social class as distinct from economic class necessarily includes a political dimension which is in the broadest sense of the term 'culturally' rather than 'economically' determined.

Class consciousness does not follow automatically or inevitably from the fact of class position. *The Poverty of Philosophy* (1847) distinguishes between a 'class-in-itself' (class position) and a 'class-for itself' (class consciousness), *The Communist Manifesto* (1848) explicitly identifies '[the] formation of the proletariat into a class' as *the* key political task facing the communists. In *The Eighteenth Brumaire of Louis Napoleon* (1852) Marx observes,

> In so far as millions of families live under economic conditions of existence that divide their mode of life, their interests and their cultural formation from those of the other classes and bring them into conflict with those classes, they form a class. In so far as these small peasant proprietors are merely connected on a local basis, and the identity of their interests fails to produce a feeling of community, national links, or a political organisation, they do not form a class. (Marx, 1974 p. 239)

The major consequence of this formulation is that social class exists in a contingent rather than a necessary relation to economic class. The process (and conceptual category) which links economic and social class is that of 'class consciousness'. This is arguably the most contentious and problematic term in the debate over class (a cogent summary of the arguments within the Marxist tradition is provided by Richard Johnson's essay 'Three problematics: elements of a theory of working class culture' (Johnson, 1979).

Re-building class Identity as a political task

To reiterate our earlier point, demonstrating the weaknesses and errors in postmodern analysis does not prove the superiority of our own class-based analysis. Beyond that, there is a gulf between first, demonstrating the theoretical validity of our own analysis, and second, translating that into an effective political strategy. For the latter to occur, we have to find a register in which we can make a class analysis relevant to those in whose name and on whose behalf we claim to perform our theorising. In short, we have to find a way of developing class consciousness in the altered political circumstances of the 1990s and the beginning of the next century/millennium.

It is necessary to find ways of articulating and representing a class analysis as part of the process of rebuilding class consciousness. This form of class consciousness must recognise practically and theoretically the heterogeneous nature of the working class, as well as its common experience—of being in exploited wage labour. In particular, it must address the problematic relationship between class, gender, 'race', religion, sexuality, disability and other aspects of subjectivity, and seek to build solidarity on the basis of respect and toleration for difference rather than its obliteration. In order to achieve this it is necessary to develop an understanding of class as a political identity capable of uniting the largest amount of people for the purposes of progressive change. Most of the necessary work will be (and is being) done in the sphere of practical politics at a variety of levels from the grassroots to the international. There are, however, a number of specific contributions that can be made by workers in the sphere of intellectual production—there is, as always, a battle of ideas which contributes to the war of the classes.

One of the most influential contributions made by postmodernist/post-structuralist thinking has been in the area of 'identity'. It would not be inaccurate to say that poststructuralist accounts of fragmented, de-centred subjectivity are intellectually dominant. In some respects we recognise this as an advance on former monolithic 'vulgar Marxist' accounts of social class which substantially ignored questions of ethnicity, sex and sexuality in both theoretical terms and in terms of political action and mobilisation. However, as argued above, Marxist theory and practice have recognised the complexity of subjectivity. Thus we would argue that the concept of decentred subjectivity is both correct and possesses useful explanatory power when we come to confront the question of declining 'class consciousness'. Having recognised the utility of this concept of 'decentreing' we challenge arguments and theories proclaiming 'the death of class', and those proclaiming that there is a qualitative equality, a sameness, between oppression and exploitation based on 'race', gender, and social class. Our contention is that of class exploitation is *fundamental* to capitalist economy, as opposed to the (admittedly near universal) sex or 'race' exploitation). We see social class exploitation as fundamental to the continuation of capitalism. Capitalism can (and may) survive with sex and 'race' equality—indeed, for neo-liberals, these are desirable attributes of an economy and education/training system—but to conceive of social class equality and the continuance of capitalism is a contradiction in terms.

This is not to trivialise the issue of identity and of identity politics, either in the micro-sphere of day to day personal existence, delight and dismissal, or in the macro-sphere of structural forms of positive and negative discrimination and positioning. However, we would wish to point out that the notion of an essential, unitary self was rejected, over a century and a half ago, by Marx in his sixth thesis on Feuerbach, 'But the human essence is no abstraction inherent in each single individual. In its reality it is the ensemble of the social relations' (Tucker, 1978 p. 145) Social class is clearly only one of a range of possible identifications and one which is, *on various occasions*, less immediately 'obvious' than, for example, those of gender or 'race' or religion. It is useful to compare the term 'worker' with 'man/woman', 'black/white', 'Muslim/ Christian/Jew/Non-believer', 'gay/straight' (not to mention partner/wife/ mother/daughter/son/father/husband) and its relatively abstract quality can become apparent. For many, though by no means all, people in today's society the first label (worker) describes something which they do—all the other labels, to a greater or lesser extent, describe that which they are.

However, for millions, the duality 'Worker/Boss' (or Worker/Guvner or Worker/Gaffer) is not at all abstract. Postmodernism stresses that we need to learn that a class identity is only one possible identity and that identification with it will frequently be hard-won. On other occasions it is a ready and automatic self-identifier. Where postmodernism must be resisted is by enabling and encouraging people to conceptualise in terms of class identities and identifications—and indeed by recognising that people *do* so both in their daily lives and, more specifically, at certain conjunctures (Cohen and Moody, 1998; Leys and Panitch, 1998). By postmodernism's own internal logic— class remains potentially a possible/valid identity (given that no identity is 'essential' and all are constructed). In systematically denigrating class and encouraging people to think in terms of other identifications, postmodernism is engaged in class struggle (at the level of ideas). Furthermore, it is engaged on the side of the more powerful classes—those who wish to obstruct the development of working class consciousness. In this respect postmodernism is, whatever its intentions and/or proclamations, objectively reactionary (Norris, 1992; Cole and Hill, 1995; 1996a; b; Cole, Hill & Rikowski, 1997). The absence of class in postmodern theory actively contributes to the ideological disarmament of the working class movement.

Social class analysis and education

To combat the ideological disarmament of the working class and of progressive political forces it is necessary for socialists within schools, further education colleges and universities and other higher education institutions to strive to reinscribe social class and social class awareness and consciousness wherever possible in the system, to address issues of educational 'structures' as well as of overall 'standards'. This means promoting comprehensive 3-19 education as well as addressing questions and patterns of teacher expectation. It demands critiquing and developing inclusive, critical and egalitarian curriculum content as well as paying attention to patterns and standards of academic attainment. It is not enough for the Blair 'New Labour' government to repeat and repeat the mantra of 'standards not structures' when it is those very structures which are divisive, competitive, anti-egalitarian, and hierarchicalising *and thereby* work towards penalising and suppressing the educational attainment of working class children and school students, whatever their gender and whatever their ethnicity.

Social class and education: what are the facts?

The stark relationship between social class and education success is shown in England and Wales by the annually published 'league tables' of schools and their assessment and examination results—in overall effect, a re-presenting the social map of England and Wales, the social map of each town and city. Some secondary schools manage a 98% pass rate for schools students to achieve five or more subject GCSE passes at grade C or above—other schools manage a 2% pass rate.

Schools play a major role in reproducing educational, social, cultural and economic inequality. Bowles and Gintis, in their *Correspondence Principle* suggests that,

> The educational system helps integrate youth into the economic system ... through a structural correspondence between its social relations and those of production. The structure of social relations in education not only inures the student to the discipline of the work

place, but develops the types of personal demeanour, modes of self-presentation, self-image, and social-class identifications which are the crucial ingredients of job adequacy. Specifically, the social relationships of education—the relationships between administrators and teachers, teachers and students, students and students, and students and their work—replicate the hierarchical division of labor ... By attuning young people to a set of social relationships similar to those of the work place, schooling attempts to gear the development of personal needs to its requirements ... Different levels of education feed workers into different levels within the occupational structure. (Bowles and Gintis, 1976, cited in Cole (ed.), 1988a pp. 2-3)[15]

For Bowles and Gintis, *pace* the need to incorporate a selection of the most able into supervisory and some leadership levels in the state and economic apparatuses, working class failure, the reproduction of the economic, social, cultural and ideological status quo is the *raison d'etre* of the capitalist system of schooling.

The work of Bowles and Gintis, as with the other 'Reproduction Theorists' such as Althusser and Bourdieu, has been the subject of a considerable debate, since the publication of *Schooling in Capitalist America* in 1976, most of it from within a Marxist perspective.[16] One of the main critiques has been the seeming lack of space for resistance to the reproduction of the capitalist system as described by Bowles and Gintis. Although Marxist in intent, and even though Bowles and Gintis do provide a chapter on how to resist and ultimately replace capitalism by socialism, their theoretical line of argument, has been widely criticised as functional in effect, in the way it centralises the 'inevitable' reproduction of the capitalist system within education.

However for neo-Marxists critical of reproduction theory as well as those such as Cole and Hill in the late 1990s who consider the neo-Marxist pendulum has swung too far in the Culturalist direction and too far away from the Structuralist (Hill and Cole, 1995; Cole and Hill, 1996b; Cole, Hill and Rikowski, 1997; Hill, 1999a, b, c). there has remained an acute awareness of 'what schools do to working class kids'. Individuals in classrooms and school corridors bring with them and exhibit different sets of linguistic and cultural competencies. As Giroux wrote in 1983 (in fact in his seminal critique of reproduction theory), individuals,

inherit by way of the class-located boundaries of their family. A child inherits from his or her family those sets of meanings, qualities of style, modes of thinking, and types of dispositions that are assigned a certain social value and status in accordance with what the dominant class(es) label as the most valued cultural capital. Schools play a particularly important role in legitimating and reproducing dominant cultural capital. They tend to legitimize certain forms of knowledge, ways of speaking, and ways of relating to the world that capitalize on the type of familiarity and skills that only certain students have received from their family backgrounds and class relations. Students whose families have only a tenuous connection to the dominant cultural capital are at a decided disadvantage. (Giroux, 1983, p. 268)

The school,

> takes children from every class at infant-school age, and then for years in which the child is most 'vulnerable', squeezed between the family state apparatus and the educational state apparatus, it drums into them, whether it uses new or old methods, a certain amount of 'know-how' wrapped in the ruling ideology in its pure state. (Althusser 1971, p. 147. See also Sarup's synopsis and critique of Althusser in Sarup, 1983; Giroux, 1983; Whitty, 1985; Cole, 1988a)

As Sarup summarises, 'in this system each mass of children ejected en route is practically provided with the ideology which suits the role it has to fulfil in class society (Sarup 1983, p. 13).[17]

It is worth noting that though the ISAs function predominantly by ideology, there is no such thing as a purely ideological apparatus; they also function secondarily by discipline, coercion, demotion or non-promotion, penalties and, ultimately, repression: they have a material base. Thus schools and colleges as well as churches, discipline not only their shepherds but also their flocks. It is no coincidence that Trade Union activists are often top of the list when school or college redundancies are about. Or that schools clinging to what Ofsted now regards as 'outdated' (mixed ability) methods are likely to be 'failed' at their Ofsted inspection. Or that schools, such as the Earl Marshall Comprehensive school in Sheffield can have its headteacher (Chris Searle) removed for refusing to stick to the National Curriculum (Searle, 1996, 1997).

A number of writers have stressed the role, actual and potential, of teachers and students resisting the reproduction of capitalism and agitating for progressive social change. Within this critique a number of writers (in particular Giroux, *passim* such as 1988; Giroux and McLaren, 1988; McLaren, *passim* such as 1998b; Hill, 1990; 1991a; 1994; 1997b) have developed the concept of teachers (and other cultural workers) as 'critical transformative intellectuals', using a neo-Gramscian understanding and model of critically using spaces to develop and reinforce counter-hegemonic ideologies, of developing class consciousness and an understanding and commitment to egalitarian change for social justice.[18]

Why class is still a classroom issue

In Britain Marxist analysis was, throughout the 1970s, 1980s and 1990s derided as 'neanderthal, as 'loony left', as Cold War style 'oldspeak'. But the same truths are ever new. As is the witch-hunting and suppression and sidelining of those who speak and act such Marxist/Radical Left analysis and commitment. The truths are that children and teenagers bring their social class backgrounds into school with them (as well as, of course, other aspects of their subjectivities). As such they tend to meet with socially differentiated—(i.e. social class related) teacher expectations. This is primarily through 'the hidden curriculum'—the values and attitudes and desired social and work behaviours that is expected of them. Teenagers attending Hackney Downs School in inner city London, or Ramsgate Secondary Modern in a rundown corner of Kent, or The Ridings Secondary School in Halifax, at the foot of the local 'league table' of secondary schools, tend to have different expectations, and labelling, and stereotyped work futures than those attending the selective London Oratory School or the most prestigious of private schools, Benenden or Eton.

As part of this social class based differentiation between schools via 'the hidden curriculum', there is ample evidence that the pedagogies—the teaching and learning methods used by teachers and pupils—varies according to the pupils' social class. Sally Brown, Sheila Riddell and Jill Duffield's numerous articles such as 'Classroom approaches to learning and teaching: the social class dimension' (1997) was based on following two classes in each of four schools through their first two years of secondary education, observing 204 lessons. Their findings were that children in the two working class schools spent between 3 and 6 per cent of their time in discussion compared with 17 to 25 per cent in the middle class schools. They observed that pupils in predominantly working class secondary schools appear to be given many more time consuming reading and writing tasks than children in middle class schools and have less opportunity for classroom discussions. Their two year study of four schools in a Scottish education authority demonstrated that teachers of English in the two middle-class schools were more likely to give a reading or writing assignment as homework leaving time in class for feedback and redrafting written work The long writing tasks were very much associated with control and the lack of discussion was, the writers suggested, also to do with teachers thinking that the children could not really manage to discuss things among themselves (see also Duffield, 1998a; b; c; Brown *et al.*, 1995).

Capitalist knowledge and the National Curriculum in England and Wales

The National Curriculum for schools in England and Wales has not been omitted from the concern to revamp school education in line with a capitalist society in decay (Hill, 1999a; see also Sarup, 1982:74).[19] Obviously, any curriculum that is enforced nationally takes autonomy away from potentially 'unreliable' teachers and by insisting on the prioritised inclusion of, for example Shakespeare and British history (Hill, 1999a) it may very well allow the exclusion of subjects viewed not only as non-utilitarian but potentially critical of the status quo. Hill notes that the opportunity has also been taken to influence the cultural content of the National Curriculum with the intention of reinforcing some ideological positions held by the Right such as testing, and the fetishising of "Standard English', a literary canon, 'traditional grammar' and spelling' (ibid p. 9). The National Curriculum asserts the centrality of particular definitions of 'national' culture—against the increasing tendencies to both *ethnic and social class pluralism* that were at work in schools. It is driven more, now, by a project of cultural homogeneity than by the rhetoric of equal opportunity. It is now more and more plainly the embodiment of a Conservative vision of a national culture (ibid p. 8).

Hill notes that an unashamedly culturally elitist view of the curriculum is clearly put forward by Nicholas Tate, the Government's chief curriculum adviser to both Conservative and 'New Labour' governments. In suggesting that schools must introduce their pupils to high culture, he regularly attacks 'cultural relativism' and warns that British heritage, and with it the notion of strong communities and shared values, is in danger of disintegrating unless teachers actively transmit it. Children should learn which works of art, music and literature are better than others. (The National Curriculum revision of 1995 already insists, for example, that children should read two Shakespeare plays before the age of 14 and learn mainly British history.)

At a conference in 1996 entitled *Curriculum, Culture and Society*, he proposed a series of 'big ideas' to clarify the purpose of the national curriculum. He proclaimed that the,

> fundamental purpose of the school curriculum is to transmit an appreciation of and commitment to the best of the culture we have inherited. We need a more active sense of education as preserving and transmitting, but in a way that is forward looking, the best of what we have inherited from the past. (Tate, quoted in Charter, 1996)

He challenged what he described as the growing trend towards multi-media study by saying books must remain the medium of the future. Other of the beliefs he set out were that the curriculum should be grounded in ancient Greece and Rome, Christianity and European civilisation, and that 'English English', should be taught, not 'some watered-down modern version'.[20]

Far from being a haven of diversity and creativity the educational system, from top to bottom, is now under tighter managerial control and assessment than it has been for many years with a strong concentration on business values and instrumental procedures, as evidenced, for example, by the British government's fascination with 'the School Effectiveness Movement,' a fairly mechanistic and management focused organisational perspective that concentrates on factors internal to the school and ignores questions of curriculum selection and social class intake into a school (Brown *et al.*, 1995; Chitty, 1997; Hatcher, 1998).

It remains to be seen whether, regardless of intentionality the changes implemented throughout the education system will tend to attenuate or diminish social inequalities. As far as the schooling system goes, Hill (1997a, 1999a) argues that, whilst the National Curriculum may have some positive influence on gender differences, the National Curriculum will 'increase social class differentiation' and indeed that this is an explicit aim (see also Whitty 1998, Whitty *et al.* 1998).

The changes in the organisation and content of the curriculum are, more or less, the *opposite* of what Apple has previously termed an 'advocacy' position on education.

Among the most important 'internal' stances would be that of support for student rights (and the democratic rights of teachers, oppressed groups and others). Since curriculum as a field has as one of its primary concerns the task of creating access to knowledge and tradition, especially those areas that have been victims of selective tradition, the question of a student's right to have free access to politically and culturally honest information and to public expression based on this cannot be divorced from our own pursuit of just educative environments (Apple, 1979, p. 163-4).

It is important to note that the relationship between the education system and wider social control is highly mediated and far from a mechanical response as envisaged by some the more rigid schemas of reproduction theory (Altbach, 1995 p. 235; Connell, 1995 p. 93). This is hardly surprising because, as Harris puts it:

> Eventually one has to face a realistic and unfortunately, pessimistic conclusion: education, as provided by capitalist liberal democracies,

will not change from providing structured systematic distortions of
reality by bringing people non-misrepresentative knowledge of the
world. (Harris, 1979 pp. 182-3)

As reasoning for this conclusion Harris lists two basic Marxist concerns:

> To begin with, education is an instrument of the state. Its job is to
> maintain and stabilise the social order ... second, change in education
> requires initial recognition that something is wrong followed by a long
> process of de-mystification; and it is difficult to imagine how either of
> these could occur. (ibid)

What Harris is attempting to combat here is the naïve view that education
is a 'thing in itself' somewhat autonomous from capitalist society with the
power of change, (an impetus also pertaining in some media studies). Education
is the handmaiden of capitalism and not vice versa. Far from recent changes
providing additional diversity and augmented opportunity for individual
fulfilment[21] the educational system across the spectrum has become
increasingly geared towards instrumental industrial interests. Particularly in
terms of access and student contextual choices, the educational system has
moved backwards. Of course, ruling class demands of attempting to maintain
an ideological hegemony ensure that the process of restricting access to
education and policing its content, a process which is anyway incrementally
protracted and thereby lacking strong moments of focus for oppositional
activity[22] means that there is an attempt to set an agenda of 'realism' and
developing an educational system fit for a capitalist twenty-first century.

Changes in the capitalist economy at the level of forces of production exhibit
resonances at the level of the relationships of production. Whilst these are
many and varied one of the most important for the education system is the
creation, due to technological innovations in the forces of production, of a
layer of the working class, particularly of male youth, who would have
previously gone into unskilled/semi-skilled manual work but who are simply
no longer needed.

This is nothing new. As long ago as 1982 some potential effects of youth
unemployment were noted regarding social control as work socialisation is
nullified:

> The problem of youth unemployment is connected with many fears
> that are not usually explicitly stated. There is, for example, an
> underlying fear of social and political unrest. First, could the young
> unemployed become so disaffected that they become a threat to existing
> authority structures ... There is an anxiety about future employability.

If young people begin to lose their 'motivation' their desire to be good, responsible workers, what is going to happen when jobs eventually become available? ... Could the culture of wagelessness amongst youth develop into *a refusal of all work*? (Sarup, 1982, p. 30)

Youth subcultures could form a 'cultural response, a form of resistance to the conditions young people face' (Sarup, 1982 p. 31). It is hardly very useful for the hard pressed teacher to threaten recalcitrant pupils with 'not getting the qualifications for a job' when the lived experience of the pupil is one of unemployment. Here, education, at least in any formal sense, is simply irrelevant. Whilst for some this has led to a situation of demoralisation, drug dependency or crime, for others, albeit a small minority, there has developed an alternative lifestyle with a distinct critical edge as regards environmental and animal rights issues. These provide the (sometimes full-time) personnel for the various protests against projects such as new road building.

Non-work has, of necessity, been subverted into a virtue rather than a vice. The national 'Groundswell'[23] (anti)-organisation which acts as an information network between various claimants and solidarity groups has become a subject of governmental/intelligence agency hysteria not because it is any real threat to the state, but rather because the very existence of Groundswell is a *formal* recognition that an important terrain of the class struggle now is the attempt to defend the welfare state and the social wage. The extra-parliamentary nature and direct action orientation of Groundswell also puts it beyond the political pale, and it is undoubtedly the case that the state does not relish the co-operation of three major poitical strands, Anarchists, Marxists influenced by Antonio Negri,[24] and Stalinists or 'orthodox Marxists'.

'New Labour's' 'New Deal'—from Welfare to Work

Aware that repression, the traditional Conservative response, can only get one so far, 'New Labour' has been quick to attempt to assert hegemony over the unemployed. A 'windfall tax' on the recently privatised sector has provided the finance for Labour's Welfare to Work programme, of which the 'New Deal' is a core component. There *is* a level of repression inherent in New Deal as refusal to attend after a 'Gateway' period of interrogations will result, for the vast majority of people, in a total loss of Job Seekers Allowance. At a political-theoretical level the New Deal purports to assert a link between a low level of educational attainment and a low skills level by the workforce and unemployed, especially young unemployed, and low levels of labour productivity (Donnelly *et al.*, 1998, p. xi). However, even a cursory look at the practical options on offer under New Deal enables one to note a radical divorce between the supposed theoretical legitimations and the actual practice.[25]

The New Deal is almost totally about social control exemplified by the constant refrain that staying on the dole is not an option. Typically, New Labour's programme attempts to hide any contradiction between capital and labour. At the top end of the scale University education is geared to processing large numbers of people with limited resources, (this numerical factor itself helps to minimise the nominal level of unemployment), at the other end of the scale the etymological conflation simply reflects the ideological concern of achieving hegemony over a section of the working class via the tyranny of training.

> Clearly, under the prevailing economic conditions it is necessary for the ruling class to foster ideological control by means of an intensification of constant vocational training. Not only does this shift responsibility for unemployment onto the individual, it reinforces the alliance of 'class factions' necessary to maintain hegemonic control. (Davies, 1998, p. 11)

It does appear, then, that an orthodox Marxist view of education, 'crude' and 'instrumentalist' though it may be perceived, which emphasises it as a mechanism of social control and a considerable influence on the reproduction of capitalist relations of production is borne out by empirical developments.

In short, Marxism is *optimistic* regarding the possibility of change in the human condition. This is in stark contrast to some of the perpetrators of postmodernism who see no other possibility but to, 'survive amongst the remnants' (Cole and Hill, 1995, p. 171) and have by their own account, 'nothing positive to offer educational theory, or those attempting to effect radical change in education, or finally, those attempting to rethink educational politics' (Cole, Hill and Rikowski, 1997).

The divergence between postmodernism and those promulgating a Marxist perspective is simply a reconfiguration in different terms of a tension which has existed since the origins of mass education within capitalism.

> The educational system is a site of struggle, exemplifying the tension between those who wish to transform it as part of a revolutionary process and those for whom the school is largely an agency of social reproduction and control. (Sarup, 1982:74)

Postmodernism is the contemporary form in which a *pluralist* view of education and the state is expressed.

Conclusion: the way forward

So far, we have been very critical of the way in which schools and education systems are run. We would like to finish on a positive and creative note. We believe that students in schools, in further education and in higher education should be made aware of all the major possible ways that have been suggested to run local, national and international economies and societies. But we believe more than that. We are not proposing or representing a liberal pluralist or a postmodernist pluralist perspective (critique and policy programme) for education. The Marxist tradition challenges the restrictive ethos of current conservative developments in schools (whatever the name of the government in power) and replacing it with one that encourages rather than obstructs critical thinking, and, furthermore, one which sets out an analysis and programme based on an understanding of the salience of social class reproduction in capitalist schools (as well as recognising the specific oppressions of 'race', gender, sexuality and disability).

We are not suggesting that only Socialist/Marxist/Radical Left theories be given critical attention in schools. This would amount to propaganda, just as we believe that in Britain and the United States, and in capitalist systems in general, present curricula and hidden curricula systems amounts to systematic, longstanding, and depreciating bias. What we are suggesting is that schools should encourage critical thinking and critical reflection, based on and predicated on a meta-narrative of social justice and a morality and ethic of egalitarianism.

We share the concerns of tens of thousands of teachers, student teachers, and others involved in education, that, in terms of the consideration of alternatives, and in terms of the development of 'critical thinking'.[26] British schooling, and, indeed, further and higher education is in danger of being 'dumbed down'. Although there are some differences in policy, we see New Labour's education policy as being essentially the same as that of the Conservative government.

At present, the ongoing education revolution in England and Wales[27] initiated by Margaret Thatcher and continued with a vengeance by 'New Labour' (Cole and Hill, 1997; Hatcher, 1998; Whitty, 1998; see also Hall, 1998; Hobsbawm, 1998, Jacques, 1998 for a wider analysis) accords very much with the theoretical tenets of functionalism, not only in terms of educational policy (globalised capitalism is taken as given and schools and teachers are required to function efficiently to prepare pupils/students for their future roles in the division of labour in capitalist Britain) (Cole, 1998), but also in terms of content (again the free market economy is taken as given and debate about alternatives is stifled). Through the hidden curriculum, via the expectations of teachers and other school staff, by the respective roles of staff in the schools, schooling reflects and reinforces the social class hierarchy of the wider society.

As Hill and Cole (1999a, b) suggest, schools, or other parts of the education system, do not have to be places where students are encouraged to think uncritically and uni-dimensionally. Schools, and further and higher education can and should be arenas for the encouragement of critical thought, where young people engage with a number of ways of interpreting the world, not just the dominant forms. We are doing young people and societal futures a serious disservice if, through our teaching, market capitalism, with its hierarchies of social class, of gender, of 'race' and ethnicity, of able-bodied and able-mindedness, and of sexuality is presented as God-given, natural and uncontested; if, for example, possible alternative systems, such as socialism (e.g. 'state interventionist', on the one hand, and 'democratic workers' control', on the other) are not fully addressed, then school students are being denied an effective, meaningful choice—with alternative social, political and economic systems being, in effect, *hidden from history*. All students have a right to know that market capitalism is simply one way, albeit globally the dominant one, of running economies, nationally and globally. In order to begin to understand the changes occurring in industry and in the economy and society in general in any meaningful way, students need a thorough awareness of the significance—conceptually, empirically and programmatically—of social class.

Acknowledgement

This is to acknowledge with thanks the comments on various drafts of this chapter by Mike Cole, Jane Kelly, David Limond, Jane Martin, Ann Monroe, Glenn Rikowski and Tim Waller.

Notes

1.   For expositions of 'The Third Way' in politics, 'beyond socialism and capitalism' see Blair, 1998; Giddens, 1998. For critical commentaries, see Cole and Hill, 1997; Cole, 1998; Hall, 1998; Hobsbawm, 1998; Jacques, 1998, Hill (ed.), forthcoming, 2000. The journal *Education and Social Justice* and the education magazine *Forum for Comprehensive Education* regularly set out socialist critiques of New Labour's 'Third Way'.

2.   Most of this change was caused by the rise in unemployment. The unemployed in the 1970s averaged around 700,000; in the 1980s and 1990s there have rarely been less than two and a half million of them and on the old basis of calculation over 3 million—nearly 15% of the workforce. More than a million of those registered for work have been without work for over a year. Even among those employed,

some 13 million, over 60% of the workforce, receive pay that is below half the national average, the average being pulled up by the smaller number above them, but with much higher incomes

David Brindle, writing in *The Guardian,* in October 1998, reporting on the Department of Social Security figures for Households Below Average Income, noted that on average incomes since 1979 (the election of the first Thatcher government) had grown by 44 per cent after allowing for housing costs, but that the highest tenth of earners have enjoyed an increase of 70 per cent. By contrast, the poorest tenth of the population have suffered a cut in real income of 9 per cent (Brindle, 1998).

3.   Cole and Hill, 1995; 1996a; b; Hill and Cole, 1996; Cole, Hill and Rikowski, 1997; Rikowski, 1996; Cole and Hill in this volume; Kelly in this volume; McLaren and Farahmandpur, in this volume.

4.   See also the criticism of Postmodern Feminism and some of its leading writers such as Patti Lather, Valerie Walkerdine and Judith Butler in Cole and Hill, 1995; 1996a; b; Hill and Cole, 1996 and Cole and Hill in this volume. See also McLaren and Farahmandpur in this volume, with reference to United States feminist critics of postmodern feminism, and Jane Kelly's chapter in this volume.

5.   Aijaz Ahmad's *In Theory* (1992) offers a cogent analysis of this particular postmodernist aporia, see in particular his 'Introduction' and opening chapter.

6.   Caution, however, needs to be exercised regarding the veracity of this claim. For example 'the proportion of [British] voters believing there is a 'class struggle' in Britain rose from around 48% in the early 1964 to 81% in the 1995, according to Gallup' (Deer 1998). Similarly a *New York Times* poll in 1996 'found that 55% of Americans now defined themselves as working class' (Leys and Panitch, 1998, p. 20-21).

7.   It is pertinent to note that in the USA, often given as an example of a nation with a proletariat who have a low level of class consciousness, that a major successful strike by the Teamsters at United Parcel Services in 1997 won permanent status for many temporary staff. In mid-1998, the most significant strike to hit General Motors since the Great Flint Sit Down Strike of 1936-1937 took place under the auspices of the United Auto Workers union bringing one of the world's largest corporations to a standstill. Coverage, of these not insignificant events, in the British media has been absolutely minimal (*Workers Vanguard,* passim.). See Cohen and Moody 1998 for an analytical description of these struggles.

8.   The Left press in Britain has catalogued and highlighted such struggles on a weekly basis. *Militant* (now *The Socialist*), *Socialist Worker*, and *Tribune* throughout the period have been the highest circulation socialist weeklies, and the (formerly Soviet subsidised) *Morning Star* the only socialist daily newspaper.

9.   In the words of Harman/Socialist Worker,

the early and mid 1980s were the grimmest years the working class movement had known since the 1930s. The Thatcher government introduced new anti-union laws, allowed the recession to destroy about a third of manufacturing jobs until the real level of unemployment was close to four million, began to slash social benefits, and began a carefully thought out strategy of isolating and then defeating key sections of workers—first the steel workers, then the rail workers, then the miners, then the printers (1993, p. 177-178).

10.   For a left description and analysis of these struggles see Livingstone, 1987; Hatton, 1988; Taaffe and Mulhearn, 1988; Harman/Socialist Worker, 1993; Benn, 1996; Cliff and Gluckstein, 1986; Wright and Carter, 1997. Tony Cliff, Donny Gluckstein and Chris Harman are leading members of the Trotskyist 'Socialist Workers Party', Derek Hatton, Peter Taaffe and Tony Mulhearn were leading members of 'Militant' (renamed 'The Socialist Party' following its expulsion from the Labour Party in the late 1980s). It was, during the eighties, one of the two most significant Trotskyist groups in Britain, having two of its members elected as Members of parliament, controlling dozens of Constituency Labour Parties, and controlling Liverpool City Council through the mid 1980s. Tony Benn and Ken Livingstone can be depicted as two of the leaders of the democratic socialist (or 'hard') left through the 1980s and 1990s. They remain, at the time of writing, Labour MPs. Tony Wright and Matt Carter are 'Blairite' loyalists, supporting Blair's 'Third Way'.

11.   Our use of Althusserian concepts here does not imply an uncritical acceptance of his theoretical and party political trajectory and corpus of actions. The same applies to others cited in this chapter.

12.   Perspectivism is defined by the Pan *Dictionary of Philosophy* as, 'The view that the external world is to be interpreted through different alternative concepts and systems of beliefs and that there is no authoritative independent criterion for determining that one such system is more valid than another' (1979, p. 247).

13.   See Cole, Hill and Rikowski, 1997 and Rikowski 1996 for evidence of such alliances accepted by and participated in by the Radical and Marxist Left. See the account of Ken Livingstone, the 'hard left' leader of the Greater London Council in the 1980s, in Livingstone, 1987, *If Voting Changed Anything, they'd Abolish it.* Which is precisely what Margaret Thatcher did. She abolished the Greater London Council in March 1986. The Inner London Education Authority followed into oblivion as part of the Education Reform Act of 1988. What they had in common was that they were both enormously popular with Londoners, that they were well funded and mounted anti-Conservative government campaigns, and that they were both controlled by 'the hard left', the socialist wing of the Labour Party.

14.   The most obvious and profound consequence in Britain of a modification in the social composition of the workforce is the vast numerical diminution of the manual working class in line with the collapse of manufacturing industries such as steel, shipbuilding and coal—the proletariat, and the substantial increase in the professional and managerial strata. In making this internal distinction it is important to note that the designation of 'proletarian' identifies only that section of the working class who are *directly* involved in the production of surplus value. Members of the proletariat are by definition part of the working class whilst most working class people in Britain are no longer proletarians (Gordon, 1995, p. 36).

There are manifestly different layers, or strata among the working classes. Skilled workers, (if in work, and particularly in full-time, long-term work), in general have a higher standard of living than semi-skilled or unskilled, or unemployed workers. Their weekly and annual income is likely to be considerably higher. And their wealth is likely to be higher. They are more likely, for example to have equity, or surplus value, on an owner-occupied home. In contrast, poorer families, in poorer sections of the working class, may have no wealth whatsoever, and are far more likely to live in private rented accommodation or in Council housing.

Another important 'internal' class distinction, and one which is inevitable as many workers no longer directly produce surplus value is the growth of a professional and managerial stratum. That is those who are 'between capital and labour' in the sense that whilst being entirely dependent on capital, often in the shape of the national or local state, they exercise *supervisory functions* over the working class (Walker, 1979:5; *Subversion,* 1998). Examples of this category would be social workers, teachers, lecturers in further and higher education, probation officers, Employment Service workers and so forth. Many of them have a consciousness of status in which they place themselves above other, especially manual, sectors of the working class. (Indeed, the Ehrenreich's talk of a professional and managerial *class,* (PMC) (Walker, 1979, p. 5).) Some, of course, though not many, retain a working class consciousness, family, social and political affiliations while, *pace* casualisation and proletarianisation of many managerial and professional jobs, at the same time benefiting from superior income, conditions of work, and wealth. Of course, whilst class positional location might allow one to make broad generalisations it does not automatically determine individual consciousness and activity. For example, workers on a temporary contract can do the work on a minimalist basis and get out, or attempt to curry favour with management as being 'reliable' in the hope of being offered secure employment.

15.   It should be mentioned that since the publication of *Schooling in Capitalist America,* Bowles and Gintis have moved their position theoretically from revolutionary socialism to what they describe as post-liberal democracy (see, for example Bowles and Gintis, 1986; for a discussion, see Cole, 1988).

16.   See for example, in the USA, Apple *passim* e.g. 1993, Giroux *passim* during the 1980s; in Britain, Sarup *passim.* See also, in North America, Shor (1986); Liston, (1988); McLaren, (1998a), and in Britain, Cole, (1988a, b); Hill, (1990a); Livingstone (1997); Rikowski (1996); Cole, Hill and Rikowski, (1997).

17.   See note 11 on Althusser above.

18.   See Cole, Hill and Shan, 1997; Hill and Cole, 1999 for detail on how all curricular subjects can be used for egalitarian purposes and used to reinscribe class within the curriculum. See also the two Hillcole Group books, Hillcole Group 1991; 1997. The Fall 1998 issue of *Education Theory* comprises a neo-Marxist justification of Marxist educational analysis together with a critique of postmodernism by Peter McLaren. The remainder of the issue is taken up with attacks on his argument by, for example, Patti Lather, Gert Biesta, Wendy Kohli and Ilan Gur-Ze'ev. Kelly, Cole and Hill mount a critical defence of McLaren's position in Kelly *et al.,* 1999.

19.   Whilst people still do think that social goals can be won within capitalism, and to some extent and for some individuals they can, the long-term social prognosis

for capitalism is decay. By 'decay' in this sense is meant economic decline with the corollaries of persistent unemployment, an increase in 'flexible' working conditions, cuts in the social wage which impact disproportionately on the poorer sections of the population, increasingly repressive measures to maintain social control, the increasing militarisation of society, a gradual degradation in the level of popular culture leading to the paradox of mass ignorance in an information rich society.

20.   Tate continued,

> The final big idea is that we should aim to develop in young people a sense that some works of art, music, literature or architecture are more valuable than others ... by the post-modern view there are no differences in value between, say, Schubert's *Ave Maria* and the latest Blur release, or between Milton and Mills & Boon ... The final big idea therefore is that a key purpose of the curriculum is to introduce young people to some of the characteristics of what traditionally has been known as 'high culture', the pursuit of knowledge for its own sake. I am not saying that young people should spend all their time studying Jane Austen and Shakespeare or listening to Bach and Mozart. What I am suggesting is that we, their educators, should give these things their proper value as, in the words of Matthew Arnold, 'the best that has been known and thought' (Tate, quoted in Charter, 1996).

21.   A fulfilment which in some cases can be profound:

> When I was paroled in 1978, the Prison Department described me as one of the most remarkable cases of 'conversion' that it had ever witnessed. From recapture until release I did virtually nothing except study—through 'O' and 'A' levels, a Social Science Certificate, a sociology degree. I was paroled, in fact, to take up a place at Leicester University to continue with the post-graduate degree, an M.Phil. which I'd begun a year earlier'. (McVicar, 1979, p. 205)

22.   Which does not mean that there have not been protests regarding such impositions as cutting student grants or implementing tuition fees for Higher Education, but, to some extent, these have had an air of ritualism rather than real expectation of even forcing concessions. There is no alternative, 'TINA', seems to be as powerful an ideological tool, that is, pragmatic acceptance, for 'New Labour' as it was under the Thatcher regime.

23.   Groundswell is a national network of heterogeneous local groups, claimants groups, anti-Jobseekers Allowance campaigns, against, for example, poverty pay, all of which retain their autonomy, but can also run campaigns via the network. Marxist groups such as the Socialist Workers Party and the Socialist Party (formerly Militant) have also a long history of organising local and national campaigns.

24.   Negri was remarkably prescient in identifying the 'social wage' provided by the welfare state as an increasingly important terrain of struggle for the working class. As early as 1975 his, 'The State and Public Spending' essay provided a critique of the Italian 'Historic Compromise'—the formal co-habitation with the bourgeoisie of the Communist Party.

25.   Apart from self-employment which was added to the New Deal at a very late stage there are four options:

- A subsidised job. Depending on the hours worked the employer will receive from £40 to £60 weekly. This must be every capitalists dream: they receive payment for allowing a worker to work for them! (Donnelly *et al*, p. 53);
- Environmental task force. This is the heavy manual work option on the New Deal and past projects (on the Project Work pilots) included tree planting, restoring canal towpaths, etc. Employers are to be encouraged to pay a wage but if not the unemployed worker, (if that is not a contradiction in terms), will receive just over £15 weekly in addition to benefit plus some travelling expenses (Donnelly *et al.*, 1998, p. 60-67). Essentially the unemployed person will be doing work that previously was carried out by volunteers concerned for the environment. The whole notion of 'volunteer' is degraded;
- The Voluntary Sector Option. On Project Work this involved people working as sales assistants in various charity shops, Barnados, the British Heart Foundation etc., who obviously saw no contradiction between their concern for their particular clientele and their exploitation of British workers. The financial arrangements for this option are similar to the one immediately above and in similar manner it negates the very notion of altruistic behaviour inherent in some voluntary work. Both of these latter options emphasise control at work via a concentration on such aspects as teamwork and time management (Donnelly *et al.*, p. 61);
- Full-time education and training. This is an option, *but* only up to the extremely basic level of NVQ level 2 whatever the abilities or aspirations of the student. The intention here appears to be to train people to a standard where they may be of use in an operational capacity to capitalism without giving them any of the intellectual tools required to make a critical analysis of their situation. In reality there is no genuine educational opportunity available on the New Deal and an etymological transformation has been enacted where education is deliberately conflated with vocational training. There is no extra £15 available on the training option (Donnelly *et al.*, 1998, p. 50).

26.   For an elaboration of the concept and practice of 'critical thinking' see Zeichner and Liston, 1987; Hill 1991; 1994; 1997b; 1999b. See also the works of Giroux and of McLaren through the 1980s and 1990s such as Giroux, 1988; Giroux and McLaren, 1988; McLaren 1998b.

27.   By this we mean the establishment of a competitive market in schooling, the imposition of ever more prescriptive curriculum guidelines for the National Curriculum core subjects (Numeracy Hour and Literacy Hour) and for what 'New Labour' insists on emulating the Conservatives in calling 'Teacher Training' (rather than Teacher Education).

CHAPTER 7

Racism, Postmodernism and the Flight from Class
Jenny Bourne

In the same week that we learnt how, in Britain, young Stephen Lawrence's racist murderers had gone free because of the 'benign neglect' of the police force and how, in the US, a young black man was tied to the back of a truck and bounced to a dismembered death, Routledge announced the publication of a learned journal, *Interventions*, which would carry articles such as 'The veil: postcolonialism and the politics of dress'. In the US, the revamped *Social Identities: Journal for the study of race, nation and culture* advertised itself as 'a forum for contesting ideas and debates concerning the formations of, and transformations in, socially significant identities, their attendant forms of material exclusion and power, as well as the political and cultural possibilities opened up by these identifications'.

On the one hand, we have palpable, violent, crushing racism. On the other, an academy retreating further and further into esoteric sophistry and rarefied language. How has this massive gap between the impact of racism on the ground and its theorising developed?

Radicalising the study of race

The theorisation of race in Britain has always been highly contested—not least in the struggles, over a quarter of a century ago, to transform the Institute of Race Relations (IRR), from where I now write. That struggle at the IRR, examined in detail elsewhere (Sivanandan, 1974), was important for articulating, for the first time in Britain, a radical approach to 'race relations' and the role that academics could play. (Till then 'race relations' studies had been divided between trained anthropologists now studying 'natives' in a British habitat and a bevy of lay social analysts advising government on how to assimilate the said natives into British society (Bourne, 1980).) The impetus for transforming the production of knowledge at the IRR came from the radical Left, which was already challenging every aspect of learning in the universities, from curriculum to examination. Robin Jenkins, himself a researcher in the international unit of the IRR, in his address to the Race and Neo-imperialism Section of the British Sociological Association in January 1971, denounced the IRR's widely-acclaimed race relations bible, *Colour and Citizenship* (Rose *et al.*, 1972) as helping to make 'the power elite more powerful' and 'the subject (immigrant) population relatively more impotent and ignorant'. In future, when IRR's researchers came knocking on black people's doors, they should be told to 'fuck off' (Jenkins, 1971). Already, in 1970, two London School of Economics researchers had attacked the book's ideological bias. In particular, they condemned its 'social problem' framework, its emphasis on studying prejudiced attitudes, and its suggested solutions, which took as given an economic system based on exploitation in which blacks played the part of an oppressed international proletariat (McGreal and Corrigan, 1970).

'Bourgeois interpretations' of 'race relations' came increasingly under attack, and Marxists began to analyse racism itself within the overall context of capitalist accumulation in western economies. Marios Nikolinakos, professor of economics at the Free University in Berlin, looking at the position of migrant labour, declared that:

> the migratory mechanism of late capitalism in Western Europe is supported by an institutionalised system of discrimination which is anchored in legislation regarding foreigners and in inter-state agreements ... Discrimination raises the rate of exploitation. Capital succeeds in maximising surplus value through dividing the working class and granting privileges to a section of it. (Nikolinakos, 1975, p. 12)

A. Sivanandan, in the seminal *Race, class and the state*, produced the first analysis of the black presence in Britain in terms of Britain's labour needs, on the one hand, and the cost of social control, on the other. He also explained how immigration laws, by turning black people into second-class citizens, had put the state's imprimatur on racism, and how administrative edicts and court rulings, taking their cue from such laws, helped to *institutionalise* racism (Sivanandan, 1976).

The impetus to change race theory might have come from 'traditional' Marxist academics and those who, like Nikolinakos and Sivanandan, were strongly influenced by militant trade union organising among Europe's migrant workers[1] but they would have made little impact had they not resonated with the immediate experiences of black working-class communities in Britain. Police brutality, Paki-bashing, ESN-schooling, criminalisation of young people were everyday occurrences for black families. Yet the old-school race academics and the IRR 'experts', prompted by government concerns, continued researching on how 'they' could be taught to 'adjust' or be made to 'disperse'.[2] And it is in that context that the battle to transform the IRR in 1972 by rank and file staff became significant: it fired the first broadside against institutional racism and declared that racism, not race relations, was the field of study. It was not black people who should be examined, but white society; it was not a question of educating blacks and whites for integration, but of fighting institutional racism, and that was not about changing attitudes but taking on state power.

The IRR's struggle and change had a salutary effect on the academy. Gone was the genteel 'let's hold a coffee-morning' approach to racial understanding; gone the psychological tolerance scales and attitude surveys; gone the innocence that social scientists were somehow objective and impartial. Academics had been put on their mettle, and those on the Left, seeing how racism affected black people's lives, decided to fight that racism both as individuals and as academics.[3]

That is where we were in the mid-1970s. But many of today's academics, influenced by post-structuralism and postmodernism, would take issue with most of the central themes of the last three paragraphs. First, they would probably contest the concept of institutional racism, putting *racialised discourse* in its place as the key concept of study. Second, they would object to the term black people (because it is 'essentialist') and replace it with *ethnic identities*. Third, they would consider the idea of engaging in a political fight against racism *passé*. Fourth, they would object to the use of the term anti-racism and indeed the anti-racist project, calling instead for the acceptance of *difference*.

The whole of race thinking has been turned on its head—depoliticised, whilst keeping the trappings of politics. Every aspect of Left race theorising: the relationship of race to class, the fact of institutional racism, the importance of black struggle, the emphasis on the structural as opposed to the individual, has been overturned.

The path to postmodernism

Discontent with orthodox Left analyses, however, began long before postmodernism gained ascendancy. Already, in the 1970s, black activists were taking issue with a Marxism which relegated racism to the superstructure and demanded affiliation to a party which would deal with 'their' problems after the class war had been won.[4] At the same time, feminists (and, later, gay activists) were resisting the macho definition of blackness emanating from black political parties. The growth of the black feminist movement in Britain and networks like the Organisation of Women of Asian and African Descent (OWAAD) attested to the limitations to be found within both black theorising and black practice.

But what was significant then was that, by and large, critics who saw limitations in the orthodox Marxist position of subsuming race to class or the traditional black position of subsuming gender to race chose not to ditch Marxism or black struggle but to try to change or augment them. Hence, black activists tried to 'blacken' Marxism and, to some extent, managed to get changes (such as the fight against immigration controls) on to the Marxist agenda. And black feminists, while forming their own groupings to discuss their own issues, expressed, simultaneously, a commitment to the struggles of the black community as a whole[5] Marxism and black struggle had their discontents, but there was a kind of tacit understanding that contradictions were to be worked through.

The rise of cultural studies

Meanwhile, elsewhere in academia, cultural studies (which had, under the influences of Richard Hoggart and Raymond Williams, been created to extend the teaching of literature and root it in the popular) was, under the influence of Stuart Hall, beginning to examine the cultural inscape and impact of race and racism. It was no longer enough, to look at black workers in class terms or measure racism in terms of fascist activity. Racism was not just some kind of aberrant false-consciousness. The old model, with its economic base and cultural superstructure, was wanting. Racism was, as Gramsci had indicated in his treatment of ideology, in general, being structured into society culturally, and reproduced in everyday life. And the publication of Hall *et al. Policing the Crisis: mugging, the state and law and order* from the Centre for Cultural Studies (directed by Stuart Hall) signalled these changes in the study of racism. The book's aim was, in the words of its authors: 'to examine why and how the themes of *race, crime and youth*—condensed into the image of 'mugging'— come to serve as the articulator of the crisis' that society was slipping into (Hall *et al.*, 1978: viii). Why and how was a 'moral panic' being created and used by the state, around the imported concept of mugging, to police its crisis?

But if the early work of the Centre was a necessary corrective to those on the Left who continued to ignore the autonomy of the cultural superstructure, its later *oeuvres* tended to emphasise the cultural to the exclusion of everything else. And Hall himself, in his subsequent writings, seems to have emerged from the shadow of Gramsci and Althusser to come under the more dubious influence of Foucault, Derrida, Laclau, Lyotard *et al.* (you name it and he was there) to end up a fully blown post-Marxist in the vestibule of *New Times*, of which he himself was the supreme architect (Hall and Jacques, 1989).[6]

The hokum of New Times

Neither thesis, nor concept, nor ideology, *New Times* was a hall of mirrors, reflecting the moving picture show of the social and cultural upheavals of our time. Everything was in flux, making life uncertain, destroying old realities, creating new ones that were equally ephemeral. 'All that is solid melts into air' declared the New Timers, citing Marx in a last ditch attempt to sound radical, and went on to describe (not analyse) how 'our world is being remade by the shift from the old mass-producing Fordist economy to a new, more flexible post-Fordist order based on computers, information-technology and robotics' (Jacques, 1988)—i.e.: the technological revolution; the qualitative leap in the productive forces; and the economic imperative. But they had already thrown out 'economic determinism', cause and effect, analysis. Hence they juxtapose the social, cultural and economic changes in society without seeing them as interdependent and interactive. Hence the politics they arrive at is not structural, systemic, but cultural, personal, subjective. But then, according to Stuart Hall, 'all interests, including class ones are [now] culturally and ideologically defined' (Hall, 1988). And 'far from there being no resistance to the system, there has been a proliferation of new points of antagonism, new social movements of resistance organised around them and, consequently, a generalisation of 'politics' to spheres which the Left assumed to be apolitical: a politics of the family, of health, of food, of sexuality, of the body' (ibid.).

'Thatcherism in drag' is how A. Sivanandan characterised this complete break with class politics in his searing critique of New Times (Sivanandan, 1990). Noting the influences on Marxism of linguistics, semiotics, psychoanalysis, post-structuralism and deconstruction, he showed how this section of the 'Left', in throwing out the bath water of 'economic determinism' and 'class reductionism', had thrown out the baby of political struggle against capital and the state. In its stead, there was now a 'cultural politics' which challenged 'social blocs' in civil society.

The personal and the political

Eschewing collective political struggle opened the gates to a whole supermarket of different quasi-political brands of fashionable thinking on what used to be called racism. Prominent among the ideas being sold was that power itself was no longer to be conceptualised in terms of 'the state' or 'the ruling class' but as something that operated everywhere, 'horizontally as much as vertically, internally as well as externally' (Brunt, 1988). It could therefore be taken on at a 'multiplicity of points of resistance' which included creating new discourses (ibid.). Thus, politics was not something done 'out there' in meetings and parties but here in the person.

New Times also put its pseudo-left seal on the feminist construct that the personal is the political. When that maxim gained currency in the race field and came to inhere as holy script in the race policies of Left-wing councils, the results turned out to be disastrous. Racism, divorced from its institutional definition,[7] was no longer to do with practices, laws or state power, but with individuals: the personal is the political personalised power, personalised the enemy. The white person was the enemy of the black person. And all whites were racist. Thus official racism was the combination of power plus prejudice. 'Remove the prejudice and you remove the cutting edge of power; change the person and you change the office'.[8]

This personalising of racism (and the racism awareness training [RAT] classes that were set up to counter it) ended up by instilling guilt in white people and hampering anti-racist action.[9] Worse, where 'action' did take place, it was often at the level of language and discourse alone—taking issue with the term 'black' in nursery rhymes, having children's books revised, images reworked, streets renamed. And because such anti-racism was tokenistic and often imposed from above, it lent itself to pillorying by the Right-wing media, and provided the basis for the creation of the popular image of the loony Left and, later, for the creation of the bogey of political correctness (Murray, 1989; Bourne, 1995).

Identity is all

The 'personal is the political' also helped to shift the centre of gravity of struggle from the community and society to the individual. 'What has to be done?' was replaced by 'who am I?' as the blacks, feminists and gays, who had been part of the pressure groups in Left parties or in social movements campaigning for rights, turned to Identity Politics. Articulating one's identity changed from being a path to political action to being the political action itself (Bourne, 1987a). In the event, all kinds of people and groups claimed some kind of oppression, some kind of victim status which would allow them an in to an 'identity'.

And some, by purloining Derrida's concept of *differance* and other currents in the emergent postmodern critique of the Enlightenment emanating from French philosophers, posited 'difference' and 'otherness' to rationalise Identity Politics.[10] 'In these Postmodern times', wrote Pratibha Parmar, 'the question of identity has taken on colossal weight ... Being cast into the role of the Other, marginalised, discriminated against and too often invisible within the 'grand narratives' of European thought, black women in particular have fought to assert ... our sense of self.' (Parmar, 1990 p. 106). For Hall, 'the play of identity and difference which constructs racism ... fundamentally *displaces* many of our hitherto stable political categories (Hall, 1992 p. 255).

The politics of identity and difference were now being clearly used to justify the break with class politics and, indeed, with the concept of Left politics altogether. 'Identity is a key motif of post-consensus politics because the post-War vocabulary of Left and Right and centre ... has been shot to pieces,' asserted Kobena Mercer (Mercer, 1990 p. 50). 'This 'Left' is now so diverse', agreed

Jonathan Rutherford, 'that its constituent parts have no underlying shared logic, values or politics.' He went on, 'We can use the word difference as a motif for that uprooting of certainty. It represents an experience of change, transformation and hybridity' (Rutherford, 1990:10).

Reclaiming ethnicity

Although on the surface these writers appeared to be extending democracy by giving new groups a voice, what they were in fact holding out was nothing more than a debased pluralism. Theirs was a view of society which had no horizontal divisions of class but only vertical divisions of gender, sexuality, ethnicity, religion, etc.—and class did not enter into those gender or ethnicity divisions either.

But pluralism as a solution to the race problem had, in effect, been rejected both by the Black Power movement and the strugglers at the IRR in the 1970s. Black writers like Sivanandan had pointed to the destructive nature of state policies which encouraged the fragmentation of black politics with ethnic programmes and ethnic funding (Sivanandan, 1983). Reducing black people's problems to cultural or religious needs, was, he explained, to side-step both racism and poverty.

A rescue package was at hand for the Identity Politics school. In a talk on film at the ICA, London, in 1988, Stuart Hall explained how we need to recognise 'the end of the innocent notion of the essential black experience' and 'the extraordinary diversity of subjective positions, social experience and cultural identities which compose the category 'black'.' He predicted 'a renewed contestation over the meaning of the term 'ethnicity'.' A new conception of ethnicity would emerge which would be 'a new cultural politics which engages rather than suppresses *difference*.' Ethnicity needed to be 'decoupled' from the way it functioned in dominant discourse so that we could 'represent a non-coercive and a more diverse conception ... a positive conception of the ethnicity of the margins ... of the periphery ... a recognition that we all speak from a particular place, but of a particular history, out of a particular experience, a particular culture ...' (Hall, 1992:253-258).

Cultural difference was a world apart from cultural diversity, concurred Homi Bhabha, drawing on post-structuralist thinking, psychoanalytic concepts and a critique of Western universalism. What he was attempting, he explained to an interviewer, was 'to begin to see how the notion of the West itself, or Western culture, its liberalism and relativism—these very potent mythologies of 'progress'—also contain a cutting edge, a limit. With the notion of cultural difference, I try to place myself in that position of liminality, in that productive space of the construction of culture as difference, in the spirit of alterity or

otherness.' (Babha, 1990 p. 209). The obscurantist had succeeded the word-
smith.

Full-blown postmodernism

Writers like Hall and Bhabha, coming from cultural studies and literature,
might be expected to analyse race on a culturally rarefied level. But what is
surprising is that so many sociologists, including erstwhile serious Marxists,
have forsworn what might be called a political economy of race or racism in
favour of culturalist interpretations using postmodern concepts.[12]

One of the most full-blown defences of the shift can be found in the work
of sociologist Ali Rattansi. In *Race, culture and difference, a postmodern
anthology*, he edited with James Donald, they explain that '[g]etting to grips
with the dynamics of 'race', racism and anti-racism in Britain today means
studying an everchanging nexus of representation, discourse and power. And
that requires a critical return to the concept *culture* .[12] 'Critical', for them,
means taking in the impact of Saussurian semiotics, Althusserian and post-
Marxist theories of ideology, Lacanian psychoanalysis, Foucault's concern
with discourse and power, the British cultural studies school and 'various
strands of feminism'—in what appears to be a rerun of Stuart Hall's own
journey, but this time as farce. Rethinking culture means discarding 'the claims
and comforts' of concepts like community or 'the black experience' to
understand that 'race' and identity are 'inherently contestable social and
political categories'. According to Rattansi, the new thinkers have re-posed
the question 'in terms of cultural authority and individual agency' to require a
'careful analysis of contemporary political struggles over questions of
representation, symbolic boundary formation and identification'.

But he wants us to discard yet more of the old baggage. 'Racism', 'ethnicity',
'nationalism' are no longer part of 'a viable taxonomy'. For they belong to
that era of creating 'convincing, all-encompassing explanatory frameworks'.
Today, in postmodern times, there is a 'loss of confidence in the West's meta-
narratives'. Nor could he accept the European Enlightenment's confidence in
Reason with Progress that emanates from 'Western Man'. On the contrary,
racism is connected to the sub-conscious and the irrational. Besides, how can
we use the concepts of a modernity which has been associated with colonialism,
genocide, slavery and the Holocaust? If Enlightenment-derived values of
human universalism installed 'western man' as the norm, how can we use
these same tainted values to mobilise for human rights 'against racialized
discrimination, inequalities and violence?'

In a largely undigested and indigestible chapter of a book *on Racism,
Modernity and Identity*, which Rattansi again co-edited, this time with Sallie

Westwood, he romps through the range of authors—Bauman, Giddens, Foucault, Derrida, Laclau and Mouffe—who have helped him construct his postmodern frame. The language in which he introduces his chapter conveys some of the topics he covers as well as his convoluted approach:

> the 'postmodern' condition [is] a reflection on the nature and limits of Western modernity; an analysis of modernity which focuses on its typical dualities, for example the chronic disembedding and reinvention of traditions and collective identities; the marginalization of Western modernity's Others in the construction of Western identities; the impact of new forms of globalization; the decentring and de-essentialization of both subjects and the 'social'; an appreciation of temporality and spatiality as constitutive of identities and the 'social'; a consideration of the relation between the 'psychic and the 'social'; and an engagement with questions of sexuality and sexual difference. (Rattansi, 1994:4)

Taking issue with postmodernism

On difference and universalism

To mock the postmodernists for their pretentiousness, though, is not enough. The project reflects far more serious political dangers. Kenan Malik's first objection to the postmodernists rests on the fact that they use the very same assumptions as racists: the notion of difference and a hostility to equality. 'The postmodern critique of racial discourse flows out of its hostility to universalism and in its embrace of the particular and the relative, postmodernism embodies the same notions of difference as are contained in nineteenth-century Romantic racial theories'.[13] He acknowledges that it is important to see identities as socially constructed and not naturally given but, he explains, 'by insisting that society is inherently and irreducibly heterogeneous and diverse and by rejecting any idea of 'totality' that might allow us to see the commonalties or connections among heterogeneous and diverse elements, poststructuralist discourse has undermined its own capacity to challenge naturalistic explanations of difference.' Postmodernists deny the idea of an essential identity, stressing instead multiple social identities, which suggests that everything from colour, gender, to music or clothes are matters of style. Yet difference is not a coat you choose to put on. Different, for Malik, is what society has systematically made you, if you are black in Brixton or a Jew in Nazi Germany. Blackness is a social distinction, not a personal choice.

And without a human 'essence' how can one, asks Malik, call for equality between groups? Without some totalising universal principle of equality or racial justice, how can one respect the difference of others or ask them to respect one? Most critically then, the anti-essentialism of postmodernism disables the anti-racist project.

For Aijaz Ahmad, too, 'no struggle against racism or any kind of collective oppression is possible without some concept of universality' (Ahmad, 1997a). Contrary to what Rattansi says, Ahmad holds that, '[t]he fact that men have historically had more rights than women does not turn us against the concept of rights ... Anti-imperialism itself will be merely xenophobic if it breaks with the idea of universality' (ibid.). Asked how to grant recognition to human 'difference' without giving up the universal principles that used to underlie socialism, Ahmad concludes that, just because struggles 'of both universal and particular rights' have not produced socialism, people tend to note only what they failed to achieve. 'We also need to have memories of the traditions of mercy and the struggles for justice' if we are to affect a real reconciliation between the universal and the particular (Ahmad, 1997b).

Against culturalism

Sivanandan critiques postmodernism not so much in terms of the inward-looking self-referencing type of debate beloved of academics as in terms of the danger it spells to anti-racist practice. First, he takes issue with those intellectuals who, at a time when racism against the black working class is getting worse, have 'retreated into culturalism and ethnicity or, worse, fled into discourse and deconstruction and representation—as though to interpret the world is more important than to change it, as though changing the interpretation is all we could do to change the world'. And in an acerbic aside he adds: 'Marxists interpret the world in order to change it, postmodernists change the interpretation'.[14]

Second, Sivanandan shows how the emphasis on culturalism and ethnicism is in fact a retreat from the struggle against racism. Struggling *for* culture is not struggling *against* racism. Cultural politics 'does not have to confront economic power (including the state), only cultural power... And such power can be personal, individual. Hence the personal is the political: the fight for my blackness, for my Asian-ness, as they would call it, is also my fight against racism. Granted, but the converse is not necessarily true: the political is not necessarily personal: the fight against racism does not necessarily help my Asian-ness. The one is about cultural politics as it affects some sections of society, the other is about political culture as it affects the whole of society.'

Third, he shows how the postmodernists, by maintaining that experience itself is nothing till it is 'linguisised, discoursed, represented' remove the ordinary person's ability to act out of the authority of her/his experience and puts it in the hands of her/his discoursist interpreters. But then, for the postmodernists, 'there are only processes and provisionality and ever-changing perspectives through which subjects are 'constituted', identities are 'negotiated', problems 'represented'. By the same token, 'there is no racism in schools, only a 'racialisation process', no ghettos but a 'racialisation of space', no 'binary oppositions' such as old racism/new racism but all sorts of racisms feeding off and into each other...'

Fourth, Sivanandan argues, the postmodernist intellectuals, who are the real betrayers of the Left, blame modernity for having failed them. 'And to justify their betrayal [they] have created a whole new language of their own which allows them to appropriate struggle without engaging in it.'

Applied postmodernism in education

Fortunately, most postmodern theorists on race are confined to the lecture theatre and so rarely contaminate 'the real world'. But when their ideas become applied more widely, by constructing a kind of postmodern pedagogy, of which Phil Cohen is the foremost proponent, the results are dangerous.

Phil Cohen was, in the 1970s, a worker with disaffected youth and, in the 1980s, a researcher in cultural studies and anti-racist curricula at the Institute of Education. More recently, he has been instrumental in setting up a New Ethnicities Unit at the University of East London. Based in the heart of London's East End—an area unique in its mix of migrant communities and a breeding ground for fascist movements—the Unit boasts an interdisciplinary forum where 'cultures of racism and anti-racism can be investigated' with an emphasis on 'the question of identity and cultural empowerment'. Cohen himself, keened to the growing concerns in Europe about organised racism within youth cultures, has targeted the study of white working-class boys' attitudes—an area which till now has been relatively neglected in British research. And his ideas, straddling as they do, the academic postmodern race arena, cultural studies and the development of educational pedagogy,[15] are becoming increasingly fashionable both in education and youth work.

In brief, Cohen's position is that all types of educational anti-racism are: a) wrong because they rest on a *theory* of racism; and, b) will fail because they appeal to *reason*.

Inevitably, he rejects historical materialism because 'it has proved quite incapable of grasping the micro-foundation of racist ideologies' (Cohen, 1992:96) and 'offers a rationalist pedagogy which fails to engage with the structures of feeling and belief through which children relate to history and racism' (Cohen, 1991:38). And he is opposed to any attempt, Marxist or otherwise, to analyse society by making 'certain *a priori* assumptions about origins, causes, meaning and effect' which 'correspond to particular forms of experiences of racism' (Cohen, 1992 p. 83). He attacks the 'totalisation rule', substituting instead a rule of 'relative autonomy', where 'different sites or forms of racism have their own conditions of existence and articulation' (ibid p. 95). (I have no quarrel with that if, by it, he is saying what we all know: racism is not one-dimensional or static but complex and dynamic.) For 'the relationship between race, class and gender is not a fixed eternal correspondence' but 'one of shifting internal articulations between specific discourses and technologies of power, producing uneven and indeed contradictory effects' (Cohen, 1986). (Here he loses me, but I am left wondering at the sophistry that so readily transforms a common-or-garden platitude into high-faluting thought.)

There is no such thing as racism for Cohen, only racialised discourses. And how they are constructed is 'an integral part of the power they exercise in and through material practices of discrimination' (Cohen, 1992:68). Thus his work as an educationalist is to 'decode and deconstruct racist representations' and 'to elicit and give expression to cultural materials which resist or are repressed by racist discourses' (Cohen, 1986). Why, in fact, the whole of anti-racist education founders is because it starts from the premise that reason can overcome racist ideas.

Anti-racism, for Cohen, is a catch-all term which brings together everything he dislikes—whether it is tame multiculturalism which merely teaches children about cultures, religions, artefacts, mores, etc., or the kind of radical anti-racism set up in opposition to multiculturalism to situate racism in the British history of slavery, colonialism and imperialism.[16] Indeed, he goes out of his way to destroy the philosophical foundation of the type of anti-racist education that the Institute of Race Relations and others have battled for in schooling. He ignores the genesis of anti-racist education as a response to a biased curriculum which gave all children—black and white—a partial and sanitised view of history in which racism was divorced both from the black presence in Britain and Britain's history as a colonising power.

Cohen parodies attempts (by IRR and others) to write an account of how racism was written into exploitation and different modes of production, terming it a 'teleology of the oppressed'.[17] According to him, an account is being constructed around the oppressions faced by certain 'privileged' groups: Blacks, Irish, Jews. In other words, the producers of this kind of history, by picking their groups and their moments, write the inevitability of racism into history, producing a narrative of victimhood. His analogy is a mystery story which always has the same culprit. He mocks anti-racists in an article entitled, *It was racism what dunnit*, supposedly a real remark made to him by a white pupil.

On the other hand, when progressive writers—usually Marxist with a black perspective—try to redress this tale of eternal victimisation,[18] they are equally derided. These 'Roots Radicals', he claims, are just turning the 'teleology of the oppressed' inside out and upside down to construct an over-glorifying 'triumphalist narrative' of the fights against racism. (Cohen fails to see that such works of reclaiming black working-class history were necessary exercises for the struggle on the ground—and a counter, at the same time, to the dominant pedagogies which either wrote anti-colonial struggles and black people's fights out of working-class history or personalised history to individual black achievers.)

Cohen states that he is against such anti-racist narratives because of the teleology involved. Yet there is evidence that he is actually antagonistic to the emphasis on black history itself. In his early work, he queries why anti-black racism is privileged over anti-Semitism or anti-Irish racism. And he is emphatic that racist discourses do not have their roots in Britain's colonial and slave history but that 'its essential idioms are generated from within certain strategic discourses in British class society' and the codes of breeding which grew up (Cohen, 1988; 1991).

But Cohen's niggle, today, is reserved for any anti-racist education which attempts to reason young people out of their racism. For this is a practice that comes straight out of the eighteenth century's Enlightenment project, with its belief in the progress of 'Man' from barbarism to civilisation. Anti-racist education 'locked into a 'civilising mission', which is itself founded on a hidden curriculum of middle-class racism', will naturally be resisted by working-class pupils (Cohen, 1988 p. 2). And teachers on this mission commit another cardinal sin in trying to silence racism in the classroom. 'Resentments against the pedagogic form compound resistance to the ideological content' (Cohen, 1991:49). You cannot, he says, shut down racism 'by order'. (Although he does state that serious acts of racism cannot go unpunished, he is unclear on how a teacher is to distinguish between acts to be punished and those to be allowed, or prevent one slipping into the other, or how a teacher in a mixed classroom can prevent minority group children from feeling vulnerable and open to attack.)

Why does reason fail, punishment provoke? Because, says Cohen, racism thrives in the imagination and 'unless the inner workings of the racist imagination are properly understood there is little chance of challenging its 'common sense" (Cohen, 1988:2). We ignore at our peril, 'the deeper reaches of the racist imagination, the structures of feeling and phantasy which are embedded in even the most rationalised forms of racist argument and action' (Cohen, 1992 p. 82). It is 'the failure of humanist arguments' to 'engage with the subtle dialectics of the racist imagination', in Cohen's view, which keep young people one up on the anti-racist movement (Cohen, 1991:19).

The issue, therefore, is not about whether racist myths are true or not, but why an individual needs the myths. It is psychological fear over sexuality and identity, states Cohen, drawing on Foucault's work and various psychoanalytic theories, that leads the individual to find solace in racist ideas. And, today, the most insecure and identity-less is the white working-class male who 'has been written out of the script' by anti-racist teachers. Being a 'working-class racist is something to be' because it addresses 'a profound sense of dislocation'. For 'one of the more seductive ruses of racism, its secret pleasure principle, is the way it reduces ontological insecurity'.[19]

Cohen like others at the cultural end of the postmodern spectrum loves his tropes, puns and word-plays. Most of all, though, he relishes his iconoclasm. 'Look at me!' he seems to shout out of every article, 'I am really at the cutting edge of the *avant garde*.' But he is in fact one of the most defeatist of writers on racism. He has locked racism firmly in the subconscious where it cannot be reached by reasoned argument or rational analysis. He has taken racism from the structured part of society, where it could be combated, and located it solely in discourse, where it could be negotiated. He has not merely written morality out of the discussion, he has also ditched equality. And, for an anti-doctrinaire postmodernist, he is remarkably doctrinaire about his own 'theories'. He does not seem to care how many hostages he offers the enemy. Or, perhaps, he is the enemy. How else to explain his joining the New Right's cause in defining anti-racists as the cause of racism and white working-class boys as its true victims?

Postmodernism has come full circle. It had its roots in the genuine shortcomings of Marxism and Left politics, especially in relation to issues of race and gender. But, in the process of pulling the rug from beneath 'complacent certainties' and prying open 'some paranoid totalities', it has also surrendered to 'a politically paralysing scepticism, a flashy populism and a full-blooded moral relativism' (Eagleton, 1997 p. 24). It has pulled the rug from under itself too. There is no reason to resist racism. There is nothing to choose between its perpetrators and its opponents.

Notes

1.   The Pan-European Conference of Migrant Workers (which both Nikolinakos and Sivanandan helped to organise) was held in the Netherlands on 21 November 1974. See *Race and Class*, XVI (2) October 1974, pp. 207-213.

2.   Of the studies carried out by the domestic policy wing of the IRR in the early 1970s, one was called 'The Adjustment Study' and the second was on how to encourage the dispersal of black people to the New Towns.

3.   The influence of the IRR's struggle could be seen in the work of people like Robert Moore, Lee Bridges, Anne Dummett, John Downing *et al.*

4.   At this time numerous black papers and magazines such as *Samaj, Mukti, Black Struggle, Flame* emerged from the ranks of black socialists impatient with the blindness of the Left parties to the race issue. Socialist feminists were making similar critiques of the gender-blindness of Left parties and showing the way to new forms of organisation engendered by the women's movement. See, for example, *Beyond the fragments* (1979) written by Sheila Rowbotham, Lynne Segal and Hilary Wainwright.

5.   This dual consciousness can be seen in FOWAAD, the magazine of OWAAD and in Beverley Bryan *et al., The Heart of the Race.*

6.   As Ellen Meiksins Wood points out, 'Hall's theoretical statements are sufficiently ambiguous and his movements in an NTS [New True Socialism] direction are so often accompanied by qualifications and disclaimers that it is not always easy to know exactly where he stands.' (1986 p. 3, footnote).

7.   The fact that Metropolitan Commissioner Condon was able, during the Lawrence Inquiry of 1998, to deny institutionalised racism in his force (since that, he said, would be saying that all his officers were guilty of racism) is partly a legacy of the personalised definition of racism which was popularised during these times.

8.   A. Sivanandan, 'All that melts', op. cit. An example of the disastrous implementation of this as policy was the suspension of head teacher Maureen McGoldrick. See A. Sivanandan, 'Race, class and Brent', *Race and Class,* 29 (1) Summer 1987.

9.   See Jenny Bourne (1987b), Towards an anti-racist feminism (London: IRR) and A. Sivanandan, 'RAT and the degradation of black struggle' *Race and Class,* XXVI (4 April 1985).

10.   Derrida's *differance* seems to derive from the combination of the verbs to defer and to differ.

11.   This is not to say that I or others who write for the IRR's magazine, *Race and Class,* think that there is no place for examining aspects of racialised discourse or how things are represented. In fact, many of the articles already cited above from *Race and Class*—on race strategies, feminism, the media, anti-racism etc.—have been doing just that. But we examine discourse as just one arena where racism can be analysed. And we look for strategies that would change racism's material operations (which might well later be reflected in discourse). For the postmodernists, however, the emphasis is quite different. They seek to change, not the world, but the word. Stuart Hall, for example, draws attention to the way that 'scenarios of representation' are increasingly being given 'a formative, not merely an expressive, place in the constitution of social and political life.' (New Ethnicities in Ali Rattansi and James Donald (eds.) (1992), p. 254.)

12.   All quotations in this section are taken from Ali Rattansi and James Donald (eds.) (1992) Introduction. In *'Race', culture and difference* (London: Sage).

13.   All references to Malik's argument can be found in Kenan Malik, 'The mirror of race: postmodernism and the celebration of difference', in ed. Ellen Meiksins Wood and John Bellamy Foster, *In defense of history: Marxism and the postmodern agenda* (New York, *Monthly Review*, 1997). See also Kenan Malik, 'Universalism and difference: race and the postmodernists' in *Race and Class*, 37 (3) Jan-Mar 1996.

14.   All quotations in this section are taken from A. Sivanandan, 'La trahison des clercs', *New Statesman*, 14 July 1995, pp. 20-21.

15.   He even went so far as to publish a whole paper on how Althusser and Foucault might have deconstructed the East London football supporters' chant, 'We hate humans'. See *Monstrous Images, perverse reasons* (Cohen, 1991). London: Centre for Multicultural Education, University of London Institute of Education.

16.   'Just to learn about other people's cultures is not to learn about the racism of one's own. To learn about the racism of one's own culture, on the other hand, is to approach other cultures objectively,' explained A. Sivanandan in the introductions to two anti-racist educational books—*Roots of racism* (1982a) and *Patterns of racism* (1982b). London: IRR.

17.   See Cohen (1991), (1992).

18.   See, for example, Sivanandan (1982c) and Fryer (1984)

19.   Ibid. And for a longer critique of Cohen's tendency to focus on white racist youth as the new victims, see Liz Fekete, 'Let them eat cake', *Race and Class,* 39 (3) Jan-March 1998.

CHAPTER 8

Postmodernism and Feminism:
The Road to Nowhere.
Jane Kelly

Introduction

During the 1980s and 1990s feminism has been profoundly affected by postmodern and poststructuralist ideas and this influence is still pervasive today. In its turn Women's Studies has suffered from the same ideas. While it flourishes today in most academic institutions, it has developed during a period of the decline of the women's liberation movement, from which it had its inception. The deepening division between theory and practice in the 1980s has become solidified in this decade so that not only is most theory devoid of the experience of practice, but feminist campaigns and activities, while often militant in themselves, have been less and less informed by theory.

The growth in the influence of ideas described as postmodern has sidelined socialist and Marxist feminism, which in the 1970s, in a variety of forms, had dominated feminist thinking in Britain. Initially, with the shift to the right in Britain and the United States, especially after the election of Thatcher and Reagan, the attack on socialist feminism came from an influx of ideas contained in books from the United States which were essentialist in their framework. But although they used a radical feminist rhetoric—against pornography, against male-dominated language, against rape, for the celebration of motherhood—their politics was bourgeois.[1] Rather than basing themselves on mass campaigns and trying to build alliances with the organisations of the working class, as had to some degree happened in Britain in the 1970s, these writers, often using a civil rights agenda, were oriented towards the use of the state to enact legislation.[2]

With socialist feminism on the defensive in the 1980s, the ideas of these writers had some influence in Britain. But there were other changes in feminist theory too. Increasingly the writings of the French female psychoanalysts Luce Irigaray and Julia Kristeva, who had been students of Jacques Lacan, were adopted, along with the writings of Michel Foucault, Jacques Derrida, and Roland Barthes. These writers have stressed the instability of the subject, the negative entry of women into the conscious world, the decentredness of power which is located within the individual rather than emanating from the state, or recognisable authority, and the impossibility of attaining knowledge or of judging truth from falsity.

These pessimistic attacks on what they called Enlightenment thought, against the idea of any overarching theory by which the world could be understood, have had particular significance for feminism and Women's Studies. For Women's Studies was never just another academic discipline, it always crossed institutional boundaries and it always had implications for everyday life, and in particular how to change it. While it was set up as 'another' academic discipline, Women's Studies was and is different from others subjects like English Literature, French Studies, Art History, Maths or Physics. It was and is both broader in its remit—anything to do with women and the way we live—and much more dangerous—this can change your life! Women, especially mature returners to education, have found it a subject that they can bring all sorts of experiences to bear upon—work, motherhood, sexuality, race, class, trade unionism, abortion, etc. despite what they might see as a lack in their own formal education. So while it makes demands on women to generalise from and theorise their experiences, its evidence often rests on everyday life, on the real lives of women. In such a context the moves to postmodernity and poststructuralism in feminist theory have had profound consequences which are negative rather than positive.

One such consequence is the development of theoreticism, endemic in much postmodern writing, which makes the writing inaccessible and often unreadable. Another consequence is the lack of obvious connection between much of this theory and ordinary womens' lives, which makes it seem irrelevant.[3] Third, and most importantly, postmodernism's refusal to think about the whole world and its relationships, to be replaced by the contingent, the local, the specific, is thoroughly pessimistic when it comes to changing the lives of half the world's population—namely women.

The 1990s have seen various developments within feminism, from the post feminism of those who think the battles have been won to academic feminists who have built their careers out of an engagement with theory, increasingly devoid of any practice other than theory itself,[4] and especially the development of a wide range of positions which are more or less critical of, but place themselves within postmodernism. What all these have in common is a rejection of the concepts of socialist and Marxist feminism. In this piece I am not going to deal with the post-feminist agenda, nor with those feminists who adopt postmodernism hook, line and sinker; both of these are easy targets. Rather I want to concentrate on feminist writers who take a critical stance towards postmodernism, but who try to draw out from it what they regard as useful to a feminist analysis and discard what is not. What I hope to show is that by engaging with the terms of postmodernity, albeit critically, and rejecting the possibility of any overarching analysis of the oppression of women, these writers get caught up in circular arguments which tell us little of the sources of our oppression nor how and where to fight it. I believe such developments have done and continue to do a disservice to women, including those who study the issues through Women's Studies courses, many of whom are also fighting against their oppressions, but without the help of useful knowledge and theory.

Against those who say that Marxist and socialist theory is gender—and colour-blind, that it 'has used the generalising categories of production and class to delegitimise demands of women, black people, gays, lesbians, and others whose oppression cannot be reduced to economics', (Nicholson 1990 p. 11) I want to argue for a return to the ideas of socialism and Marxism, to reject the criticism that it ignores and is ignorant of the position of women (and other oppressed groups), in order to discuss the position of women today in Britain. I think it is important to relate the ideological offensive against women, carried out by the Tory Governments since 1979 and continued by New Labour, to the real position of women, at home and in the paid workforce and to sketch out some areas of fruitful campaigning activity for the development of feminism and women's liberation.

Theoretical chaos:
Postmodern feminism—the road to nowhere

The characteristic of many feminists who have rejected Marxism is to damn with faint praise. In her book, *Feminist Practice & Poststructuralist Theory*, Chris Weedon summarises the positions of Marxist feminism quite accurately. She points to its understanding of the historically specific aspects of oppression, including the interrelationship between different forms of oppression (capitalism, patriarchy, racism); its acknowledgement that the meaning of biology is also historical and social; its recognition that the psychic dimension too is historically produced and that Marxist feminists correctly argue that,

> ... while the family is a key site of all these issues, it cannot be seen in isolation from broader social relations of work, leisure and public life, all of which require transformation. (Weedon, 1987 p. 18)

Weedon then goes on to elaborate the implications for socialism of these understandings: the need to eliminate the sexual division of labour, to achieve reproductive rights, the freedom to define one's own sexuality, and so on. Later in the chapter she elaborates Marxism's contribution to an understanding of human consciousness,

...early Marxist writing decentred the sovereign, rational humanist
consciousness of liberal philosophy and economics, making
consciousness not the origin of social relations but their effect. As such,
consciousness is always historically and culturally specific ...
determined ultimately by the conflict of interests between capital and
labour. (Weedon, 1987 p. 27)

It is this linking of ideology with material interests that is, she argues, so
important for feminism, for it is where in struggle these material conditions
can be reproduced or transformed. So far so good. But then comes the
bombshell: she continues,

However, experience for Marxism as for poststructuralism, is a
linguistic construct. The dominant liberal account of the experience of
capitalist relations of production is one way among others of
interpreting the world and, for Marxism, a false one which helps
reproduce oppressive power relations by misrepresenting the real
relations of capitalist society. Marxist discourse is able to use the terms
'real' and 'false' because it has a concept of historical materialist *science*
which can offer a true explanation of capitalism, guaranteed by the
Marxist principle of the ultimate determining power of the relations of
production. Poststructuralist discourses reject the claim that scientific
theories can give access to the truth. (Weedon, 1987 p. 28)

So for Weedon, utilising an Althusserian Marxism informed by structuralism,
experience 'is a linguistic construct' and seeking 'truth' a belief in 'false
objectivity'.

Despite some rigorous critiques of Lacanian psychoanalysis, including the
writings of Irigaray and Kristeva which she says, 'offer little space for feminist
appropriation', (Weedon, 1987 p. 73) and a sharp attack on radical feminism
which she says fixes difference and 'rejects the need to engage politically',
(Weedon, 1987 p. 135) she argues in her last chapter 'Feminist Critical Practice',

From a feminist poststructuralist perspective the process of criticism
is infinite since meaning can never be finally fixed. Every act of reading
is a new production of meaning. Positions from which to read and the
discourses with which to read are in principle infinite and constantly
changing. At any particular historical moment, however, there is a finite
number of discourses in circulation, discourses which are in competition
for meaning. It is the conflict between these discourses which creates

the possibility of new ways of thinking and new forms of subjectivity. (Weedon, 1987 p. 139)

Although Weedon admits to a limit to the possible available meanings, it is the conflict between *discourses* which she proposes as the motor force of change. Quite how this happens except at a level of ideas and intellectual work is unclear. For, despite her understanding of Marxism, this is far from the Marxist concept of the class struggle as the motor of change. Her ideas are founded on the Althusserian notion that theory is a political practice in itself. This is a distortion of Marx for whom praxis—the unity of theory and practice— meant that actual political activity informs and is informed by theory in a dialectical relation, neither one has precedence or priority.

Weedon combines an Althusserian Marxism with the postmodern notion that 'truth' is only ever a momentary reading in a chain of meanings:

> Modes of subjectivity, like theories of society or versions of history, are temporary fixings in the on-going process in which any absolute meaning or truth is constantly deferred. (Weedon, 1987 p. 173)

This means that despite the final paragraph of her book which calls on women to adopt her poststructuralist framework and 'use it in the fight for change', (Weedon 1987 p 175) it can only be change at the level of the individual and ideas—in the end a liberal and idealist project.

While Weedon's work does not in the end use a classical Marxist method, despite her apparent understanding of its theories, many other postmodern feminist writers dismiss Marxism altogether by caricaturing it. In 'Feminism and the Politics of Postmodernism',[5] Linda Nicholson cites Lyotard in her rejection of what she terms 'foundationalist' philosophy, finding, 'problematic the requirement that philosophical claims be grounded in basic, or foundational, truths.' (Nicholson, 1994 p. 70). She continues, 'Marxism's inadequacies for feminism [are] a consequence of Marxism's reliance on a single category to explain social life across history and diverse culture ... it had become ... politically oppressive.' (Nicholson, 1994 p. 70). This single category is apparently production.

> Like many feminists, I had come to see that this focus on production within Marxism provided a crucial obstacle in Marxism's abilities to explain and to help remove many forms of women's oppression... While theoretically the term referred to any activity conducive to human reproduction, Marxists most frequently understood it in accord with its predominant meaning in capitalist societies: as an activity taking place outside the home in the form of wage labour. Such a use situated

oppression outside the home. Moreover, since the theory claimed to account for all aspects of social life, this use constructed Marxism as not only irrelevant to explaining important aspects of women's oppression but, indeed, as an obstacle in the attempt to develop such explanations. (Nicholson, 1994 p. 71)

While it may be true that some left wing currents have adopted such economistic and workerist politics in the past, including in Britain the Socialist Workers Party and the Socialist Party in its previous incarnation, the Militant, it is not good enough to reject a whole theory on the basis that you do not agree with some of its self-proclaimed proponents, who themselves have had only partial understandings of the ideas. Nicholson makes no reference to the writings of Engels[6] and so leaves one of the key texts of Marxism out of the account of what she calls 'oppressive Marxism'.

Engels' analysis of the family entails a belief that the equality of bourgeois marriage is like the equality between the bourgeoisie and the proletariat: a false 'equality' hiding a reality of oppression in which the woman is a proletarian and the man a bourgeois (Engels, 1978). Nor is it the case that later Marxists forgot the work of Marx and Engels on these questions. Among the members of the Bolshevik Party, Alexandra Kollontai had much to say about how to overcome women's oppression *after* the revolution and Trotsky too believed that socialism could not be achieved without the liberation of women from unpaid domestic labour. He wrote in 1924, 'In order to change the conditions of life, we must learn to see them through women's eyes', (Trotsky, 1973 p. 8) and in his polemic against the effects of the Stalinist counter-revolution on the family he writes:

> How man enslaved woman, how the exploiter subjected them both, how the toilers have attempted at the price of blood to free themselves from slavery and have only exchanged one chain for another—history tells us much about this. In essence, it tells us nothing else. But how in reality to free the child, the woman, and the human being? For that we have as yet no reliable models. All past historical experience, wholly negative, demands of the toilers at least and first of all an implacable distrust of all privileged and uncontrolled guardians. (Trotsky, 1973 p. 73)

Far from being 'gender-blind' Marxism has a long history of interest in, theories about and practical attempts at overcoming the oppression of women. It is true that there are problems with Engels' book on the family.[7] It fails to theorise the interrelationship between the spheres of production and reproduction, a relationship which ensures women's secondary entry into the labour market, and it underestimates capitalism's ability to structure women's oppression through production. He also underestimated the capacity for survival of the monogamous nuclear family amongst the working class. Nonetheless, his understanding of the bourgeois nuclear family both as the place of women's oppression and as a historically specific form and therefore open to change, were major insights into the recognition that women's oppression resulted not from biology but was (and is) a problem of history.

Nonetheless Marxism, along with any other so-called 'monocausal' theory is rejected by the majority of feminists who have adopted poststructuralist or postmodern positions. Thus Kate Nash in an article entitled 'The Feminist Production of Knowledge: Is Deconstruction a Practice for Women?' and Nancy Fraser and Linda Nicholson in 'Social Criticism Without Philosophy: An encounter between feminism and postmodernism',[8] both adopt, more or less critically, Lyotard's critique of the Grand Narratives of Enlightenment thought, the central motif of all postmodern writers.

In her argument for the usefulness of deconstructive theory for feminism, Nash says,

> ...the importance given to detail and context in the theory and method of deconstruction is readily appreciated by feminists at the moment because of the way we have come to distrust the grand monocausal theories of women's oppression. (Nash, 199 p. 68)

Fraser and Nicholson are more circumspect: while they reject, along with Lyotard and postmodernism, 'foundational' philosophy, they nonetheless want to retain some aspects of socio-theoretical analyses, and note that Lyotard,

> ... throws out the baby of large historical narrative with the bathwater of philosophical metanarrative and the baby of socio-theoretical analysis of large-scale inequalities with the bathwater of reductive Marxian class theory. (Nicholson, 1990 p. 25)

Both articles reject Marxism as the basis for 'socio-theoretical' analysis. Nash cites Michelle Barrett's *Women's Oppression Today* (1980) to confirm her statement that the attempts to ally feminism with Marxism failed because,

> ...the central categories of grand theories are simultaneously too abstract and too specific, and also too fixed in their theoretical framework, to allow the specific position of women to be considered. (Nash, 1994 p. 68)

Fraser and Nicholson paraphrase Lyotard in their caricature of Marxism. He presents it as one-dimensional and both historically and economically determinist,

> ... and most importantly, Marx's drama of the forward march of human productive capacities via class conflict culminating in proletarian revolution. (Nicholson, 1990 p. 22)

As in Nicholson's later article of 1994, Fraser and Nicholson do not here actually deal with Marxist theory *vis-à-vis* feminism, and their discussion of Lyotard's dismissal of it is critical only in so far as he refuses (or is unable) to replace the 'Marxian conception of capitalist society as a totality traversed by one major division and contradiction' by a 'better social theory' (Nicholson, 1990 p. 24). But they are caught in an impossible contradiction themselves for they recognise that,

> ... a phenomenon as pervasive and multifaceted as male dominance simply cannot be adequately grasped with the meagre critical resources to which they [the postmodernists] would limit us. (Nicholson, 1990 p. 26)

Indeed when trying to construct a social theory that is adequate to the task, they catalogue a range of sociological methods, producing an incoherent and contradictory list,

> ... an array of different methods and genres ... large narratives about changes in social organisation and ideology, empirical and socio-theoretical analyses of macrostructure and institutions, interactionist analyses of the micro-politics of everyday life, critical-hermeneutical and institutional analyses of cultural production, historically and culturally specific sociologies of gender ... The list could go on. (Nicholson, 1990 p. 26)

Mainly notable for its use of long words to disguise the appalling lack of understanding of the role and place of theory, this is a sort of 'pick an' mix' method, which might be all right when choosing sweets in Woolworths, but is hardly adequate when faced with the task of achieving the liberation of women. They seem to suggest that we can adopt one way of looking at the realm of institutions, another method to analyse everyday life (as if the two were not connected), and as for gender—'historically and culturally specific sociologies'—will be the means. We could use a bourgeois feminist framework to discuss legal rights, a radical feminist theory to analyse pornography and socialist feminism to look at women and work. Suitably postmodern in its variety it might be, but incoherent and chaotic if you are trying to link together different elements of women's oppression in order to understand them and so be in a position to develop strategies for change.

Both articles accept that feminism is, by its very nature, political and therefore inevitably about change, making strategic ideas a necessity. Yet both also adopt versions of postmodernism which, because of their adherence to the local, the contingent and the specific, disallow precisely that necessary strategic thought.

To overcome the contradiction between their recognition that feminism is political and their rejection of any totalising theory, the two articles adopt tactics which gloss over the problems. Having dismissed Marxism from the frame, Fraser and Nicholson continue by exposing what they call the essentialist and monocausal explanations of women's oppression in the work of Shulamith Firestone, Michelle Zimbalist Rosaldo, Nancy Chodorow, Carol Gilligan[9] (Nicholson, 1990 pp. 27-33). Equating essentialism with monocausality, they ignore the several different uses of this word available to feminism. Essentialism has traditionally been used to describe a radical feminist framework which proposes something *essentially* female about women, usually biologically determined, though sometimes developed as psychological characteristics. In British feminism it has nearly always been opposed by a social construction theory (sometimes socialist, sometimes Marxist)[10] which rejects biology as the source of oppression whilst recognising women's reproductive capacity as an element in the equation. In these articles, however, essentialism is used to describe any theory which has what Nash terms a 'monocausal' theory of women's oppression: as such she dumps Marxism, and presumably socialist feminism as well, in with it.

This is really a sleight of hand. All but one of the writers referred to by Fraser and Nicholson are radical feminists, but theirs' is an essentialism shot through with a strong dose of bourgeois politics, mostly because all are North American where bourgeois and radical feminism has been dominant, while socialist and Marxist feminism has always been weaker there than in Britain. But these articles neither prove nor disprove the redundancy of a socialist or Marxist feminist approach—it is just not dealt with.

The inconsistencies in the article by Fraser and Nicholson are revealed in the short final section, 'Towards a Postmodern Feminism'. The prescription of a theory which, '... would be explicitly historical, attuned to the cultural specificity of different societies and periods, and to that of different groups within societies and periods' (Nicholson,1990 p. 34) seems to me not at all at odds with a Marxist framework, which at its non-Stalinist best is both coherent, consistent and flexible, has different levels of analysis, and has been developed by many in this century to take account of changes which its originators could not have foreseen.

However the second part of this final section does rule out Marxism, for while the writers adopt terms such as class, like the 'movementist' politics[11] redolent of the 1980s and the slightly later 'identity'[12] politics of the 1990s, this is just one other category along with others such as 'gender', 'race', 'ethnicity', 'sexuality', none of which has any priority over any other. Moreover they seek a postmodern feminism which is,

> ...pragmatic and fallibilistic. It would tailor its methods and categories to the specific task at hand, using multiple categories when appropriate and forswearing the metaphysical comfort of a single 'feminist method' or 'feminist epistemology'. In short this theory would look more like a tapestry composed of threads of many different hues than one woven in a single colour. (Nicholson, 1990 p. 35)

The political purpose of such a postmodern feminism is unclear. They propose that it should be, 'a practice made up of a patchwork of overlapping alliances' which would find 'its theoretical expression in a postmodern-feminist form of critical inquiry' (Nicholson, 1990 p. 35). But who these alliances would be with and what 'postmodern-feminist critical enquiry' would be like (apart from more confused and confusing articles in academic journals) is not answered.

In some ways however this earlier article is a model of coherence compared with the one published in *Feminist Review* in the Summer of 1994. Although they concur on their rejection of Marxism, this later article by Kate Nash goes much further down the road of dismissing all possibility of objective knowledge, adopting a Derridian deconstruction theory and arguing for its compatibility with feminism. Although the writer tries to put both sides of the argument—for and against its usefulness—and recognises a tension between the two, it is clear she thinks this can be a productive tension. Describing deconstruction as 'anti-essentialist' she argues that,

> ...anti-essentialism, the demonstration of the inadequacy, incompletion and undecidable nature of every characterisation of 'woman', or even 'women', has been an important feature of second-wave feminism and deconstruction would seem to be closely related. (Nash, 1994 p. 75)

Apart from lumping together the feminism of the 1970s with that of the 1980s as 'second-wave feminism' as though those decades were identical,[13] such argumentation is clearly inadequate. Even if we accept the related interests of deconstruction which 'aims to show how every identity is contingent, provisional and incomplete' (Nash 1994 p. 75) with feminism as in the quote above, this only deals with half the problem, for what each may wish to do about this apparent collision of interest may be totally different. Indeed 'collision' is perhaps a clue to the whole sorry mess, for maybe deconstruction and feminism are colliding because they are coming from and going in two different directions! The 1970s feminist slogan 'the personal is political' did not imply that only personal experience was valid; on the contrary, it stressed the interconnectedness of the personal with the political. It was this tension that was so productive in developing an understanding of the causes of women's oppression and by inference an analysis of how to move forward against that oppression.

The acceptance by Nash and others of the theories of deconstruction, poststructuralism and postmodernism have been very damaging for feminism. Her uncritical adoption of Barthes' idea that 'texts and discourses always escape their authors' intentions' (Nash, 1994 p. 68) disregards the relation between theory and practice, which has been central for feminism in the past, and was based, sometimes unconsciously, on the method of historical materialism. Indeed the deepening division between theory and practice has been one of the most negative features of the 1980s and early 1990s—damaging both to feminist theory which has not been tested out in action, and to feminist campaigns and activities which have been less and less informed by theory.[14]

Moreover, her acceptance of Foucault's notion that knowledge, 'positions subjects within certain discourses' (Nash, 1994 p. 69) is always partial and incomplete and cannot be objective, leads her to deny the validity of anything feminists might say. Surely this is a worse option than the use of theories which women have had to fight to be included in.

> ... deconstruction emphasises how knowledge is *always* partial and incomplete, always produced from a particular perspective. In this way it helps confound a rigid distinction between subjective and objective knowledge and releases us from the burden of trying to show how knowledge produced from an overtly political position—feminism— is really *more objective* than (androcentric) research results achieved using neutral methods and theories. (Nash 1994 p. 69-70)

This is the theoretical equivalent of saying something and then laughing— 'don't listen to me, I'm only a woman'. In any case Marxists, better than most, are aware of the way writers and thinkers always come from a certain position or perspective which will influence what they argue—this understanding is by no means the prerogative of deconstruction.

Finally her use of the concept of rhetoric to defend her definition of knowledge tells us little,

> We can never have certain knowledge according to the theory of rhetoric but we can, and do, have good reasons for the beliefs we hold ... knowledge consists in having, at best, good reasons for holding the beliefs one holds about the world and, at least, no good reasons for giving them up. (Nash, 1994 p. 72)

This vague and woolly definition is followed in her next paragraph by an implicit negation of much of her earlier argument by assuming a *unified* feminism,

> As feminists, then, we need not scare ourselves with the prospect of falling into relativism; we have good reasons for preferring feminist to non or anti-feminist beliefs, for preferring one feminist definition of women to another and for whatever short or long-term political strategies we propose or support. (Nash, 1994 p. 73)

This use of 'we' not only confounds her own adoption of the strategy of the contingent and partial but also confuses the real political interests of and differences between feminists, precisely those expressed in different positions, bourgeois, radical, socialist and Marxist feminism. For these differences do matter. A bourgeois feminist analysis of and the answer to the changing patterns of women's (un)employment will not be the same as a radical feminist analysis and answer: and they will both differ from that proposed by socialists and Marxists.

Useful theory: Marxism, socialism and the liberation of women

In order to understand the situation of women in the here and now, the real lives of women, our role in society, our position in the family and in the labour market, we have to analyse these as a whole. Postmodern theory is incapable, by its very nature, of doing this. By contrast, Marxism and the method of historical materialism can start to explain how the different aspects of women's lives are connected together. It can show the ways in which the oppression of women (as well as other oppressed groups) is linked to the exploitation of the working class by capital; that the bourgeois nuclear family, the historically specific form most appropriate to capital's needs, is also the site of women's oppression. It reveals how women's position in the workforce is structured by her assumed role in the family. It can investigate the ways in which changes in the labour market and especially changes in the employment of women, responding to the needs of capital, are linked to an ideological offensive pursued by both Conservative and Labour Governments against women and their position in the family. And, most importantly, it can suggest the alliances that have to be forged, between women and between women and men to fight these oppressions as well as the issues on which these alliances will be brought together.

Any socialist or Marxist analysis will be based on the idea that there can be no socialism without the liberation of women and other oppressed groups, but also that there can be no such liberation without socialism. This basic premise was well understood in the 1970s, even if today it has been submerged by a welter of postmodern theory on, amongst other unhelpful notions, the unstable nature of female subjectivity. At that time there were links made by the women's liberation movement with trade unions and other working class organisations and these had an impact far beyond the ranks of women organised in the Women's Liberation Movement.

Traditionally the divisions between women and men in the working class have been used by capital to weaken any struggle against it, but the late 1960s and early 1970s brought changes. Women at Fords went on strike over equal pay, night cleaners went into battle over the right to join a trade union. These and other struggles gave birth to the Women's Liberation Movement in Britain. In 1972 miners' wives organised in support of the striking miners. In 1974 a media-orchestrated demonstration of wives of workers at the Cowley car plant in Oxford, arguing for a return to work of striking car workers, was defeated by an alliance between women from Oxford Trades Council, the Oxford socialist feminist movement, women working in the trim shop at Cowley and some wives of striking car workers, in a formation called 'Women in Support of the Union' (Thornett, 1998 pp. 38-55).

This type of alliance was evident again in the Miners' Strike of 1984-5, where socialist feminists worked in solidarity with the relations and friends of miners to sustain the strike. Moreover many of the tactics adopted by the Women Against Pit Closures groups had been learnt from feminists at Greenham Common in the early eighties in the peace camp against Cruise Missiles—tactics like non-violent direct action and sit-ins. More recently the Liverpool Dockers' strike (1995-98) was supported by a women's group, Women of the Waterfront, as was the Magnet Strike (1996-98). Socialist feminism has always understood that divisions in the working class are dangerous and lead to defeats. This has been learnt by women who do not see themselves first and foremost as feminists, but who have recognised the centrality of solidarity in the working class.

Here and now: women, work and the family

The alliances built in struggles like these were ultimately based on ideas rooted in Marxist theory and it is to this that I now want to turn. Marxism has analysed the intimate connections between women's position in society, in the family and in the paid workplace. Postmodernism, whether through lack of interest or the inadequacy of its theories, ignores analysis of these related issues. The exclusive interest in subjects cultural rather than directly political or economic, has meant that postmodern writers, including feminists, seem unaware of the major changes affecting the position of women at home and at work, as well as the population as a whole, and have little to say about the connected ideological offensive in relation to the role of women in the family as wives, mothers and sisters.

It is a commonplace that women's waged work is underpaid, in poor conditions and in a segregated labour market, a market that depends on the assumed skills derived from domestic labour—caring, cleaning, repetitive tasks. In addition, because looking after a family is seen as the central role carried out by women, part-time work with flexible patterns, including homeworking, is seen to appropriately fit in with domestic responsibilities.

Over the last fifteen years or so there have been major changes in the workforce which have affected all workplaces. A combination of the closure of much heavy industry and engineering, deskilling and the introduction of new technology, has led to a steep decline in traditional 'male' jobs in heavy industry such as engineering, steel, mining, etc. At the same time there has been an increase in traditional 'female' work. Women now make up around half the workforce in Britain, the highest percentage ever. But there has not been a straight swap of jobs between men and women—nearly one million skilled, industrial, unionised, male jobs have been lost, while women have gained a similar number, but mainly part-time, temporary, fixed contract jobs often in the service sector, with flexible work patterns and usually non-unionised.

This shift is evidenced by reports on the make-up of the labour market. According to *Labour Market Trends*, March 1997, 71 per cent of women between the ages of 16 and 59 were economically active at the start of 1996, of whom 44 per cent were working part-time (compared to 8 per cent of men). This represents 82 per cent of the 5.8 million people working part-time. In addition women's work is confined to several key sectors, just over half (52%) were working in three major occupational groups—clerical/secretarial, personal and protective services, and sales—areas where only 18 per cent of men worked.[15]

Along with the changes in the labour market there have been increasing cuts in the welfare state,[16] in provision for child care, in the National Health Service, in education, in community services for the old, the ill (including the mentally ill), the disabled, in social services. These cuts affect women twice over, first as workers in the caring professions and secondly as users. Where services have been closed down women have both lost their paid work and been left to pick up the pieces from a failing welfare state. It has been estimated that by the mid 1990s, 6.8 million people in Britain were carers for relatives or friends. Seventeen per cent of women are carers saving the state an estimated £24 million.

Alongside these structural changes in the workforce and in the state provision of welfare there has been an ideological offensive against women. The nuclear family, that contradictory place where love and intimacy flourish beside violence and dependency, has been promoted by all post-war British governments—indeed for Thatcher, the family was more important than society—in fact, for her, the latter did not exist. While less than 30 per cent of the population now live in such a nuclear family, it is still promoted as the ideal model, and anyone living a different lifestyle, especially if there are children involved, is castigated. Single parents (predominantly women) have been scapegoated for every social evil from petty crime to drug addiction, from truancy from school to low levels of literacy and numeracy. What began under the Conservative Governments has been continued by the Labour Government. The Child Support Act, while it did not attempt to 'glue' families back together, tried to force women to identify the father of their child so that the agency could force the father to pay for the child's upkeep, thus reducing state benefits.

How are we to understand this process? In the late 1970s several socialist feminists (Beechey, 1987 and Bruegel, 1986) adopted the Marxist concept of a Reserve Army of Labour to analyse the ways in which women were being used by capital. According to Marx, the reserve army of labour is a pool of the unemployed, especially young people and women, characterised by its capacity to depress wages, which through the threat of unemployment and competition in the labour market, enables capital to increase the rate of exploitation, and therefore the rate of profit. Marx notes the tendency of capital to substitute from this surplus labour the unskilled for the skilled, youth for adults and women for men.

Although initially used to analyse male unemployment, it seemed a useful concept to look at the way women had been historically used in the labour market, for example during the early years of industrialisation and in both world wars. It also goes some way to explaining why male trade unionists have seen women as a threat to their jobs—not simply because they were, and probably still are, inherently sexist towards women, but because they knew women could be used to undermine their wage levels and even take their jobs. This antagonism exacerbated existing gender divisions in the workforce to capital's advantage.

Moreover the whole process of women being drawn into and then expelled from the workforce, according to the needs of capital and industry, has happened in the context of a gradual increase of working women throughout the twentieth century: in 1918 women made up about 30 per cent of the labour force, while today it hovers around 50 per cent.[17] But as noted before women tend to work in different sectors to men. Despite that it does look as though women have been used as a reserve army in the last fifteen years or so. Not that they have been drawn into and then expelled from the workforce as happened during and after the second world war, but instead their cheaper labour has depressed wages and helped change working conditions.[18] Not only has there been a decrease of 3 per cent in the number of working men and a similar increase in the number of women, but the kinds of conditions and contracts of work women have traditionally had to suffer—part-time, flexible, unskilled with few fringe benefits—are increasingly being applied to male employment. Right across the labour market short-term, even zero-hours contracts, compulsory overtime, draconian work practices are being introduced. The percentage of men working part-time has doubled between 1986 and 1996 to 8 per cent, while the number of part-time women has gone up only 1 per cent in the same decade. Even more striking, the number of women in temporary jobs has increased by 23 per cent while the increase for men is 74 per cent. We can be sure not only that these figures are an underestimate, but that the trend is continuing, despite an upturn in the economy in the past eighteen months (Labour Market Trends 1997 p. 99).

But how is it possible to use women and their labour in this way? Why does it seem to have been relatively easy to remove women from 'male' jobs after 1945, when returning soldiers needed employment, even though women had spent the war years in munitions factories and heavy engineering plants? How has capital been able to use women to introduce widespread part-time and temporary work in the last ten years?

The answer lies in the fact that women, whatever their real position, are primarily seen as carers in the family and breadwinners only second. Although the term 'pin money' is now outmoded, the misconception that it described has not gone away. Despite the reality of women making up around half the workforce, their wages are a necessary component of the family income, and many families headed by single mothers, whether widowed or separated, the assumption remains that the woman's earnings are an addition; secondary to the main male wage.

To understand this it is useful to look again at Engels' writings on the family and women's role in it. To the centrality of production, Engels added the importance of reproduction, '...the decisive element of history is pre-eminently production and reproduction of life and its material requirements' (Engels, 1978 p. 4). Engels analysed the position of women within these two spheres separately, noting that the role of women within the bourgeois family was part of the private sphere of reproduction, whilst her entry into production, into the paid labour force, into the public sphere, was a precondition for her liberation; although this was not an inevitable process. Key to this understanding was that women who took on paid work outside the home would become increasingly financially independent, with the social and collective organisation experienced through paid work replacing her isolation within the family.

More recent writing on the subject by feminists (e.g. Beechey, 1987) has shown that these two spheres, production and reproduction, the private and the public, are in fact interconnected. It is precisely the position of women in the family, whose domestic labour reproduces the labour force, both daily and generationally, which determines her entry into paid labour. The concept of the 'family wage' adopted in the late nineteenth century by the bourgeoisie and supported by the male-dominated trade union movement, still today underpins gender divisions in the workforce. The cost of reproducing the woman is deemed to be included in the male wage, so that if a woman works that cost is deducted and she receives a lower wage.

All of these changes in work are having a profound effect on many aspects of our lives, both as women and as men, but the process also has contradictions for capital which we need to be able to analyse and understand in order to resist capitalism's logic. These contradictions include the conflict between the need to develop the forces of production including the paid labour of women with the private reproduction of labour power, including fulfilling the functions once carried out by the welfare state; the conflict between women's childbearing capacity and her role as wage labourer; and the potential conflict between the tendency to remove tasks of domestic labour such as cooking, laundering, sewing, education and health care, into the profit-making sector, thus drawing more women into the workforce. Furthermore there is an increasing mismatch between ideological assumptions about the nuclear family and lived reality. High levels of male unemployment paralleled by an increase of working women has led to some redistribution of domestic labour—men taking children to and from school is no longer an uncommon sight, especially in those areas devastated by de-industrialisation. The increased participation in the public world by women also means that as the isolation of domesticity is overcome women are more and more able to organise together and with men to fight for their rights (Vogel, 1983).

More specifically the increasing numbers of women in the workforce conflicts with cuts in the welfare state which depend on the unpaid work of women to replace these lost services. It is possible that once the kinds of jobs women have traditionally done have been accepted by men—including the poor conditions women have suffered—there will be attempts to cut back on women's work. The European Union Inter-Governmental Conference in Cardiff in June 1998 adopted a set of working conditions based on the flexibility achieved in Britain over the last ten years, the annualisation of hours being one example of the regulations which will become mandatory across Europe. This will give employers the right to impose working conditions on the whole workforce which so far mostly women have endured.

The response must not be to accept these changes and allow women to be forced back into the home to provide free labour to replace the welfare state. This suggests the areas of activities feminists should be developing. First of all it is important to recruit women into trade unions so that the existing gender divisions can be fought. Second, in order to facilitate women's paid work, we should campaign for free creches and nurseries, for both maternity and paternity leave and for women's reproductive rights. Third, we should be fighting against any cuts in the welfare state, to retain what are mainly female jobs and also to ensure that women are not forced into the role of unpaid carers.

Conclusion

These issues are distant indeed from the preoccupations of postmodernism. It may be interesting to debate how knowledge is always relative, how subjectivity is fragmented, how women's identities are formed from a multitude of different experiences, but while we do, the lives and working patterns of ordinary women and men (including those of the very people who are engaged in the debate) are radically changing and most of us remain ignorant of it. Without the use of a theory that can link together the different aspects of the lives of women, analyse and develop strategies to overcome elements of our oppression, we will remain commentators on the sidelines. Careers can be built from these commentaries, but progressive change will not happen. If feminism has at its core the understanding of the need for such change, then postmodernist theory has to be rejected in favour of more useful theory.

For Women's Studies as an academic subject, the actual lives of women, including working class women, have always been an impetus both to study itself and to the development of theories to understand oppression. Without that link between real experience and ways of understanding it—praxis—we are on the road to nowhere.

Acknowledgement

This chapter is indebted to the support of my companion David Packer. His knowledge of Marxism and its implications for a political practice are an inspiration.

Notes

1. Socialist feminism was never as strong in the United States as it was in Britain, which can partly be explained by the lack of a mass party of the working class and a less powerful trade union movement in the United States.
2. Anti-pornography campaigners Andrea Dworkin and Catherine McKinnon attempted to get states to legislate for what they called 'Porn-free zones'.
3. I am not arguing here against theory, but against theory for its own sake, rather than theory to make a difference, to change things.
4. This is based on the notion put forward by Louis Althusser, that theory is a practice in itself.
5. Nicholson, L. 'Feminism and the Politics of Postmodernism', in Ferguson, M.and Wicke, J. (1994).
6. Nor does he appear anywhere in Nicholson (1990).
7. I am grateful for the ideas of Gill Lee in the following critique of Engels.
8. Fraser, N. and Nicholson, L.J. (1988) 'Social Criticism Without Philosophy: An encounter between feminism and postmodernism'. This was first published in *Theory, Culture and Society* (1988), 5 (2-3) pp. 373-394 and republished in Docherty (1993) pp. 415-432, and in Nicholson (1990) pp. 19-38.
9. They discuss Firestone, S. (1970) *The Dialectic of Sex*. New York: Bantam; Rosaldo, M.Z. 'Woman, Culture and Society: A Theoretical Overview' in Rosaldo, M.Z. and Lamphere, L. (eds.), (1974) *Woman, Culture and Society*. Stanford: Stanford University Press; Chodorow, N. (1978) *The Reproduction of Mothering: Psychoanalysis and the Sociology of Gender*. Berkeley: University of California Press; Gilligan, C. (1983) *In a Different Voice: Psychological Theory and Women's Development*. Cambridge, MA: Harvard University Press
10. There is some confusion between these two types of feminism. I use socialist feminism to describe feminists whose political framework is ultimately reformist, although they may often adopt Marxist terms such as class, ideology, etc.; Marxist feminists, by contrast, would see women's liberation intimately tied to (but not an inevitable consequence of) the achievement of socialism, resulting from the revolutionary overthrow of capitalism. The two terms are used differently by different people at different times and so definitions are much argued over.
11. 'Movementist' politics can be defined as a politics which aligns itself with any progressive social movement fighting the status quo on any issue (such as gay

rights, anti-racism, peace protesters) without trying to link the campaign to the organisations of the working class, such as trade unions. *Marxism Today*, that ill-named journal of the Communist Party in Britain, most influential during the 1980s, was a good example of 'movementist' politics, giving, as it did, at least equal weight to the social movements of the oppressed as to the labour movement. Sometimes, as in the writing of Bea Campbell, these were even counterposed to each other. For a stimulating critique of the impact of *Marxism Today* on political ideas in Britain in the 1980s, see Callinicos, A. (1989).

12.   'Identity' politics develops the position outlined in n.11 above, emphasising difference against commonality. Thus separate analyses of lesbians, black women, older women, Irish women would be promoted as against what all women have in common. While it is of course imperative to promote the right to autonomy (each oppressed group having the right to discuss and develop demands based on their specific oppression), this does not mean that each group should fight alone for its liberation: separatism should not be the goal.

13.   An emphasis on difference and identity is characteristic of the 1980s and early 1990s, but not of the 1970s.

14.   For example the anti-pornography campaigns of the 1980s which mistakenly called for censorship without realising the damaging impact this would have on the availability of, amongst other things, gay and lesbian material.

15.   All figures from *Labour Market Trends*, March, 1997. I am grateful to Dave Shepherd for his help in searching out these figures for me.

16.   Governments are attempting cuts in welfare and benefits across Europe as they try to reach the convergence criteria for admission to the Single European Currency.

17.   *Labour Market Trends*, March 1997 reports 44 per cent of the labour force as female. The discrepancy between this and the reported 50 per cent of the workforce being female is due to different reporting criteria.

18·   Women still only earn about 70% of full-time pay: Low Pay Unit, *The New Review* (1997) (Nov/Dec) p. 6.

CHAPTER 9

Critical Pedagogy, Postmodernism, and the Retreat from Class: Towards a Contraband Pedagogy
Peter McLaren and Ramin Farahmandpur

Division of labour only becomes truly such from the moment when a division of material labour appears. From this moment onwards consciousness can really flatter itself that it is something other than consciousness of existing practice, that it *really* represents something without representing something real; from now on consciousness is in a position to emancipate itself from the world and to proceed to the formation of 'pure' theory, theology, philosophy, ethics, etc. But even if this, theory, theology, philosophy, ethics, etc., comes into contradiction with the existing relations, this can only occur because existing social relations have come into contradiction with existing forces of production ... (Karl Marx, 1976, p. 159)

Capitalism can not be gradually replaced or removed piecemeal; it must be transformed in its entirety or not at all. (J. K. Gibson-Graham, 1995, p. 190)

From whose point of view do you then read history? From the standpoint of capital that circulates globally, or from that of labor which is everywhere in chains? (Aijaz Ahmad, 1997, p. 102)

The economic anarchy of capitalist society as it exists today is, in my opinion, the real source of all evil. (Albert Einstein, 1998, p. 5)

Introduction

As we lean into the gusty winds of the approaching millennium, squaring our shoulders and lowering our heads against an icy unknown, we discover much to our surprise that the future has already arrived; that it has silently imploded into the singularity of the present. We are lost in a crevice in the 'wrong side' of history, in a furious calm at the end of a century-old breath, doing solitary confinement in the future anterior. Time has inhaled so hard that it has lodged us in its lungs, compressing us into shadowy, ovaloid spectres out of the horror classic, *Nosferatu*. Capitalism has authored this moment, synchronizing the heartbeat of the globe with the auto-copulatory rhythms of the marketplace; deregulating history; downsizing eternity.

Contemporary global capitalism signals the revival of idolatry in the deification of the marketplace. With its new degree of mobility (yet with no fundamental change in the mode of production), its mixture of flexible accumulation and older Fordist formations, its growing mobility, its increasing autonomy of financial markets, and greater flexibility of labour markets, and its financial gutting of those regimes foolish enough to place barriers in its profit-seeking trajectories, capitalism has banalized all serious oppositions to its robust presence. Its sacerdotal power is derived, in part, both from the vulnerability of the worker within the new forces of globalization and the capitalist's unslakable thirst for power and profit. Capitalism has become a surrogate for nature and a synecdoche for progress. Having confuted the socialism and Marxian optic of the Eastern bloc nations with a triumphal 'end of history' mockery, capitalism has found its most exalted place in the pantheon of quintessential bourgeois virtues celebrated by the apostolate of that great factory of dreams known as 'America'. The 1994 Bretton Woods conference at the now-famous Mt. Washington Hotel, Bretton Woods, New Hampshire, that created the World Bank, the International Monetary Fund, and shortly after, the General Agreement of Tariffs and Trade, established the framework and political architecture necessary for the United States to acquire free access to the markets and raw materials of the Western Hemisphere, the Far East, and the British Empire (Korten, 1996). The vision that emerged from this historical meeting laid the groundwork for the lurid transmogrification of the world economy into a global financial system overrun by speculators and 'arbitrageurs' who act not in the interests of world peace and prosperity and the needs of real people but for the cause of profit at any cost (Korten, 1996).

As the world's 'mentor capitalist nation' the United States has not only become detached from the struggles of its wide-ranging communities but betrays an aggressive disregard for them. Of course, capitalism has not brought about the 'end of history' as the triumphalist discourse of neo-liberalism has announced. Historically, capitalism has not carried humankind closer to 'the end of ideology' or 'end of history.' Rather, as Samir Amin comments,

> in spite of the hymns to the glory of capital, the violence of the system's real contradictions was driving history not to its end as announced in triumphalist *belle époque* proclamations, but to world wars, socialist revolutions, and the revolt of the colonized peoples. Re-established in post-First World War Europe, triumphant liberalism aggravated the chaos and paved the way for the illusionary, criminal response that fascism was to provide. (1996, p. 3)

As social agents within a neo-liberal capitalist regime, one whose link between international competitive forces and neo-liberal state policy tightens as market forces gain strength (Moody, 1997), we seem to lack substance. Capitalism's history appears to have written us out of the story, displacing human agency into the cabinet of lost memories. The world shrinks while difference swells into a forbidding colossus, bringing us face-to-face with all that is other to ourselves. Global capitalism has exfoliated the branches of history, laying bare its riot of tangled possibilities, and hacking away at those roots which nourish a socialist latency. As capital reconstitutes itself *à discrétion*, as traditionally secure factory work is replaced by the feckless insecurity of McJobs, as the disadvantaged are cast about in the icy wind of world commodity price fluctuations, as the comprador elite expands its power base in the financial precincts of the postmodern necropolis, and as the White House redecorates itself in the forms-fits-function architectonic of neo-liberalism, capitalist hegemony digs its bony talons into the structure of subjectivity itself. Communications networks—the electronic servo-mechanisms of the state—with their propulsions and fluxes of information that have grown apace with capitalism, make this hegemony not only a tenebrous possibility but also an inevitability as they ideologically secure forms of exploitation so furious that every vulnerability of the masses is seized and made over into a crisis. Neo-liberalism is not simply an abstract term without a literal referent. The current corporate downsizing, outsourcing, deregulation, and the poverty it has left in its wake is neo-liberalism *in flagrante delicto*. Look at the faces of the men and women who line up for food stamps in South Central and East Los Angeles, the slumped shoulders of the workers lining up at the gates of the *malquiladores* in Juarez, Mexico, and the wounded smiles of children juggling tennis balls, breathing fire, and washing car windows in the midst of a traffic jam in Mexico City, and you will have come face-to-face with the destructive power of neo-liberalism.

The global death rattle that announces this *fin-de-siècle* moment joltingly alerts lost generations whose subjectivities have been melded into capitalist forms of such pure intensity that time and history do not seem necessary. We are always already shaped by the labyrinthine circuits of capitalist desire, a desire that hides catachrestically behind the veiled dystopianism of postmodern bourgeois rhetorics. It is a desire so ruthless, that it thirsts even for the tears of the poor. Accumulation in the name of profit has become the *acta sanctorum* of the age of desire.

In the United States we have lost our yearning to know ourselves by recognizing what we are not. Investing in the singular culture we call 'American' by means of echoliac rhetorical proclamations that bind us together as one nation indivisible, many cling only to the familiar or the promise thereof, fearful that all acts of knowing *who* we are sooner or later become acts of destroying *what* we have become. To know who we are is, after all, to recognize the slack-jawed, low intensity democracy despoiled by the lesions of greed that now pockmark the unconquerable visage of the holiest of U.S. monuments, the Statue of Liberty. It is also to acknowledge the United States' total propinquity with inventing ways of exploiting the wealth of the globe and razing the fragile infrastructures of the most poor and powerless of nations.

The political punditocracy of that same Washington elite who boasted that the United States was 'the only remaining superpower' and who—conveniently ignoring the United States' two trillion dollar debt to the outside world and the fact that 60 percent of its population is sinking into penury—has been zealously promoting by way of neo-liberal monetary orthodoxy the merits of deregulated markets, is now finding its triumphalist proclamations in dangerous conflict with reality. August 13, 1998 marked the sixteenth birthday of the lavish bull market of the 1980s and 1990s (decades when 'foreign' policy finally became recognized as a code word for 'trade' policy) but it was anything but sweet. Considering the collapse of the Russian, Mexican, and Asian markets, it came closer to a wake. In the face of the current 'global paroxysm' of worldwide deflation and what has been described as the 'crises of an entire economic model' (Henwood, 1995, p. 5), the United States government continues its draconian welfare reforms, maintains its shameful and callous punishment of defenseless children (as in the repeal of the federal guarantee of Aid to Families with Dependent Children), weakens civil rights initiatives, enacts dangerously cruel legislation against immigrants, and imprisons, and puts to death African-Americans and Latino/as in unprecedented numbers.

Over the last several decades the social, economic, and political metamorphoses in Western industrial nations and developing Third World countries have culminated in an increasing interest in Marxist social theory within various critical traditions of educational scholarship. While some critical educators are rediscovering Marxism, recognizing its rich historical and theoretical contribution to social theory and acknowledging its invaluable insights into the role of schooling in the unequal distribution of skills, knowledge, and power in society, others are riding the fashionable currents of the postmodern *soi-disant Quartier Latin* (see McLaren, a, b).

Among educational scholars there has been a growing interest in melding various strands of postmodern social theory with elements of Marxist theory, a project that would be too otiose to summarize here. However, many theorists who straddle the postmodernist-Marxist divide have failed to formulate a sustained and convincing critique of the prevailing social and economic inequalities within advanced Western industrial capitalist nations. Too often such attempts have witnessed social relations of production becoming buried in the synergistic swirl of theoretical eclecticism.

We believe that it is urgent task to locate educational theory more securely within a Marxist problematic than we have done so in the past in order to explain in more convincing fashion the dynamic mechanisms that ensure the production and reproduction of capitalist social and economic relations, as well as to unravel the complex ways in which schools participate in the asymmetrical distribution of technical knowledge and skills. This is not an argument against eclecticism *per se*, but a cautionary reminder that much conceptual ground already covered can get lost in the laboratory of theory when trying to meld models into some grand synthesis in an attempt to reveal what has been hidden.

The intensification of international competition among multinational corporations under the flagship of neo-liberal economic policies has the threatening tendency of colonizing everyday life. It has created conditions in which declining living standards and increasing wage inequalities between the poor and the wealthy have become the norm. The new global economy is regulated by the growing service and retail industry that relies significantly on the exploitation of unskilled immigrant labour in the Western industrial nations and workers in Third World countries. As a means of decreasing production costs, manufacturing jobs are exported abroad to Third World developing countries where a combination of cheap labour markets and weak labour unions create a ripe mixture for a massive accumulation of capital in a frictionless, deregulated industrial milieu. The 'K-marting of the labour force' has yielded unprecedented record profitability for transnational corporations, especially in Third World countries where a combination of cheap labour markets and weak unions has created extremely ripe conditions for economic exploitation of the working-class (Zukin, 1991). Kim Moody (1997) reminds us that today's transnational corporations 'are clearly predators waging class war to expand their world-wide empires and restore the legendary profit-rates of decades ago' (p. 287).

The replacement of the United States manufacturing industry by low wage employment in the service and retail industry has contributed in no insignificant way to the increasing social and economic inequalities and has witnessed 10% of the population taking ownership of more that 90% of the nation's wealth. Much of the recent evisceration of social programs and the vicious assaults against trade unions by the neo-liberal comprador elite can be traced to the 1980s, when the capitalist class was given a dose of corporate Viagra through massive deregulation policies. According to Robert Brenner:

Capitalists and the wealthy accumulated wealth with such success during the 1980s largely because the state intervened directly to place money in their hands—enabling them to profit from their own business failure through lucrative bailouts, offering them massive tax breaks which played no small part in the recovery of corporate balance sheets, and providing them with an unprecedented array of other politically constituted opportunities to get richer faster through fiscal, monetary, and deregulation policies—all at the expense of the great mass of the population. (1998, p. 207)

Of course, after the initial surge, the economy went flaccid, which put the lie to the myth of deregulation. Brenner remarks:

If, after more than two decades of wage-cutting, tax-cutting, reductions in the growth of social expenditure, deregulation and 'sound finance,' the ever less fettered 'free market' economy is unable to perform half as well as in the 1960s, there might be some reason to question the dogma that the freer market, the better the economic performance. (1998, p. 238)

Moody reports that at a global level we are witnessing the production of a transnational working class. He warns that 'the division of labour in the production of the word's wealth is more truly international that at any time' (1997, p. 308). In tandem with these economic shifts has been the unceasing virulence of neo-liberal attacks against social programmes, educational opportunities, and the civil rights of working class women and minorities. The globalization of national economies—something that is not really new, but as old as capitalism itself (see Marx, 1976)—through deregulation, free marketisation, and privatization has become an open door policy to the unrestricted movement of finance capital from national to international markets, creating flexible arrangements suitable for capitalist exploitation. As globalization has dramatically intensified over the last several decades, its lack of an ethical foundation or warrant has never been so apparent. Michael Parenti writes:

Capitalism is a system without a soul, without humanity. It tries to reduce every human activity to market profitability. It has no loyalty to democracy, family values, culture, Judeo-Christian ethics, ordinary folks, or any of the other shibboleths mouthed by its public relations representatives on special occasions. It has no loyalty to any nation; its only loyalty is to its own system of capital accumulation. It is not dedicated to 'serving the community'; it serves only itself, extracting all it can from the many so that it might give all it can to the few. (1998, pp. 84-85)

The growing numbers of undocumented immigrants in Los Angeles and throughout the Southwestern United States is being examined by the general public as the probable result of miserable social, political, and economic conditions in so-called Third World countries. What the media persistently fails to report is that the root of this situation can be traced to the downgraded manufacturing sector in the United States and the growth of new low-wage jobs in the service sector where the growth industries—finance, real estate, insurance, retail trade, and business services—come equipped with low wages, weak unions, and a high proportion of part time and female workers. These workers are more than likely to be immigrants who are forced to work for low pay, have little employment security, possess few technical skills and little knowledge of English (Sassen, 1998). Of course, the growing high-income professional and managerial class in the major metropolitan centers has created a need for low-wage service workers—restaurant workers, residential building attendants, preparers of speciality and gourmet foods, dog walkers, errand runners, apartment cleaners, childcare providers and others who work in the informal economy 'off the books' (Sassen, 1998).

In the face of the changing dynamics of world capitalism, Moody argues that there is persistent continuation of three aspects of today's economic, social, and political world that resembles the world of a century ago. First, there is no existing social system that competes with capitalism for the future, whether pre-capitalist regimes or bastions of post-capitalist, communist, bureaucratic collectives. Second, capitalism has retained its market-driven form to create uneven development on a world scale. Third, the state and institutions of capitalist politics have been captured by neo-liberal/conservative movements and politicians; the objective power of international markets continue to impose severe limits on reform projects for those unwilling to struggle (1997, pp. 296-297).

Yet while much remains the same about capitalism, there does exist a profound difference. Social provisions within the working class have worsened and resistance to the regime of wage labour is much more difficult than at any other historical moment. David Harvey (1998) reminds us that

the barriers to that unity are far more formidable than they were in the already complicated European context of 1848 [publication of the Communist Manifesto]. The workforce is now far more geographically dispersed, culturally heterogeneous, ethnically and religiously diverse, racially stratified, and linguistically fragmented. The effect is to radically differentiate both the modes of resistance to capitalism and the definitions of alternatives. And while it is true that means of communication and opportunities for translation have greatly improved, this has little meaning for the billion or so workers living on less than a dollar a day possessed of quite different cultural histories, literatures and understandings (compared to international financiers and transnationals who use them all the time). Differentials (both geographical and social) in wages and social provisions within the global working class are likewise greater than they have ever been. (p. 68)

Addicted to its own self-induced adrenaline rush, capitalism's reckless gunslinging frontierism and goon squad financial assaults on vulnerable nations has brought itself into a naked confrontation with its own expanding limits, the *ne plus ultra* extremity of accumulation, turning it upon itself in a cannibalistic orgy of self-destruction. The collapse of the former Soviet Union and Eastern European state-sponsored bureaucratic socialism, following in the wake of a speeded up process of globalization[1] and its unholy alliance with neo-liberalism, has fostered hostile conditions for progressive educators who wish to create coalitions and social movements that speak to the urgent issues and needs inside and outside our urban schools. These include growing poverty, racism, and jobless futures for generations of increasingly alienated youth. Confronted by the fancifully adorned avant-garde guises worn by postmodernists as they enact their wine-and-cheese-party revolution, the education left is hard-pressed to make a case for Marx. It has become exceedingly more difficult to mobilize against capital which is conscripting the school curriculum and culture into its project of eternal accumulation.

Postmodern theory has made significant contributions to the education field by examining how schools participate in producing and reproducing asymmetrical relations of power, and how discourses, systems of intelligibility, and representational practices continue to support gender inequality, racism, and class advantage. For the most part, however, postmodernism has failed to develop alternative democratic social models. This is partly due to its failure to mount a sophisticated and coherent opposition politics against economic exploitation, political oppression, and cultural hegemony. In its celebration of the aleatory freeplay of signification, postmodernism exhibits a profound cynicism—if not sustained intellectual contempt—towards what it regards as the Eurocentric Enlightenment project of human progress, equality, justice, rationality, and truth, a project built upon patriarchal master narratives that can be traced to seventeenth century European thinkers (Green, 1994). Perry

Anderson (1998), paraphrasing Terry Eagleton, aptly describes the phenomenon of postmodernism as follows:

> Advanced capitalism ... requires two contradictory systems of justification: a metaphysics of abiding impersonal verities—the discourse of sovereignty and law, contract and obligation—in the political order, and a casuistic of individual preferences for perpetually shifting fashions and gratifications of consumption in the economic order. Postmodernism gives paradoxical expression to this dualism, since while its dismissal of the centered subject in favour of the erratic swarming of desire colludes with the amoral hedonism of the market, its denial of any grounded values or objective truths undermines the prevailing legitimations of the state. (p. 115)

Challenging such ambivalence is one reason that Marxism has come under trenchant assault in recent years by postmodernist theorists of various stripes.[2] Postmodernists have taken Marxism to task for its perceived lack of attention to issues of race and gender. Leaning heavily on the idea of the incommensurability of discourses, some intellectual apostles of postmodernism such as Patti Lather (1999) offer a tired and hidebound caricature of Marxism as a patriarchal totalising discourse in order to reinvent the all-too-familiar assertion that Marxist educational theory is quintessentially hostile to feminist theory. This is, of course, an gross overstatement, ignoring much that has gone on within Marxist theory over the last several decades (see McLaren, 1995; 1997b; Ebert, 1995; Cole and Hill, 1995; Cole, Hill, and Rikowski, 1997). For Lather, the so-called subsumption of Marxism under the superior model of deconstruction has not been a *créve-coeur*. Contrary to Lather's grievous misapprehension that links Marxism to modernism's boy's club, Marxism recognizes that the greatest threat to equality on the basis of race, class, gender, and sexual orientation is capitalism itself.[3] As Aijaz Ahmad (1998) notes:

> Marxism is today often accused of neglecting all of kinds difference, of gender, race, ethnicity, nationality, culture, and so on. But it is not Marxism that recognizes no gender differences. These differences are at once abolished by capitalism, by turning women as much as men into instruments of production. These differences are also maintained through cross-class sexual exploitation, not to speak of the differential wage rate, in which women are paid less than men for the same work, or the direct appropriation of women's labour in the domestic economy. Similarly, it is not communism that sets out to abolish nationality. It is abolished by capitalism itself, through imperialism, through circulation of finance and commodities, through the objectivity of the labour

process itself, while nation-states are maintained simply as mechanisms for the management of various units of the world capitalist economy in the context of globally uneven and unequal development. Finally, the bourgeoisie is already a universal class, transnational in its operations and with a culture that also tends to be globally uniform. (p. 22)

Bourgeois critics who condemn Marxism as too 'deterministic' often advance an ideology of unfettered capitalism that is even more deterministic. Samir Amin remarks:

> It is rather amusing to see managerial types who dismiss Marxism as unduly deterministic proffering this rather vulgar absolute kind of determinism. Moreover, the social design they seek defend with this argument, namely the market-based management of the world system, is utopian in the worst sense of the term, a reactionary, criminal utopia, doomed in any case to fall apart under the pressure, of its own highly explosive charge. (1997, p. 151)

Bourgeois liberal educational theorists in the United States have enjoyed a long-standing apostolic advantage to Marxist scholars who for the most part are characterized as political extremists, idealists, untrustworthy and intransigent intellectuals, and rogues and renegades. The works of Marx and his heirs have been placed on *the librorum prohibitorum*. Regrettably, too few Marxist analyses are published in U.S. education journals, and even fewer works by Marxist educators appear in the syllabuses of teacher education programs. With the exception of works by Apple (1993; 1996), Brosio (1994), Giroux (1988, 1992), Whitty (1985, 1997), and a handful of others, very few social and cultural theorists in the field of education appear to recognize the extent to which political economy shapes educational curriculum and policy decisions. Although we acknowledge many of the inherent weaknesses in the reproduction and correspondence theories and models of schooling that surfaced in the 1970s and early 1980s (see for example Cole, 1988, ed.), we nevertheless believe that, *mutatis mutandis*, schools still wittingly and unwittingly participate in reproducing social and economic inequalities in the name of freedom and democracy. Further, they function in the thrall of capital more overwhelmingly today than at any time in history. Acknowledging the brute and intractable reality of capitalist schooling, Carol Stabile asserts that

> capitalist education is organized and has a purpose, which is held in place by a number of other institutions and their ideologies. In a word, the educational system in the United States reproduces and maintains

division between capitalists and workers, thereby producing ... capitalist relations of production. This organization and purpose are manifest in the historical link between educational institutions and industry, with the former being directed by the needs and interests of the latter. (1995, p. 209)

We apologize to those conservative postmodernists, neo-Nietzscheans, deconstructionists, Gallo-poststructuralists and the like, who find this observation too crude for their academic taste. We follow our apology with an historical materialist alternative.

The naughtiness of postmodernism

The incursion of French social theory into North American academic precincts over the last thirty years is foregrounded against a lack of leftist political coalitions poised to effectively resist the expanding power of capital orchestrated by organized multinational corporations. Many liberals and progressive intellectuals on the left now seek post-Marxist frameworks for explaining the current disorganization of capitalism in order to avoid the so-called reductionism of conventional Marxist theories. These leftists are often quick to comfort themselves with the debonair gestures of avant-garde social critics that emerged from the fashionably elegant apartments of Paris during the last several decades.

During the Khruschev era, it became quite clear that the social and economic models that had been put forth by the former Soviet Union and Eastern European countries had failed to offer promising alternatives for developing democratic social life. And by the late 1980s it became clearer that Soviet-style state capitalism was doomed. Shortly thereafter, neo-liberal politicians in the West pledged the demise of the welfare state to its anti-socialist constituencies, while liberal politicians continued to sing the praises of humanism and envision a pluralistic democracy built on happy consensus. Marxism, however, was relegated to the dank and garbage strewn gutters of failed revolutionary and popular struggles, often due to political fragmentation and ideological differences among its proponents, and the role played by the international capitalist cavalry—the marines and the CIA (Dave Hill, personal communication). Rarely did these liberals stop to think that reforms correspond to a certain period of the capitalist mode of production, represent at best an imposed amelioration of the worst effects of capitalism, fail to challenge the basic principles or contradictions of capitalist exploitation, serve as mere state mandated accords, and fail to free the working-class from complete dependence on the labour market or change the fundamental relations of ownership in society (Teeple, 1995).

Moody (1997) touches on a key issue of contemporary politics when he remarks that socialist thought over the last century has separated the idea of economic struggle from political struggle. This dualistic counter-position of the economic and the political has posed some serious problems. For instance, traditional mass parties of the working class and the political left are now more removed from the idea of socialism than ever before. There has rarely—if ever—been a time when the revolutionary socialist left has been so fragmented. Many socialists were slow to realize that all aspects of social life involved both the economic and the political and that there existed no such dichotomy in the world of everyday social life.

That a lack of a coherent political platform against global capitalism contributed to the increasing factionalism among the United States Left should come as little surprise to those who have lived through decades of sophisticated anti-socialist cold war propaganda and, a sacerdotal celebration of neo-liberal free enterprise practices, and the deregulation of markets propagandized as the advance guard of democracy. James Petras and Chronis Polychroniou (1996) refer to the crisis of Marxism as a 'crisis of the intellectual nerves', which 'is rooted in the failure of the Left to resist the ideological pressures from the Western mass media and states (as well as their intellectuals in uniform) to amalgamate Marxism with the bureaucratic collectivist regimes and to reproduce history from an anti-socialist, anti-working class perspective' (p. 101). Petras and Polychroniou provide three explanations for the prevalent crisis: many intellectuals on the left erroneously equated bureaucratic socialism with Marxism; the Left was largely subservient to the political and ideological support it received from the former Soviet Union and Eastern European socialist countries; and the mass media and intellectuals in Western capitalist countries succeeded in portraying the demise of bureaucratic socialism as the end of Marxism. Yet the crises of Marxism can also be considered a deepening. intellectual malaise brought about by the disorganization of global capitalist relations. The intellectual crises is perhaps most evident in the 'post-Marxist' attack on Marxism as a decidedly modernist enterprise rooted in the imperializing project of the Western Enlightenment tradition.

Globalization binds people together through the economic-political machinery of new technology, the media, and new circuits of production, distribution, and consumption within the culture industry. Yet globalization also creates new divisions and hierarchies of difference, style, and taste. To be sure, consumer culture industries have intensified 'sign value' and exchange value through the processes of commercialization. Following in the wake of the globalization of capital, is the globalization of culture, a process that creates as many new differences as it does patterns of sameness. Noting that 60 percent of the revenues of all feature films are made in overseas mass markets, Disney has brought Henry Kissinger to Hollywood to advise on its projects in China (with all its potential movie-goers). If there is already a McDonalds near Tiananmen Square, why not envision a movie theatre in the Great Hall of the People? (Gardels, 1997).

Yet it would be a mistake to agree with the postmodernist claim that sign value has superseded use value. Such a claim rests on a mistaken realist assumption and truncated conception of use value that argues that use values have been replaced with exchange values, meaning with money, and human needs with profit (Fornäs, 1995). We claim that all capitalist commodity production rests upon the production and reproduction of needs and use values. Specific needs and desires have been inflected in certain directions—a process that is certainly visible in the aesthetic surfaces of everyday consumer culture. But Marx anticipated the heterogenization of needs in his commodity theory. We need to stress that sign value does not exceed use value but rather is constitutive of it. What we regard as the new postmodern empire of signs actually belongs to the material reality of use value, even though we concede, as did Marx, that the relationships between needs and use values have been historically and intersubjectively defined. While the aestheticization of everyday life gives the illusion that sign values are epiphenomena of use values, this is decidedly not the case. As Johan Fornäs has put it, 'symbols and aesthetics are more than simple effects of commodification and more than a secondary aura above a firm material base' (1995, p. 220).

Under the impact of rapid technological innovations over the last half of the century in computers and communications devices, some ludic postmodernists have argued that the hierarchical distinctions between reality and its representations have been erased (Green, 1994). Teresa Ebert (1996) identifies two variants of postmodernism: 'ludic' and 'resistance' postmodernism. Ludic postmodernism celebrates the free-floating articulation of signifiers in the construction of lifestyle discourses that are viewed for the most part as decapitated from external determinations. Resistance postmodernism draws upon poststructuralist advances in understanding signification but views language as the product of history and links signification to class struggle through the Formalist linguistics of Mikhail Bakhtin, V. N. Volosinov, and a sociological analysis of language associated with Lev Vygotsky and G. Plekhanov. Ebert explains that while ludic postmodernism is the result of material and historical contradictions inherent within capitalist social relations of production, resistance postmodernism exposes those contradictions by linking social, political, and cultural phenomena with the existing asymmetrical social and economic relations. Resistance postmodernism and critical postmodernism reveal that the base and superstructure are not independent of one another as ludic postmodern thinkers such as Baudrillard, Derrida, and Lyotard are wont to argue.

Jean Baudrillard's *faux pas* begins with the belief that a Marxist emphasis on production is no longer relevant in a consumer-driven capitalist culture. Baudrillard's 'spectral superstructuralism' privileges cultural production (i.e. images, texts, simulations) over economic production. While postmodern theory swimming in the currents of Baudrillard's renegade vanguardism dismantles meaning in brilliant and manic flashes of hyper-theorizing, it too often ricochets off anti-capitalist critique, angling towards a politics of representation whose progressive inertia eventually log jams in a centerless cesspool of floating signifiers.

Postmodernists refute meta-narratives and participate in an unequivocal rejection of universal truths (Cole and Hill, 1995). However, critics of postmodernism point out that de-centering grand-narratives and rejecting universalism in favour of heterogeneity and a plurality of truths is feasible only if postmodernism constitutes itself as a totalising narrative. As Rick Joines comments:

> One of the founding principles and shibboleths of the postmodern academic left is the disavowal of totalising master narratives (which are coded as 'totalitarian') and the conjoined belief that Marx's so-called predictions have failed as the world of class struggle becomes a world of discursive representations and linguistic play. This discourse, which cannot admit its own totalising, has abandoned thinking about labour and exploitation in favour of textuality and body: desire is hot—economics and class struggle are not. (1997, p. 30)

Even journals that profess a leftist agenda are succumbing to the lure of postmodernist perspectives. In a recent article in the journal *New Left Review,* Boris Frankel (1997) deftly exposes several post-Marxist intellectual movements as liberalism in disguise. The American journal *Telos* is criticized for advocating postmodern populism as a way of confronting corporate capitalism. Frankel notes that postmodern populism falls short of developing a persuasive critique of capitalism since it remains trapped within a Keynesian welfare economics. Similarly, Frankel criticizes the British journal *Economy and Society* for supporting a neo-Foucauldian form of *realpolitik* influenced by the works of Max Weber and Frederick Nietzsche and for rejecting Marxism and socialism on the basis of its putative political romanticism. Frankel traces the roots of these contemporary postmodern and politically conservative intellectual movements in the works of early twentieth century bourgeois classical elite theorists such as Mosca, Pareto, and Michels. Postmodernists and classical elite theorists both share a rejection of universalism and totalising theories while failing adequately to critique class inequalities in capitalist societies. Although both journals see themselves as politically progressive, they recuperate the project of globalization and the politics of neo-liberalism.

We agree with Amin (1998) when he asserts that modernism has not been surpassed by the fictional period known as 'postmodernism' Rather, modernism has yet to be finished:

> Modernity is still unfinished, and it remains so as long as the human race continues to exist. Currently, the fundamental obstacle setting its limits is still defined by the social relationships specific to capitalism. What the postmodernists refuse to see is that modernity can progress further only by going beyond capitalism. (1998, p. 103)

We are not suggesting that the Marxist problematic that informs our work cannot greatly benefit from criticism by postmodernist, feminist, or critical multiculturalists. We continue to advocate for feminist theory and anti-racist and anti-homophobic perspectives as an extension and as a deepening of many aspects of the Marxist project. This is far different, however, from abandoning the Marxist project *tout court* in favour of identity politics.

Surely it is undeniably a good idea to follow anti-essentialism in disbanding, dispersing and displacing the terms that claim to represent us in a shared field of representations premised on the mutual imbrication of 'us and them' that we give the term 'Western identity'. Anti-essentialism[4] has, above all, enabled researchers to criticize the notion of the unsullied position of enunciation, the location of interpretation free of ideology, what Vincent Crapanzano refers to as a 'lazy divinity ... contemplating its creation in order to observe it, register it, and interpret it' (cited in Da Cunha, 1998, p. 243). Yet identity politics grounded in an anti-essentialist position has not focused sufficiently on the material preconditions for liberated ethnic identities that have been undermined by the dramatic intensity of historical events irrupting across the landscape of advanced capitalism. While displacing our historical selves into some new fashionably renegade identity through a frenzied spilling over of signifiers once lashed to the pillars of conventional meanings might reap benefits and help to soften the certainty of the dominant ideological field, such postmodern manoeuvres do little to threaten material relations of production that contribute to the already hierarchically-bound international division of labour.

We are not against the development of self-reflexivity directed at issues in popular culture, or cultural criticism in general. We are interested in finding *common ground* between cultural criticism and the movement for a transformation of productive relations. Our position is that postmodern cultural criticism—that mainly addresses specific logics of non-economic factors— for the most part has not addressed the liberation of humankind from economic alienation linked to capitalist economic logics that serve as the motor for transnational oligopolies and the reproduction of established social relations. Samir Amin (1998b) sets forth a non-economic-determinist interpretation of Marxism that we find convincing. In Amin's model, the capitalist mode of production is *not* reduced to the status of an economic structure. In other words, the law of value governs both the economic reproduction of capitalism *and* all the aspects of social life within capitalism. Unlike the concept of 'overdetermination' famously articulated by Althusser, Amin counterposes the concept of 'underdetermination', in which the determinations of economics, politics, and culture each possess their specific logic and autonomy. There is no complimentarity among logics within the systems of underdetermination; there exist only conflicts among their determining factors, conflicts which allow choice among different possible alternatives. Conflicts among logics find solutions by subordinating some logics to others. The accumulation of capital is the dominant trait of the logic of capitalism and provides the channels through which economic logic is imposed onto political, ideological, and cultural logics.

Precisely because underdetermination rather than overdetermination typifies the conflictual way in which the logics governing the various factors of social causation are interlaced, all social revolutions must of necessity be cultural revolutions. The law of value, therefore, governs not only the capitalist mode of production but also the other social determinants. In order to move beyond— to overstep—contemporary capitalism that is defined by its three basic contradictions of economic alienation, global polarization, and destruction of the natural environment, Amin charts out social transformation that would initiate through its political economy, its politics, and its cultural logics, a social evolution bent on reducing these contradictions rather than aggravating them. Amin convincingly argues that postmodern criticism for the most part capitulates to the demands of the current phase of capitalist political economy in the hope of making the system more humane. Marxists perceive the humanization of capitalism to be a contradiction in terms. Efforts such as those by Bill Clinton to create a 'third way' have rightly been dismissed as 'neo-liberalism with a smiley face' (Ehrenreich, 1998, p. 13).

Within the precincts of postmodern theorizing and in the absence of universal *criteria* for evaluating the validity of truth claims, we are forced to accept politically ambiguous positions when confronting the privileging hierarchies of capitalist social relations. In our view concepts such as universal rights are *central* to the development of a democratic society and should not be placed in philosophical quarantine as the postmodernists believe. While we may agree with those postmodernists who claim that truth does not have a pre-determined or fixed meaning, embedded as it is within the specificity of social, political, and historical contexts, this in no way implies the validity of every truth-claim, since truths-claims conceal asymmetrical social and economic relations. Teresa Ebert (1996) elaborates on this idea:

> The question of knowing the 'truth' is neither a question of describing some 'true' metaphysical or ontological 'essence' nor a matter of negotiating incommensurable language games, as Lyotard suggests. Rather it is a question of dialectical understanding of the dynamic relations between superstructure and base: between ideology— (mis)representations, signifying practices, discourses, frames of intelligibility, objectives—and the workings of the forces of production and the historical relations of production. Crucial to such a dialectical knowledge is ideology critique—a practice for developing class consciousness ... (1996, p. 47)

Conservative postmodernism—epitomized by that *bien-aimé* of postmodern pseudo-transgressors, Jean Baudrillard—leaches attention away from the messy, conflictual, and power-sensitive materiality of everyday life by refusing to differentiate between image and reality, surface and depth, discourse and ideology, and fact and fiction. Postmodern epistemology is based not so much upon critical inquiry in which 'objectivity' is pursued, but rather is constructed in relation to the tropicity and rhetoricity of discourse. The fixed dualism of reality versus fiction does not apply. Carl Boggs (1997) captures this absence of any substantive counter-hegemonic agenda beneath conservative postmodernism's façade of avant garde bohemianism:

> In politics as in the cultural and intellectual realm, a postmodern fascination with indeterminacy, ambiguity, and chaos easily supports a drift towards cynicism and passivity; the subject becomes powerless to change either itself or society. Further, the pretentious, jargon-filled, and often indecipherable discourse of postmodernism reinforces the most

faddish tendencies in academia. Endless (and often pointless) attempts to deconstruct texts and narratives readily become a façade behind which professional scholars justify their own retreat from political commitment ... the extreme postmodern assault on macro institutions severs the connections between critique and action. (1997, p. 767)

Similarily, Hilary Wainwright (1994) argues that:

> Postmodernism ... does not ... provide adequate tools to answer the radical right ... the tools of postmodernism produce only a more volatile version of the radical right... . Postmodernism cuts the connection between human intention and social outcome. While for the radical right the incompleteness of our knowledge means that society is the outcome of the blindfold and therefore haphazard activities of the individual, for the postmodern theorist, society in an equally haphazard plethora of solipsistic statements of various sorts. (1994, p. 100)

Sardar (1998) makes the cogent claim that postmodernism suffers from a 'paradoxical dualism' or double coding. It claims that nothing is real, yet it also claims that reality represents something real: simulated *images*. Postmodernists view history as a collection of necessarily fragmented narratives where the notion of determinate relations is made anemic by the haemorrhaging of signifiers and their bleeding into each other (Eagleton, 1996; McLaren, 1995; Green, 1994). Historical events are too often transformed into a Disneyesque theme park of fantasy and play where the distinction between fact and fiction is barely—if at all—perceptible. History is sequestered away in a grammatologist's laboratory where it can conjure a metaphysics of disappearances and invent reality as a nightmare where all attempts at objectivity suffer the fate of Dr. Frankenstein and his monster.

And what about the postmodernist aversion to master narratives that guide global struggles for liberation? We find that the postmodernist alternative—the stress on local struggles and regional antagonisms—often subverts the anti-capitalist project necessary to bring about social democracy. The development of world capitalism as an imperializing force, as a means of subjugating labour, as a system of unequal and combined development, as a means of superexploitation and the repression of democratic aspirations, needs more than monadic local efforts at improving resource allocation and warning the public against excessive consumptive practices. Local efforts fail to take advantage of reform at the level of the state. The fact that the state is more dependent on capital than ever before suggests that it could potentially serve as an instrument in reform efforts if these are organized with broad national support. According to Ahmad (1998):

> The currently fashionable postmodern discourse has its own answer: it leaves the market fully intact while debunking the nation-state and seeking to dissolve it even further into little communities and competitive narcissisms, which sometimes get called 'multiculturalism'. In other words, postmodernism seeks an even deeper universalization of the market, while seeking to decompose 'social humanity' even further, to the point where only the monadic individual remains, with no dream but that of, in Jean-François Lyotard's words, 'the enjoyment of goods and services.' Or, to put it somewhat differently: the postmodern utopia takes the form of a complementary relationship between universalization of the market and individualization of commodity fetishisms. This, of course, has been a dream of capitalism since its very inception. (1998, pp. 21-22)

According to Amin, postmodernism gives theoretical legitimacy to a retreat from revolutionary momentum. He further claims that

> these retreats go exactly counter to the sincere wishes of the postmodernists for a strengthening of democratic practices in the administration of everyday affairs. They give fodder to conformity and hatred, contempt for democracy, and to all sorts of chauvinisms ... Postmodernism, therefore, is a negative utopia (in contradistinction to positive utopias, which call for transformation of the world). At bottom, it expresses capitulation to the demands of capitalist political economy in its current phase, in the hope—the utopia hope—of 'humanly managing the system'. This position is untenable. (1998, p. 101)

Postmodernists rarely elevate facts from anecdote to history, a practice which is commensurate with following the latest top-of-the-line designer narratives. At the same time they ritualistically weave together post-Marxist and end-of-history claims into a seamless genealogy in an attempt to mummify historical agency and seal the project of liberation in a vault marked 'antiquity.' It is worth quoting Sardar (1998) again:

> In designer history any choice can be fitted with a tradition by associating it with a chosen historical pattern of ideas or events or characters that are selectively assembled. History returns not to its fictional, putative father—Herodotus—as he was constructed by

nineteenth century historians, but to the spirit that moved the civilisation that produced him: history becomes myth-making. (1998, p. 86)

Educational theorists working in the Marxist tradition such as Mike Cole and Dave Hill (1995) and Glenn Rikowski (1996) view postmodernism as altogether reactionary and serving only to reinscribe capitalist social relations. They reject leftist appropriations of postmodernism (i.e. critical postmodernism, radical postmodernism, resistance postmodernism) as basically a *trompe-l'oeil* in which capitalism is able to masquerade as a necessary condition in order for democracy to flourish. In contrast, we are more sympathetic to limited aspects of these radical variants of postmodernism, at the very least, for their ability to analyse intersecting relationships among race, class, and gender in late capitalist societies without falling prey to epistemological reductionism. Yet as we mentioned at the beginning of this essay, some forms of postmodernism that attempt to incorporate a Marxian problematic often fall prey to an obfuscating eclecticism in which the priority of anti-capitalist struggle is subsumed under a concern with identity politics in consumer society.

An anti-foundationalist cynicism surrounding the telos of human progress often leads ludic postmodernism to reject narratives about history's inevitability that have emerged out of the Marxist tradition. However, Marxism's emphasis on teleology—is non-teleological; it arches towards an eradication of social injustice, poverty, racism, and sexism while recognizing that history is mutable and contingent. We must emphasize that Marx did not believe history as altogether progressive. He understood that historical progress is never secured or guaranteed, but moves in and between contradictory and conflicting social spaces and zones of engagement. Alex Callinicos (1989) explains this further by arguing that

> historical materialism is a non-teleological theory of social evolution: not only does it deny that capitalism is the final stage of historical development, but communism, the classless society which Marx believed would be the outcome of socialist revolution, is not the inevitable consequences of the contradictions of capitalism, since an alternative exists, what Marx called 'the mutual ruination of the contending classes' ... (1989, p. 36)

Contrary to the criticism of Marxist teleology advanced by some postmodern critics, 'Marx doesn't describe the overthrow of capitalism as marking the end of history but rather the end of the *prehistory* of human society' (Callinicos 1995, p. 39).

Terry Eagleton (1996) similarly confirms Marx's opinion that historical regression is more probable that historical progression, since the outcome of historical progress depends upon the development of social forces and social relations of production. Moreover, he adds that the 'point for Marx is not to move us towards the telos of History, but to get out from under all that so that we may make a beginning—so that histories proper, in all their wealth of difference, might get off the ground' (p. 65). Postmodern theory too often discounts class struggle and underestimates the importance of addressing economic inequality for fear of succumbing to an implicit teleology of progress. At the same time, it continues to recite the satanic verses of capitalist ideology represented by free-market economics and political neo-liberalization which is fast becoming the governing ethos of our time.

We want to be clear that we are not trying to privilege class relations over those of gender, race, ethnicity, or sexual orientation. We remain aware, however, that the law of value under capitalism plays a formidable role in coordinating these relationships and their interrelations. We acknowledge the complex and mutual constitutiveness of race/ethnicity, gender, and sexual orientation as an ensemble of social practices that, while interconnected, to a certain extent constitute different logics. Our point is to underscore the ways that the state makes use of 'difference' and 'diversity' and the militant antagonisms that play out in the theatre of identity politics in order to break up the unity of popular forces.

Postmodernism's petit-bourgeois driven movement away from a 'represented exterior' of signifying practices renders an anti-capitalist project not only unlikely but firmly inadmissible. Not withstanding the slippage between Marxist categories and some poststructuralist categories, we believe that postmodernist theories, in effectively delinking identity politics from class analysis, have damagingly relegated the category of class to an epiphenomena of race/ethnicity, gender and sexuality. Class solidarity has often been replaced by ethnic solidarity and an uncritical rehabilitation of difference that defines ethnicity and race in essentialist ways (see Gilroy, 1991). This does not mean that we take the position that history is shaped by the infallible laws of economics. Far from it. Amin rightly argues that history 'is the product of social reactions to the effects of these laws, which in turn define the social relations of the framework within which economic laws operate' (1997, p. 103). History in this view becomes more than an effect of a specific logic inherent in the accumulation of capital; in fact it is given shape by the refusal to subordinate society to the absolute needs of economic laws. Such a politics of refusal admittedly takes many forms, including struggles involving gender, race, ethnic, and sexual liberation. Yet we believe, along with Amin, that 'the postmodernist critique, pitched short of the radical perspectives attained by Marxist thought, fails to provide the tools needed to transcend capitalism' (1997, p. 137). Despite postmodernism's ability to deconstruct the metaphysical nature of post-Enlightenment bourgeois discourse and socialist thought, and to reveal its economistic rationality while exposing its teleological prejudices, Amin argues that its

> penchant for the uncritical adulation of difference and the glorification of empiricism make it quite compatible with conventional, economistic management practices designed to perpetuate capitalist practices, still considered the definitive, eternal expression of rationality. That leaves the way open for neoconservative communalist ideologies of the kind common in Anglo-Saxon traditions of social management. In extreme cases, it may also lead to nihilistic explosions. Either way, the result is an ideology compatible with the interests of the privileged ... (1997, p. 137)

Within the United States, postmodernism's contribution to the dominance of categories of identity politics over those of class is due, in part, to the demise of the once vigorous Marxist culture that thrived in the United States before the McCarthy Era. One thinks immediately of the Critics Group of New York, the work of Granville Hicks, V. F. Calverston, Edmund Wilson, Joseph Freeman, John Reed, John Dos Passos, James T. Farrell, and others. In the 1960s the work of Michael Harrington, and Norman Mailer captured national attention. Despite the fact that the work of bell hooks, Cornel West, Henry Louis Gates, Barbara Ehrenreich, Michael Parenti, Noam Chomsky, and other thinkers are appearing more frequently in popular publications, contemporary leftist intellectual life makes very little impact in public debates.

Sherry Ortner remarks that 'class exists in America but cannot be talked about, that it is 'hidden', that there is no language for it, but that it is 'displaced' or 'spoken through' other languages of social difference—race, ethnicity, and gender' (1998, pp. 8-9). We agree with Ortner that while to a certain extent class, race, and ethnicity are separate but interacting dimensions of United States social geography and while they operate at least in part on different logics, '*at the level of discourse*, class, race, and ethnicity are so deeply mutually implicated in American culture that it makes little sense to pull them apart' (1998, p. 9). And while 'there is no class in America that is not always already racialized and ethnicized' (1998, p. 4) or racial and ethnic categories that are not always already class categories, the salience of race and ethnicity in the United States is such that when they are introduced into the discussion, they tend to override to a considerable degree that of social class. The persistent hiddenness of class means, for Ortner, that the discourse of class 'is muted and often unavailable, subordinated to virtually every other kind of claim about social success and social failure' (1998, p. 14). Given the frenetic advance of contemporary global capitalist social relations, the disappearance of class from the public discourse presents favourable conditions for the uncontested reproduction of the social division of labour.

In these times of extreme pessimism and cynicism, the *brujos* of global capitalism and neo-liberalism, with their well orchestrated Deja Voodoo wizardry, reinvent the present in the image of a luminous past, harkening back in Panglossian fashion to an earlier period of capitalist expansion under Reagan and Thatcher. We reject *tout court* such social amnesia. Coal miners in England and air traffic controllers and General Motors factory workers in the United States to name only a few groups sacrificed at the altar of neo-liberal greed during the profligacy of Reagan and Thatcher—should put this roseate version of historical memory to rest. The aim of neo-liberal economic politics is to privatize social and public institutions while socializing the risks involved in order to facilitate the frenzied accumulation of capital. Meiksins Wood (1998) argues that the 'objective of today's neo-liberal politics is to 'privatize' anything that could be conceivably be run for capitalist profit—from prisons, to postal services, to old age pensions. But it has also set out to ensure that every public enterprise, every social service, that cannot be profitably privatized will still be subject to market imperatives' (1998, p. 34).

The cultural critique that today predominates in cultural studies and post-Marxist 'new times' critical exegesis and that assails Marxist theory for privileging social class over race, gender, and identity often constitutes a veiled essentialism. In contrast to such an accusation, Marxism emphasizes that racism, sexism, and heteronormativity are mutually informing relations and integrally linked to one another, yet they always need to be theorized *in relation to* social and economic inequalities. For anti-sexist and anti-racist struggles to move beyond the rhetoric of identity politics and take on a transformative rather than reactive role within the public sphere, they need to consider beyond simple head-nodding gestures the global shifts in the social relations of production and international division of labour. For this reason it is important to move beyond 'political standpoints that view class, gender, race, and ethnicity as discrete, mutually exclusive phenomena' (Gimenez, 1995, p. 262).

Furthermore, a closer examination of relations of class reveals, for example, how the feminisation of poverty and the oppression of women are linked with world-consolidating forces within capitalist social relations, patriarchy, and other catechism of the market. Carol A. Stabile (1995) illuminates the relationship between gender and class by arguing that reinstating 'class as a central category of analysis for feminism emphasizes the relationality of structures of oppression in politically powerful ways' (p. 289). She further adds that 'this move does not mean relinquishing the theoretical and practical gains following from feminists analysis of gender and race; instead, it provides a much more nuanced and complicated understanding of the manner in which oppressions are structurally intertwined' (p. 289). The meanings that follow from socially constructed concepts of race, gender, sexuality, identity, and ethnicity are never fixed, but historically constructed and interwoven *with* social relations of production. Martha Gimenez emphasizes this idea, arguing that in order to 'attain a fuller grasp of the relevance of gender divisions and struggles for the political future of the working class, it is necessary to leave behind the notion of gender as being primarily an individual attribute and to examine it, instead, as the observable effect of underlying social relations of physical and social reproduction' (1995, p. 258).

While the success of socialist and left-wing progressive movements in Western industrial and Third World countries in forming effective anti-capitalist revolutionary alliances has been detained (we hope only temporarily) by the onslaught of global capitalism, postmodern social theorists continue to regard themselves as the primary animateurs of a egalitarian new world order—one that will provide an aesthetic education for the *profanum vulgus* while leaning on the ideological backbone of the multi-national corporations. Having dismissed Rosa Luxemburg's alternative of 'socialism or barbarianism' as a quaint blot on the horizon of social struggles, postmodern apostles are codifying in their vulgate discourses of transgression primarily linked to an aesthetic problematic which in turn is grounded in the often *ex tempore* apostatizing pretensions of the metropolis. The conservative nature of postmodern politics has largely remained undetected, helping to keep the ideology of free-enterprise, individualism, and privatization the only real game in town.

Since postmodern theorists have been unable to offer convincing accounts of existing class inequalities, a shroud of suspicion surrounds their political motivation and jaundiced eye is cast upon their social and political objectives by the Marxist left. Postmodernists have the appearance at least of rejecting a unified political commitment to social change and transformation. Samir Amin (1998a) has offered a cogent description of the way in which neo-liberal economics underwrites the political philosophy of postmodernism (see also Habermas, 1990; Cole and Hill, 1995). He asserts that

> empty economics has its pale complement in the enfeebled social
> and philosophical theses of 'postmodernism', which teach us to be
> happy and to cope with the system on a day-to-day basis, while closing

our eyes to the ever more gigantic catastrophe which it is cooking for us. Postmodernism thus legitimizes, in its own way, the manipulative practices required of political managers for whom democracy must be reduced to the status of 'low intensity' activity even as it treats the attachment of a society to its own identity as something neurotic, empty, and impotent. (1998a, p. 38)

The treatment of class as yet another arbitrary floating signifier among race, class, and identity, and the taboo usage of concepts such as 'base' and 'superstructure', have led postmodernists to expunge the notions of capitalist exploitation and imperialism from their lexicon and replace them with more politically benign discourses of 'difference' and 'identity politics.' Even self-proclaimed progressive postmodernists fare no better in articulating a persuasive critique of capitalism. Roslyn Wallach Bologh and Leonard Mell (1995) remark that 'the best that this tradition can offer is a rearrangement of the existing distribution of power—ideally, some kind of vague hope for egalitarianism or radical democracy' (p. 85). Because postmodern politics has failed to develop a sustained critique of class inequalities, racism, sexism, and economic inequality are thus framed superficially within fragmented discourses articulated around the holy trinity of race, class, and gender. Bologh and Mell (1995) culminate their argument with the assertion that: 'If postmodernism wants to confront colonization and the production of otherness, it must confront capital. If it wants to deconstruct universal categories, it might begin with the categories of political economy—as did Marx. Those are the most universal categories in which power resides' (p. 86). It follows that we need to critically examine and re-articulate from a Marxist perspective the dynamic mechanisms that allow capitalist social relations of exploitation to persist.

Developing and envisioning an anti-capitalist pedagogy requires a common yet open-ended historical-materialist framework of equality and social justice. The meaning of equality and justice are not pre-determined nor do they float-freely in some evanescent semiotic ether; rather, they are embedded within the specificity of social, economic, and political relations. In fact, historical specificity of the concept of equality neither denies its universal quality nor its objective significance. Rather, it is a standard by which we are able to judge political arguments or social practices, and it is a measure by which we can objectively gauge historical and social progress (Malik, 1996).

The anti-essentialism and anti-universalism of conservative postmodernism considers race, class, and gender to be indeterminate and relatively unstable identities by which we represent ourselves. However, race, class, and gender are not merely fashionable costumes we wear in our daily social relations but constitute historically grounded social practices within the material relations of production. As Ahmad (1998) explains at length:

> There is the idea of *discreteness* of identities, cultural, ethnic, or national; a kind of remorseless differentiatialism, whereby I am not permitted the claim that I may understand your identity but I am supposed to simply respect whatever you say are the requirements of your identity. In this ideology, any number of people celebrate hardened boundaries between self and other, denounce, what they understand as the 'universalism' of the enlightenment, rationalism, and so on, while also fully participating in the globalization of consumption patterns and the packaging of identities as so many exhibits. At the same time and often from the same people, we also have the propagation of the idea of infinite hybridity, migrancy, choice of alternate or multiple identities, as if new selves could be fashioned in the instant out of any clay that one could lay on one's hand on, and as if cultures had no real historical density and identities could be simply *made up, sui generis,* out of the global traffic and malleability of elements taken from all over the world. (1998, p. 103)

In sum, we need to fashion identities that partake of a universal commitment to social equality. This also means that an ethics of social justice must more clearly underwrite the current work being done in identity politics (Malik, 1996; McLaren, 1997b).

We need to identify radical elements within the postmodern movement and not simply ignore postmodernism since there exists conservative, liberal, and critical variants of it. This does not imply, as many critics of postmodernism would prematurely argue, a defeatist or assimilationist position. On the contrary, we believe that class by itself cannot be the driving force for social change. This is not to argue that class is no longer central in developing a revolutionary praxis. What it does suggest is that we need to expand our struggles by way of culture, language, and discourse in order to contest the contemporary triad of social, economic, political oppression. And the scope of our struggle must be international. On this issue, Michael Parenti writes:

> Our task is not to wage a class war but to realize that class war is being waged against us constantly. More international cooperation between labor unions, progressive organizations, and other popular movements is necessary. The ruling classes have taken the struggle to the international level and we must meet them there to prevent our standard of living, our sovereignty, our rights, and indeed our planet,

from being sacrificed to a rapaciously profit-driven, monopoly capitalism. (1998, p. 94)

Class analysis needs to be deepened along the lines of its Marxist predecessors, in order to explain its contemporary connections among race, class, gender, and disability. This is, however, a far cry from the postmodern claim that 'class' is just one of the many identities by which people represent themselves. Douglas Kellner (1995) reminds us that 'it would be wrong to ignore the centrality of class and the importance of class politics, [however] a radical politics today should be more multicultural, race and gender focused, and broad-based than the original Marxian theory' (p. 37). This is not an endorsement of the radical democracy of Laclau and Mouffe (1985). Nor is it a call for a commitment to nonviolent negotiation at all costs. If war is being waged on the working class, we support the working class in their attempts to fight back. Our concern is to create the conditions for the defeat of capitalism and in so doing defining the real stakes and challenges. Samir Amin poses one of the biggest challenges in the form of the following question: 'How are we to create conditions that allow the genuine advance of universalist values beyond their formulations by historical capitalism' (1996, p. 8) Certainly the answer is not to be found in the postmodernist's call for local, specific struggles over more global ones. This strategy only plays into the hands of a culturalist, communalist solution resulting in political fragmentation. Rather than contributing to a resistance to exploitation, however, such culturalism itself becomes part of the problem. As Amin notes in the case of European capitalism:

> The European project itself is conceived in these terms as the communal management of the market and no more, while beyond its borders maximum fragmentation (as many Slovenias, Macedonias, Chechnyas as possible) is systematically sought. Themes of 'democracy' and 'peoples' rights' are mobilized to obtain results that cancel peoples' capacity to make use of the democracy and rights in whose name they have been manipulated. Praise of specificity and difference, ideological mobilization around ethnic or culturalist objectives, are the engine of impotent communalism, and shift the struggle onto the ground of ethnic cleansing or religious totalitarianism. (1996, pp. 9-10)

In sum, 'class' needs to be broadly theorized and class struggle needs to be reconsidered taking into consideration the complexity of its contradictory and shifting meaning within global capitalism. As Julie Graham and Katherine Gibson (1996) remark:

Because class is understood as a process that exists in change, the class 'structure' constituted by the totality of these positions and sites is continually changing. Projects of class transformation are therefore always possible and do not necessarily involve social upheavals and hegemonic transition. Class struggles do not necessarily take place between groups of people whose identities are constituted by the objective reality and subjective consciousness of a particular location in a social structure. Rather, they take place whenever there is an attempt to change the way in which surplus labor is produced, appropriated, or distributed. (1996, p. 59)

If we can conceive of class as the process of producing, appropriating, and distributing surplus value (which is not to displace or deny the importance of property and power in the structure of contemporary society), and if we can also consider class as types of groupings in terms of how persons perform, appropriate, or receive distributed shares of surplus labour, we will notice that allocations of power and property follow from the different relationships one has to the production and appropriation of surplus labour (Wolff and Resnick, 1986). If the class process defines the performers (productive laborers) and the appropriators (capitalists) of surplus value as the fundamental class process, we will also notice that there exists two subsumed classes: distributors and recipients of surplus value. Non-class processes also need consideration because such processes can at times and under certain circumstances compromise the conditions of existence of the fundamental capitalist class process.

Non-class processes involving race and gender relations can provide the changes necessary for a transformation of the class processes of Western capitalist societies. Using gender as one example, Wolff and Resnick (1986) remark that

specific changes in social processes concerned with gender relationships would provide conditions for a change in the class processes of Western capitalists societies today. A change in popular consciousness about what 'male' and 'female' means (i.e., a change in certain cultural processes) alongside a change in the authority distribution process within families (a change in political or power processes) might combine with a change as women sell more of their labor power as a commodity (a change in the economic process of exchange) to jeopardize capitalist class processes. With other changes in still other social processes—which our class analysis seeks to identify—such altered gender relationships might provide the conditions of existence for a revolutionary change to a new social system including a different class structure. (1986, p. 120)

It follows that our agenda for revolutionary social change does not subsume gender relations or relations involving race, ethnicity, disability, or sexual orientation beneath the class process. Rather, we are trying to call attention to the possibility of using non-class relations as part of a larger anti-capitalist revolutionary project, not by analytically isolating non-class relations, but by bringing *them into conversation* with class relations.

Critical postmodernism can generate, at best, a limited counter-hegemonic praxis to capitalism. Yet, to its credit, it can open new sites for transforming the oppressed social conditions of marginalised groups through ideology critique and consciousness raising practices. But critical postmodern will be most effective in this regard when it centres its analysis around a critique of existing capitalist social relations. We don't want to downplay the effectiveness of, say, queer pedagogy in offering a powerful critique of capitalism through a deconstruction of the social and cultural myths pervasively at work that legitimize hetero-normativity and demonises other sex/gender orientation and identities. It can challenge rather forcefully the social construction of gender/ sex roles that men and women have been forced to accept by exposing how heterosexuality supports ideologies geared towards stabilizing the social division of labour. Queer pedagogy articulates a multiplicity of gender roles, identities, and desires that exist beyond the biologically-regulated concepts of male and female—concepts that ensure the production and reproduction of labour in maintaining social inequality.

Conclusion

As we approach the third millennium, leaving behind a centuries-rich legacy of social and political history, the triumphant victories and bitter failures of revolutionary struggles remain forever sketched in our memories. Yet the fight for a socialist alternative to the current capitalist reality is taking place at a time when the manufacturing of capitalist ideologies under the banner of ludic postmodernism in academia ensures rather than impedes the flow of capital and the uninterrupted business-as-usual economic, cultural, and environmental exploitation backed by neo-liberal social and economic policies.

Marxist-Leninism's success in effectively challenging capitalism has been interrupted by the market-Leninist ideologues of state capitalism. Although its exponents cry out for the abandonment of the welfare state, the deregulation of the market, and the abolition of social programs, they argue for strident state protection in the boldest Hayekian fashion imaginable when it comes to protecting the spontaneity of the marketplace. Today few revolutions and revolutionary ideas escape the profit-hungry claws of predatory capitalism unscathed. Figures associated with Marxism have been reduced to fodder for advertisements: Che Guevara's revolutionary ideals are inverted by chainfood restaurants such as Taco Bell where, in a series of commercials, he is depicted as a Chihuahua wearing a beret and selling the new revolutionary 'Gordita' taco to the masses. A Cabezol Cerveza billboard sign on Sunset Strip in Los Angeles that reads, 'Is Stalin buried in a Communist plot?', periodically revives the murderous ghost of Stalin and the Communist party as a way of discrediting anti-capitalist struggles. Referring to the new anarchist anti-establishment rock band, Chumbawamba, which recently signed with EMI Records, Adam Bergman (1998) writes that

> multinational corporations [are] skillfully turning rebellion into profit. If the biggies can buy up leftist newspapers, black-separatist rap acts and anarchist collectives and turn them into another source of capital for themselves and their stockholders, is no one immune to their fat checks? Is it some weird, modern form of progress when corporations sell products that endorse anarchy, or another case of their unchecked dominance over every sector of the economy? (1998, p. 43)

We must not forget that even an end to capitalist social relations of production does not necessarily guarantee an end to the circulation of capital. This is because, as István Mészáros explains, 'capital is a command system whose mode of functioning is accumulation-oriented, and the accumulation can be secured in a number of different ways' (1993, p. 13). For this reason, we must also not underestimate the power of capital which possess the capacity to temporarily absorb its internal contradictions by disarming anti-capitalist ideas and socialist movements. Capitalism offers us the illusion of democracy by separating political rights from economic rights, and conceals economic inequalities by depicting itself as democratic (Bowles and Gintis, 1976). It accomplishes this by creating a democratic political atmosphere but only up to the point where it does not threaten its economic order. Ellen Meiksins Wood (1998) argues that 'Capitalism can tolerate democracy because capitalists control the labour of others not by means of exclusive political rights but by means of exclusive property' (p. 22). Wood goes on to argue that 'in its best and most democratic forms, capitalism can, and must, confine equality to a separate political sphere which does not, and must not, intrude into the economic sphere or subvert economic inequality' (p. 22).

Postmodernists and neo-liberals alike, who have temporarily succeeded in retiring the history of class struggle to the graveyard of failed social revolutions, have become customarily blind to the pale ghost of Marx still hovering protectively over the horizon of humankind's hopes and dreams. Some harbour a desperate wish that Marx be still be disinterred and brought back to life to a commodified state so he can participate in the ideological polarization of capital's rule, as a reincarnated threat to capitalism's social and economic order. The return of the demon seed of Marx would only ensure the progress of capital's expansion. If Marx had never existed, capital would have to invent him, for such ritual slayings are always, to borrow the words of Ian McKay, 'in the interests of the mental health of each new corn-fed, rosy-cheeked bourgeois generation...' (1995, p. 10). We believe that Marxist ideas will continue to play a crucial role both in the academic and political arena in the years to come.

As a counter-praxis to capital, we envision a type of social movement unionism recently discussed by Kim Moody. Social movement unionism uses the power of organized workers to mobilize the poor, the casualised workers, and the unemployed as well as neighborhood organizations. This is a far cry from the old business-union service model that is often seen as just another labour aristocracy that remains largely circumscribed by what goes on within the factory gates. Social movement unionism attempts to mobilize the less well-organized sectors of the working class. Here the members participate in shaping the union's agenda and democratic workplace organization, fighting to eliminate racial and gender inequalities in job sites and struggles to ensure social justice for the disabled. Unions must fight for common demands among workers in all countries. In fact, common cross-border activities must be designed to destroy transnational markets. What is important about Moody's vision of social movement unionism is its emphasis on becoming part of a transnational worker network.

Social movement unionism is an approach that significantly moves beyond mere reformism, as in the standard reformist attempts to overcome the fragmentation of the working class through a stress on diversity through a reform of the old mass party system. Unions must continue to defend welfare measures, health care provisions, employment benefits and existing public services and the gains of women, ethnic minorities, the disabled, and gays and lesbians. At the same time it should be recognized that the counterforce to capital's job-destroying tendencies is length of working time. An effective campaign for shorter work time must be worldwide and, as Moody asserts, must resist *de facto* wage cuts. Hourly wages must be increased proportionately as hours are reduced. Moody is at pains to point out that the social movement unionism that he endorses is critical of liberal-populist 'stakeholder' capitalism which emphasizes a social contract between capital and 'civil society' or the 'Third Sector' of non-governmental organizations.

We agree with Moody that left alternatives such as stakeholder capitalism and civil society/Third sector counterforce movements are not enough. We need an approach that prefigures a deeper and more international socialist politics such as social movement unionism. The new socialism needs to be more international, as Che Guevara envisioned, and should contribute actively to the recomposition of regional groupings capable of opposing the internationalism of people to that of capital. We need focus on the differentiations occurring in the process of capitalist expansion, precisely at the interface between the global and the national aspects of this reality, and on the tension between general struggles and particular, regional efforts.

In order to place liberation on the agenda of history again, we need to re-enchant the project of critical educational theory. As educationalists whose work is underwritten by critical pedagogy (McLaren, 1995; 1997b), we need to conscript such a rethinking into the development of a critical pedagogy that is capable of devising a transition beyond capitalism. The stakes in the debate are considerable. In order to make possible the type of dialogue needed for strategising within today's global arena the advancement beyond capitalism and towards universal socialism requires some important choices for the Left. Samir Amin (1997) has suggested some important directions: charging the World Trade Organization with planning access to the use of major natural resources of the globe and the prices of raw materials and with planning targets for inter-regional trade in industrial products; improving the incomes of disadvantaged workers; and reconciling general competitiveness with distributional criteria favouring disadvantaged regions of the globe. In addition, excess finance must be channeled toward productive investment in peripheral countries accompanied by a rethinking of the international monetary system in the direction of regional monetary systems that guarantee the relative stability of exchange rates, etc. A prerequisite requires that the bourgeois Left—largely inconscient of its own reactive theoretical moves—confront the contradictions inherent in the politics of its own theorizing.

Capitalism's supposed inevitability and history's presumed failure to de-fang existing capitalist social relations has brought about an ethos of panic and despair among the left. The conventional wisdom—even among many former members of the Marxist intelligentsia—is that there is no realistic alternative to the market. The collapse of Soviet Communism and the decline of Marxist parties and movements in many parts of the world has, in the minds of many, once and for all refuted Marx and his heirs and has contributed to the current refusal among many leftist constituencies to take anti-capitalist struggle seriously. Conveniently forgotten by our archivists of historical memory is the fact that Soviet communism was, in effect, an overly bureaucratised and cumbersome (not to mention corrupt) form of state capitalism. As Ian Birchall remarks: 'Socialism in one country' failed, not because it abolished the market, but because it failed to escape the world market that Marx so vividly described, a world market mediated through arms race and international trade, which turned the workers' state into its opposite, bureaucratic and tyrannical state capitalism' (1998, p. 120). Historical alternatives to capitalism are considered to exist only in the realm of science fiction. A politically motivated forgetfulness surrounds many examples of working-class self-activity such as the workers' democracy of the Paris Commune of 1871, the first years of the Russian Revolution; Spain in 1936-37; Hungary in 1956; the French action committees of 1968; the Chilean *cordones* of 1973; the Portuguese workers' commissions of 1974-75; the Iranian *Shoras* of 1979; and the initial rise of Solidarity in Poland in 1980.

The siren call of the postmodernists—that we should reject a systematic explanation of material reality and the world historical struggle to abolish its exploitative systems of production—follows their conviction that the social division of labour, and the surplus labour that structures it, has been replaced by information and that the circulation and the consumption of 'sign value' has superseded the practices and relations of production. In admonishing us to believe that labour has been replaced by technology as the basis of social wealth, postmodernists tread dangerously close to simply updating the ideology of the dominant regime of capital and wage-labour and facilitating its transnational expansion under the guise of exposing representation's 'metaphysics of presence.' According to Perry Anderson (1998), the 'long downswing' from post-war capitalism, to the 1980s and the 'battering down of labour in core regions, outsourcing of plants to cheap wage locations in the periphery, displacement of investment into services and communications, expansion of military expenditure, and vertiginous rise in the relative weight of financial speculation at the expense of innovative production' brought about 'all the deteriorated elements of the postmodern' such as 'unbridled *nouveau riche* display, teleprompt statecraft, boll-weevil consensus' (1998, p. 92). Anderson writes that with the advent of postmodernism, oppositional politics aligned against capitalism have all but disappeared. He writes:

> The universal triumph of capital signifies more than just a defeat for all those forces once arrayed against it, although it is also that. its deeper sense lies in the cancellation of political alternatives. Modernity

comes to an end, as Jameson observes, when it loses any antonym. The possibility of other social orders was an essential horizon of modernism. Once that vanishes, something like postmodernism is in place. (1998, pp. 91-92)

The inexorably downward spiral towards dystopian resignation brought about by the postmodernist assault on material reality and any radical attempts to change it must be confronted by radical hope. It must be confronted by a 'contraband pedagogy' that conjugates hope with revolutionary struggle in the search for an alternative to capitalist social relations of exploitation. One primary objective should be the translocation of past socialist struggles into the corridors of our historical imaginations as a condition of possibility of transformative change and a necessary prelude to our own history-making activity. Such an objective would be to overcome despair in the face of capital's destructive and imperialising force by outbidding it with an affirmation of collective solidarity.

Whilst mainstream pedagogy has conjured away the idea that education should play a central role in the struggle for social justice, contraband pedagogy rests on the twin notions that the macrostructural frameworks of capitalism do not fully annihilate possibilities for resistance and revolution and that modernity has not been fully consummated. Contraband pedagogy is not reconciled to the postmodern insight that authentic agency has been eclipsed by the systems of symbolic mediation that create desires that can only be false or always already alienating. We still remain loyal to the conviction that the responsible, self-reflecting subject can exist and that self-knowledge can lead to self-determination and eventually revolutionary praxis. Contraband pedagogy does not seek to help individuals empower themselves. Empowerment is a liberal option that enables people to gain control over the conditions of their daily lives. Contraband pedagogy is not about gaining control of the 'always already' but is about struggling and transforming the conditions that delimit the horizons of the daily life and prohibit the acquisition of the material necessities that would enable a decent and just livelihood for all the toilers of the world. Sometimes this struggle calls for armed resistance and opposition. Sometimes it calls for negotiation.

Contraband pedagogy's deployment as a weapon in the fight against globalization can benefit from an engagement with the new wave of Marxist educational scholarship in Britain, particularly the work of educationalists Mike Cole, Andy Green, Dave Hill, and Glenn Rikowski. Whilst lacking the tradition of Marxist scholarship that has benefited education scholars in Great Britain, the educational left in the United States can never the less begin to revitalize educational reform efforts by assessing the limitations of prevailing leftist paradigms built around postmodernist forms of cultural critique. Given the exacerbating contradictions of capital—seen in the growing numbers of homeless in the streets of major US cities, the increasing vulnerability of the middle-class, and in the growth of the militarized, gated communities of the ruling class—a socialist alternative may not seem as far-fetched as it does today among the vast majority of United States workers.

Like many other educators and activists, we face a daunting challenge. In Los Angeles, where we live and labour, we face not so much a bourgeois-driven apathy from our colleagues and students as an overwhelmingly active despair exacerbated by the entrenched belief that the ideological hegemony and social practices of the United States' capitalist class is far too powerful to resist (even though at some level most people recognize that all forms of hegemony are leaky). Outraged by the vainglorious attempts of politicians to propagate the myth that the United States represents the best of all possible worlds, and disgusted by the swelling numbers of United States citizens who are following in the ideological footsteps of Christian fundamentalist politicians such as Pat Robertson (whose recent televised address to millions of U.S. citizens included a warning that a gay activist event held in Florida could provoke God to send an asteroid to destroy the earth and joins similar condemnations of public schooling as an un-American socialist enterprise that is anti-family and that teaches students to reject God and the marketplace in favour of the perils of drugs, sexual promiscuity, homosexuality and union membership), many of us spend time teaching in other countries, including Latin America, where we feel our revolutionary politics has more potential to effect a measure of material change in the lives of the toilers of the world. While to a certain extent and in certain contexts this might be true, we believe that efforts to dismantle the exploitative relations of transnational capitalism have to begin here. As one Central American *campesina* activist, Elvia Alvarado, puts it:

> It's hard to think of change taking place in Central America without there first being changes in the United States. As we say in Honduras, *'Sin el perro, no hay rabia'*—without the dog, there wouldn't be rabies.
>
> So you Americans who really want to help the poor have to change your own government first. You Americans who want to see an end to hunger and poverty have to take a stand. You have to fight just like we're fighting—even harder. You have to be ready to be jailed, to be abused, to be repressed. And you have to have the character, the courage, the morale, and the spirit to confront whatever comes your way.

If you say, 'Oh, the United States is so big and powerful, there's nothing we can do to change it,' then why bother talking about solidarity? If you think like that, you start to feel insignificant and your spirit dies. That's very dangerous. For as long as we keep our spirits high, we continue to struggle.

We campesinos are used to planting seeds and waiting to see if the seeds bear fruit. We're used to working on harsh soil. And when our crops don't grow, we're used to planting again and again until they take hold. Like us, you must learn to persist. (1987, p. 144)

We are hard-pressed to find a better clarion call for the contraband pedagogy we are advocating.

Notes

1. Our claim is that while globalization is not a new phenomenon, its temporal character has been affected by instant financial transactions.
2. See Stanley Aronowitz and Henry Giroux, *Postmodern Education.* Minneapolis, MN: University of Minnesota Press; Patti Lather (1991) *Getting Smart: Feminist Research and Pedagogy with/in the Postmodern.* London, England: Routledge; William Doll, Jr. (1993) *A Post-Modern Perspective on Curriculum.* New York: Teachers College Press; Joe Kincheloe (1993) *Towards a Critical Politics of Teacher Thinking: Mapping the Postmodern.* Westport, CT: Bergin and Garvey; Robin Parker Usher and Richard Edwards (1994) *Postmodernism and Education.* London and New York: Routledge; Andy Hargreaves (1994) *Changing Teachers, Changing Times.* New York, NY: Teachers College Press; Henry Giroux and Peter McLaren (1994) *Between Borders: Pedagogy and the Politics of Cultural Studies.* New York and London: Routledge; and Richard Smith and Philip Wexler (eds.) *After Post Modernism.* London and Washington, DC: Falmer Press.
3. For powerful developments of Marxist feminist approaches, see the work of Teresa Ebert (1996), Rosemary Hennessy (1993) and Carole A. Stabile (1997). See Peter McLaren, Beyond Phallogocentrism: Critical Pedagogy and its Capital Sins: A Response to Donna LeCourt, *Strategies* (in press).
4. Anti-essentialism and anti-foundationalism can be characterized as a postmodern philosophical position that criticizes the notion that reality exists as an entity independent of appearances.

CHAPTER 10

Postmodernism Adieu:
Towards a Politics of Human Resistance
Peter McLaren, Dave Hill and Mike Cole

Under the guise of a liberal heterogeneity with a front-line value of 'democracy', the hegemonic market capitalist agenda has set in place a brutal abandonment of systems of social protection, longer working hours, reduced welfare benefits, a lessening of resources and freedom of manoeuvre, and a transformation of governments into security forces for multi-national corporations (Bauman, 1998).

Over half the largest economies on the planet are not countries but multinational corporations who relentlessly scour the globe for places where workers can be exploited for cheaper and cheaper labour. However, just as workers are being encrypted by business and government élites into a more severe form of worldwide neo-colonial status, they are at the same time being plagued by the consumer capitalist imperative to nourish recycled desires for new commodities (McLaren and Farahmandpur, this volume). Constantly pressured by capital to de-grammaticalize their sensorium and function as irrational consumer-citizens unfettered by the discomfiting propinquities of reason and self-reflexivity, the oppressed are encouraged to an unstoppable desire to consume. As a way of mitigating the pernicious malaise that accrues daily in the domains of unemployed misery and of employment in routinised and alienating jobs, in the law, in health, and in education, they dream of one day achieving a hallowed place in commodity utopia. It is in the interests of the corporations to keep this dream alive. Accordingly, many of the international accords (such as the Multinational Agreement on Investments) are negotiated behind closed doors so that the main purpose of the game—to facilitate the movement of money and production facilities across international borders in order to shore up profits and power for the few at the expense of the toil and labour of the many—can be kept out of the public eye. Others, like the Maastricht convergence criteria for the economies of the European Union, so confident of the supremacy of capitalist imperatives, are trumpeted as such— the depletion of social programs and of budget deficits being openly and publicly held to be incontestable.

At this current millennial moment, postmodernism, with all its self-propelling capacity, has found a favourable constituency among neo-conservatives and neo-liberals—who, conjoining together (as Reaganites and

Thatcherites and their successors) have enjoyed tremendous success at promoting an anti-government, unregulated markets agenda and whose representatives benefit the most from the extraterritoriality of capital. The supply-side politics of conservative politicians and their wealthy benefactors, who regularly turn a blind eye to market inequities or failure, has prompted wage stagnation, rising inequality, real and hidden unemployment, and anti-poor legislation across the capitalist world, both advanced and developing.

The growth in Britain and USA over the last twenty-five years of right-wing think tanks and their pundits, to whom the media is more than willing to give a friendly hearing, has created a powerful infrastructure able and willing to promote a social and public policy agenda fundamentally based on unregulated markets and limited government, and the excision of government from macro-economic policy (Covington, 1998). Cutbacks in social spending, which disproportionately affect the poor, have and will continue to drastically increase social tension in the years ahead (McLaren and Farahmandpur, this volume). According to Bauman, 'One of the most seminal consequences of the new global freedom of movement is that it becomes increasingly difficult, perhaps altogether impossible, to re-forge social issues into effective collective action' (1998, p. 69). We are not so pessimistic. This new global freedom may apply particularly to finance capital (e.g. Burbach *et al.* 1997, pp. 67-8), but industrial capital is not nearly as mobile (Meiksins Wood 1997; Cole 1998).[1]

Industrial action and protest action by individual social movements (and by coalitions of movements, see Sanders, Hill and Hankin, this volume) clearly has its contingently located periods of amazing strength and of quietist retrenchment. The late 1990s has seen, across the USA and Western Europe, for example, highly successful industrial and progressive action such as the UPS and Teamsters' action in the USA and the Anti-Poll Tax movement and riot in Britain (see Sanders, Hill, and Hankin, this volume; Cohen and Moody 1998, and the pages of the Left and Marxist Press, such as The Socialist (formerly Militant), Socialist Worker, and Tribune in Britain.

The right has subjectively adduced copious reasons why the poor should be held responsible for their own poverty. And their arguments become all the more powerful in an era of economic insecurity in which people are looking for somebody to blame. In September 1995, at San Francisco's Fairmount Hotel, 500 of the world's leading politicians (including George Bush, George Shultz, and Margaret Thatcher), businessmen, and scientists gathered at the invitation of Mikhail Gorbachev to spend three days of discussion on the economic future of the planet. The future was summed up by the numbers '20 to 80'. It was proposed that 20 percent of the population of the planet was all that was needed to keep the world economy going. The 'global brain trust' at the Fairmount calculated that a fifth of all job-seekers will be enough to produce all the commodities and services that the world society will be able to afford. Since business leaders argued that it would be unreasonable to expect corporations to look after the unemployed, the bottom 80 percent will be left without jobs (with the exception of volunteer services) and therefore in need of narcoticisation, of having their senses dulled down by the mass media machinery through a form of 'tittytainment' (Martin and Schuman, 1997). Europe and North America are eager to join the privatization movement and become part of that future 20 percent who will be lucky enough to be part of the ranks of the employed.

In the United States, the voucher initiative has become a neo-liberal juggernaut, smashing through the infrastructure of public education. In England and Wales, while there is no formal voucher system, the combination of per capita funding for schools and 'open enrolment' ('choice'—for some) have, in effect, instituted a quasi-voucher system (Hill 1997; Whitty, Power and Halpin, 1998).

Whilst the rhetoric of 'choice' sounds appealing (working-class families can choose to send their children to a public or private school of their choice), the reality has serious implications that threaten to eviscerate the public sphere of education and, in the USA, turn it into a theme park for Christian Sunday School banality. When an African-American student, Tenasha Taylor, gave a speech in her English class at the private University School of Milwaukee, and proceeded to criticize what she perceived as racist practices at the school, she was suspended until the following fall. She sued the school on the grounds of free speech but lost when Federal Judge Terrance Evans argued that protections afforded by the Bill of Rights do not apply to private actors such as the University School (Miner, 1998). Private schools in Milwaukee are often used to escape desegregation in a district where 60 percent of the students are African-American. In some of the private Catholic schools, the proportion is 3 to 5 percent. In addition, private schools do not have to hire certified teachers, do not have to require college degrees for their teachers, do not have to release information on employee wages and benefits. Further, private schools are not required to release test scores or attendance or suspension or dropout rates. Religious private schools can fire teachers who do not support the religious views of the school, or who support abortion, who are gay, etc. Within private schools, teachers who teach that the Holocaust did not happen, or that evolution is a lie, will have an easier job to make their case unimpeded by objectivity, and will find that fewer bureaucratic obstacles stand between them and promoting the reactionary, racist agendas of new right enthusiasts.

From the perspective of the privateers/privatisers, the democratically controlled public school system with its structure of public weight and responsibility is little more than a 'socialist' practice and is, therefore, 'demonic.' The Blair government's proposals to invite private business into the running of individual schools, groups of schools (grouped in Education Action Zones, and 'failing' (democratically accountable) local education authorities promise—or threaten—to replicate the US experience (Cole, 1998; Hatcher, 1998; Hill (ed.), forthcoming).

Covington suggests that in the USA vouchers will help to erode middle-to-upper class support for public education since parents would save more in taxes by reducing public expenditure on education than they would lose in decreased education subsidy for their children's education (Covington, 1998). Vouchers also have strong anti-union implications by offering one means to break the power of public sector unions (Covington, 1998; Molnar, 1998). Vouchers play into the ideology of the wealthy and the powerful who support a minimalist social welfare state, and effectively disguise the exploitation of the poor and the inequality of the classes. The larger ideology that supports the anti-union, anti-government, and anti-public school constituencies denies that social problems are particular conjunctural problems related to specific times and places. In other words, it denies that social problems are fundamentally structural and linked to the devastating social consequences of the free market. It denies that these social problems are directly related to institutional structures of power in society and practices such as capital flight, industrial relocation, and reallocation of state resources towards subsidizing services and suburbs and providing tax incentives for businesses (Petras and Polychroniou, 1998). The ideology that demonises the poor for their poverty and calls for 'personal responsibility' among the disenfranchised who survive in the margins and interstices of the social order effectively polarizes the class structure and undermines collective mobility among the poor. Postmodernism plays into this logic of local initiatives over collective action (McLaren and Farahmandpur, this volume).

As the essays of this volume have clearly shown, ghosted into postmodern theory is a promiscuous fascination with epistemological exoticisms, with difference, with schizophrenia and desire, with the return of the erstwhile eclipsed Other, with a subsumption of criticality within the spectacle, and with the fragmentation of unacknowledged commonalities and potential bases for oppositional force.

It is our wish to reclaim the best that Marxist analysis has to offer, as it has been able so successfully to track humanity's long and arduous journey from the extension of industrialism into what has been termed 'postindustrialism', from market capitalism, to monopoly capitalism, to multinational capitalism and derail capital's progress before it leads to oblivion. We are not concerned here with a dialectical reading of the conditions of emergence of Marxist theory, only to stress that we continue to learn enduringly from Marx. We are not disinterring Marxism from the catacombs of history—it is, if not in the USA, a vibrant, living body of political and theoretical action and analysis (Sanders, Hill and Hankin, this volume). We are taking its defining principles and theoretical texts and seeing how historical shifts may be registered in them and creatively applied to present circumstances. Marxism is the best response to capitalism that exists. At this current historical juncture we are more subordinated by capital than in Marx's time, and this should not be so much a cause for a paralysing despair as an important opportunity to articulate the contradictions of capitalism and its unfolding (Rikowski, this volume).

Somewhere between the recurring cycles of anticipated futures and reconstructed pasts, critical pedagogy needs to bid adieu to postmodernism and to accomplish more than a voguish challenge (at the level of the mandatory doctrines of mainstream culture) to those dominant Eurocentric forms of education that have been acculturated in advanced capitalism and that so ardently imprison us. And while we agree that the dominant trope of the white, Western male as the narrating subject of history must be challenged and that individualism and agency linked to the autonomous subject be made more hybrid and heterogeneous, we must at the same time safeguard those communal forms through which subjectivity can be transformed into collective political agency. Agency cannot be relinquished for the prize of cynicism. In its attachment to the idea of identity as a transhistorical unconscious plasma unconnected to social relations of production, postmodernism has already conceded too much in the struggle for liberation by denying self-reflexive agency. It also has all but eclipsed the concept of the state (Apple and Whitty, this volume). It has occluded the totality of patriarchy, virtually ignoring the intimate connections between women's position in society and in the paid workplace (Kelly, this volume). Dismissing objective knowledge in its valorization of the 'conflict between discourses' (Kelly, this volume; see also McLaren and Farahmandpur's critique of Patti Lather, this volume), postmodern feminism fails to recognize the contributions of thinkers such as Alexandra Kollontai and Leon Trotsky, who both argued that women need to be liberated from unpaid domestic labour (Kelly, this volume).

And whilst critical pedagogy must certainly partake of a politics of critical mapping that challenges hegemonic forms of representation such as Eurocentrism and Western models of identity, and whilst it must also challenge the creation of coherent, transparent identities in which verisimilitude is connected to a master narrative of certainty, it must never fail to situate such a politics in a larger narrative of liberation from the constraints of capital (Bourne, this volume). Whilst we agree that narratives of liberation cannot be settled in advance, and that the complexities of the 'concrete historical instance' must be teased out in critical detail (Apple and Whitty, this volume), all pedagogies underwritten by a politics of liberation must nevertheless be underwritten by a critical utopianism and political praxis that takes the concept of totality seriously. Supported by a conviction that inequalities are social and eliminable, critical pedagogy must remain amenable to arbitration and collective decision-making. We remain steadfastly committed to a dialectical approach, which situates reality as a process founded upon contradictions; one can understand the parts only in relation to their totality. And once such an understanding is acquired, agency is possible, if we understand agency to be the ability of people to change social structures over time.

The dialectical reality that we all face is that we are both inside of nature and outside of it. The signifier and the signified are not one and the same. Whilst one cannot understand human needs and desires outside of a symbolic frame of reference, one also cannot escape the mediations of the economy and the reproduction of material life. Ruling ideologies are those that intervene in discourse to secure particular social configurations over others, creating dependent hierarchies that serve to contain hegemonically sliding signifiers of meaning and to halt the progress of historical understanding. Articulating mechanisms are always historically contingent but are secured by the specific activity of social forces. For instance, capital and its institutions are one such force that exists to contain the power of labour (Neary, this volume). Unpaid surplus labour is extracted from direct producers, determining the relationship between capital and labour and labour to itself; labour, in capital, is constitutive of the mediation of social relations (Neary, this volume, see also Rikowski, this volume). We need a politics of representation, and a politics of identity, but even as we admit to this we also must at the same time admit to the necessity of recognizing that whilst the self is constituted through language and representation, all representation is conditioned by the history of social relations and class struggle. Postmodernism understands the first part of this proposition but ignores—sometimes willfully so—the second.

As educators who recognize that we need to build a society where socialism can flourish, we acknowledge that there are some immediate positions on globalization that critical educators and cultural workers can take. Some of these have recently been summarized by William Grieder: global expansion must be made more stable and must abide by more realistic rules; the United States must give up its commitment to neo-colonial capitalism; the new architecture for a global economy must not be fashioned mainly by bankers and economists but by social activists, poor nations, labour, and environmentalists; capital controls must moderate the behavior of investors; countries must be given sovereign self-protection; and floating exchange rates among national currencies must be abandoned. Since the persistent overcapacity in productive output has always led to the search for cheaper labour, wage incomes must be rebalanced with capital incomes; capital needs to be funnelled into domestic industrial development and not just exports; sweatshops and child labour must be abandoned; the G-7 industrial nations must adopt emergency controls on capital; central banks should temporarily relax balance sheet rules for commercial banks; pro-growth business executives should run the IMF and stop austerity plans; and the IMF and the World Bank should forgive the poorest nations for their debts.

Ultimately, of course, these perspectives sound no more satisfying that those posed by Roberto Mangabeira Unger and Cornel West. Unger and West are in favour of a productivist program designed to 'deepen democracy' while challenging 'the stark divisions between vanguard and rearguard—between advanced and backward sectors of the economy' (1998, p. 13). They call this a 'politics of tinkering'—'a broad-based and market-friendly effort to lift up the economic rearguard' (1998, p. 13). They envisage a venture capitalist enterprise that can be used to broaden the access of finance and technology through the establishment of independently administered venture-capital funds chartered to invest in the rearguard, a project that would involve diversifying investment portfolios, establishing the coexistence of private and social property, and a strengthening of labour laws. Unger and West refer to this as a form of 'democratic experimentalism' a 'motivated, sustained and cumulative tinkering with the institutionalist arrangements of the government and the economy' by an engaged and informed citizenry (p. 15).

Of course, there is something all too reformist in these proposals. Are these not unlike the strategies of the 'resistance postmodernists', (reactionary postmodernists of course eschew such questions) accommodating the imperatives of capital to the existing structures of exploitation while claiming to make minor particularistic adjustments in order to make them less harmful to those most vulnerable in our society? What, in this perspective, is to prevent neo-liberals from continuing to threaten unemployment and competition in the labour market as a means of depressing wages and increasing the rate of exploitation and profit (Cole and Hill, this volume; Kelly, this volume)? Surely this position poses a major dilemma facing the left today.

Martin Carnoy's recent introduction to Pedagogy of the Heart by Brazilian educator, Paulo Freire, captures some of the dynamics of this dilemma. Carnoy makes some complimentary remarks about Brasil's President, Fernando Enrique Cardoso, whom he claims has expanded educational enrolment and democratized educational policies, refashioning an involvement in politics of the masses of poor and marginalised, and solidifying democratic political stability. According to Carnoy, Cardoso wants to bring about equalization of income and wealth by undoing the economic debt of the 1980s, and expanding political participation even if it is tilted toward neo-liberal economic stabilisation and delays equalization. Yet according to Carnoy, Paulo Freire believes that the process of equalization itself is needed to develop the Brazilian economy outside of global neo-liberalism.

We believe that social democratic economic strategies such as those articulated by Unger, West, and Cardoso, by way of a social democratic 'tinkering' with the economy (i.e. democratically distribute the social wealth), while well-intentioned, clearly ignore the crisis-ridden nature of global capitalism and end up as little more than a capitulation to the expansion of capital and the proliferation of labour-power surrendered to capital (Rikowski, this volume). This sounds very much like the challenge of 'Third Way' politicians such as Tony Blair and Bill Clinton—'figuring out how to make accommodating to globalization consistent with progressive social values' (Panitch, 1998, p. 20). We believe that this is the wrong challenge to be pitched by the left because, as Leo Panitch notes, 'The overarching priority will remain that of fostering the penetration of capitalist values into every dimension of state-society relations as well as every corner of the globe and every facet of human life' (1998, p. 20). Panitch articulates the problem as the failure of social democracy. He writes:

> ... .an efficient capitalist state is, increasingly, what social democracy itself stands for today. It has adopted global competition as a goal, which the state must foster, rather than regarding it as a constraint which must eventually be overcome. Social democracy still recognizes the importance of liberal democratic institutions, but is has lost that broader democratic vision that originally impelled socialists to try to use those institutions as building blocks for organizing societies on cooperative rather than competitive principles. So extensive is this accommodation to globalization that social democracy (incorporating as it does now most former Communists in Eastern Europe) is largely reduced, even in the face of continuing mass unemployment in Western Europe, to undercutting social benefits in order to advance labor-market flexibility while still promoting the new 'cargo cult' of training. ('If you train them the jobs will come`.) It is as though, seeing a man on

the street, hungry and homeless, you approach his problem only through the optic of his not being motivated enough, entrepreneurial enough, skilled enough to get a job, rather than through the optic of there being something fundamentally wrong with the capitalist system. There is nothing much socialist in a value system that does not begin, morally, from the latter optic. (1988, pp. 20-21. See also Cole, 1998.)

Here we side with Freire, who writes:

The criticism of capitalism I put forth, from an ethical point of view, derives as much from the educator as it does from the activist, which I seek to continue to be in my own way. My activism can never become dissociated from my theoretical work; on the contrary, the former has its tactics and strategies formulated on the latter. The moment we recognize that food production around the world could be sufficient to feed twice its population, it is desolating to realize the numbers of those who come into the world but do not stay, or those who do but are forced into early departure by hunger. My struggle against capitalism is founded on that—its intrinsic perversity, its antisolidarity nature. (1998, p. 88)

We are aware that socialism must assume many different forms. Yet the struggle ahead must never waver from the direct overthrow of current practices of global capitalism, and it must be a universal struggle because capital itself, while from its beginning being essentially international and global always has been, but has become, to an unprecedented extent, a globalized system. In this sense it must remain fundamentally a politics of emancipation fired by forms of human resistance to the social domination of capital which simultaneously challenge social inequalities generated by capitalist markets (Postone, 1996). Exploiting the inner contradiction within the capital relation (Neary, this volume), a new class of economic actors—from grassroots activists, workers, small-scale producers, cooperatives, to peasant collectives—must jointly challenge the capitalist system. Since abstract labour creates forms of sociality that young people reject, it is imperative that young people—recognized as a specific form of human sociability (Neary, this volume)—be given the theoretical tools to develop a language of social critique and transformation. The struggle will also have to involve diverse social movements and worker-run enterprises that can wrest control of the economy from the multi-national corporations. It is imperative that community and labour forces control the means of production. This will include workers councils and trade unions but also communities of self-interest—all of which must be profoundly internationalist in character.

In order to play a role in this process, critical pedagogy will have to wrest itself away from bourgeois social theory to the extent that it recognizes some of its major danger points. One of the most confounding overstatements of postmodernism has been the notion that discourse does not correspond in any way with external reality. From this perspective it is difficult to capture the underlying structure of reality, especially in terms of its patterns and relations of exploitation, since it is not even postulated that an independently existing reality occurs at all or that the natural world exists independently of our knowledge of it. In our view, theories must in some fundamental way correspond with external reality or else they become superfluous appendages in the struggle for social justice. There are no timeless, ahistorical or pristine discourses out of which our pedagogies of liberation are to be constructed. Conversely, acknowledging that 'race' and gender and sexuality are 'socially constructed' or 'floating signifiers' does not imperil their everyday lived social reality —a reality that does not care whether 'race' and gender are social constructions or not. Postmodernists too often forget that we have become capitalized life forms (transformed into human capital) who remain centered by capital, even as self-reflexivity itself becomes inflected by capital (Rikowski, this volume).

Our knowledge must be forged out of the flux and flow of the material world, it must be tested dialectically over time in the arena of praxis. Anti-racism and anti-sexism as part of a pedagogy of liberation must employ dialectical reasoning and not be left to psychoanalytically based models (Bourne, this volume). A non-reductionist dialectical materialism provides insights into the nature of society that is unavailable from any other perspective and is indispensable as a weapon in the overthrow of the capitalist system. A theory of pedagogy can only be adequate to the struggle ahead if it takes into consideration the historical development of capitalism. Some of the insights of postmodernism can be conscripted into the struggle against globalized capital, as long as we are aware of their limitations within the broader context of theory-building in general (Apple and Whitty, this volume). Critical educators need an engagement with postmodernism since that can deepen the conceptual reservoirs of Marxist theories by pointing out the limitations of such thought. If this engagement is successful it must eventually banish postmodernist theory to the dustbin of history. Marxist theory has, for example in this volume, pungently and clearly addressed issues pertaining to feminism, trans-gendered identities, and anti-racist struggle. Yet there remains much to accomplish in these areas. Postmodern theories provide a limited explanatory power in exploring such issues. But we want to be clear that unless feminism and identity politics cultivated in the soil of poststructuralism ally themselves more squarely with a politics of class struggle, their contributions will not nourish the revolutionary praxis necessary in the struggle ahead, and will, at best, be second-order contributions.

Acknowledgements

This is to acknowledge the contribution to various drafts of this chapter made by Mike Cole and Glenn Rikowski.

Note

1.   Cole has argued that 'globalization' is used ideologically to justify competitiveness and modernization in the interests of British and global capitalism (Cole, 1998).

References

Adonis and Pollard (1997) *A Class Act, The Myth of Britain's Classless Society*. London: Hamish Hamilton.

Ahmad, A. (1992) *In Theory: Classes, Nations, Literatures*. London: Verso.

Ahmad, A. (1997) Issues of class and culture: An interview conducted by Ellen Meiksins Wood. In E. M. Wood and J. B. Foster (eds.), *In defense of history: Marxism and the postmodern age*. New York: Monthly Review Press.

Ahmad, A. (1998) The Communist Manifesto and the problem of universality. *Monthly Review*, 50 (2) pp. 12-38.

Ainley, P. (1993) *Class and Skill: Changing Divisions of Knowledge and Labour*. London: Cassell.

Altbach, P. (1995) Professors and Politics: An International Perspective. In M. Ginsburg, *The Politics of Educators Work and Lives*. New York/London: Garland Publishing.

Althusser, L. (1971) Ideology and Ideological State Apparatuses. In L. Althusser, *Lenin and Philosophy and Other Essays*. London: New Left Books.

Althussser, L. (1971) Ideology and State Apparatus. In L. Althusser, *Lenin and Philosphy and other Essays*. London: New Left Books.

Alvarado, E. (1987) *Don't be afraid Gringo: A Honduran woman speaks from the heart*. Translated and edited by M. Benjamin. New York: Harper and Row.

Amin, S. (1996) Imperialism and culturalism compliment each other. *Monthly Review*, 48 (2) pp. 1-11.

Amin, S. (1997) *Capitalism in the age of globalization*. London: Zed Books.

Amin, S. (1998a) Spectres of capitalism. *Monthly Review*, 50 (1) pp. 36-39.

Amin, S. (1998b) *Spectres of capitalism: A critique of current intellectual fashions*. Monthly Review Press.

Anderson, P. (1998) *The Origins of Postmodernity*. London and New York: Verso Books.

Ansell-Pearson, K. (1997a) *Viroid Life: Perspectives on Nietzsche and the Transhuman Condition*. London: Routledge.

Ansell-Pearson, K. (1997b) Viroid Life: On Machines, Technics and Evolution, in: K. Ansell-Pearson (ed.) *Deleuze and Philosophy: the difference engineer*. London: Routledge.

Apple, M. (1979) *Ideology and Curriculum*. London and New York: Routledge

Apple, M. W. (1993) *Official Knowledge: Democratic Education in a Conservative Age*. London & New York: Routledge and Kegan Paul.

Apple, M. W. (1995) *Education and Power* (Second edition). New York: Routledge.

Apple, M. W. (1996a) *Cultural Politics and Education*. New York: Teachers College Press.

Apple, M. W. (1996b) Power, meaning, and identity. *British Journal of Sociology of Education*, 17 (2) pp. 125-144

Aronowitz, S. (1992) *The Politics of Identity*. New York: Routledge.

Aronowitz, S. and Giroux, H. (1986) *Education Under Siege: The Conservative, Liberal and Radical Debate over Schooling*. London: Routledge and Kegan Paul.

Aronowitz, S. and Giroux, H. (1991) *Postmodern Education: Politics, Culture and Social Criticism*. Minneapolis: University of Minnesota Press.

Ash Ra Tempel (1996) Dutch Radio broadcast, November 1996.

Babha, H. (1990) Interview with Homi Bhabha, The third space. In J. Rutherford (ed.), *Identity: community, culture, difference*. London: Lawrence and Wishart.

Baker, K. (1990) 'A bright new term for London's children', *Evening Standard*, 30 March, p. 7.

Ball, S. (1990) *Education Reform: A Critical Post-Structural Approach.* Milton Keynes: Open University Press.

Ball, S. (1990) *Politics and Policy Making in Education: Explorations in Policy Sociology.* London: Routledge.

Ball, S. (1994) *Education Policy.* Lewes: Falmer Press.

Ball, S. (1994) *Education Reform: a Critical and Post-Structural Approach.* Buckingham: Open University Press.

Banks, O. (1955) *Parity and Prestige in English Secondary Education.* London: Routledge.

Barnard, N. (1997) Most research is 'waste of time'. *Times Educational Supplement,* 12th September 1997, p. 6.

Barratt Brown, M. and Coates, K. (1996) *The Blair Revolution: Deliverance for Whom?* Nottingham: Spokesman.

Baudrillard, J. (1983) *In the Shadow of the Silent Majorities ... Or the End of the Social and Other Essays.* New York: Semiotext (e), Inc.

Baudrillard, J. (1994) *The Illusion of the End.* Cambridge: Polity Press (translated by Chris Turner).

Bauman, Z. (1998) Globalization: The Human Consequences. New York: Columbia University Press.

Beechey, V. (1987) *Unequal Work.* London:Verso.

Benn, T. (1996) *The Benn Diaries.* London: Arrow Books.

Bergman, A. (1998, April 3-9). All for one: Chumbawamba sells out to help out. *L.A.Weekly,* 20 (19) p. 43.

Best, S. and Kellner, D. (1991) *Postmodern Theory: Critical Interrogations.* Basingstoke: Macmillan.

Beyer, L. and Liston, D. (1992) Discourse or moral action? a critique of postmodernism. *Educational Theory,* 42 (4) pp. 371-393.

Biesta, G.J.J. (1998) Say you want a revolution: Suggestion for the impossible future of Critical Pedagogy, *Education Theory,* 48 (4).

Birchall, I. (1998) The Manifesto remains a guide. *New Politics,* 4 (4) pp. 114-121.

Blackmore, J. (1995) Breaking Out of Masculinist Politics in Education. In B. Limerick and B. Lingard (eds.) *Gender and Changing Education Management.* Rydalmere, NSW: Hodder.

Blair, T. (1998) *The Third Way.* London: The Fabian Society.

Blake, N. (1996) Between Postmodernism and Anti-modernism: The Predicament of Educational Studies, *British Journal of Educational Studies,* 44 (1) pp. 42-65.

Blake, N. (1997) A Postmodernism Worth Bothering About: A Rejoinder to Cole, Hill and Rikowski, *British Journal of Educational Studies,* 45 (3) pp. 293-305.

Blake, N. and Smith, R. (1997) Beware a totalising society. *Times Educational Supplement,* 10th October 1997, p. 23.

Boggs, C. (1997) The great retreat: Decline of the public sphere in the late twentieth century. *Theory and Society,* (26) pp. 741-780.

Bologh, R. W. and Mell, L. (1994) Modernism, postmodernism, and the new world (dis)order: A dialectical analysis and alternative. *Critical Sociology,* (20) 2, pp. 81-120.

Bonefeld, W. (1995) 'Capital as Subject and the Existence of Labour', in: Bonefeld, W. et al. (eds.), pp. 182-212.

Bonefeld, W., Gunn, R. & Psychopedis, K (eds.) (1992) *Open Marxism,* Vols. 1 & 2. London: Pluto.

Bonefeld, W., Gunn, R., Holloway, J. & Psychopedis, K. (eds.) (1995) *Open Marxism* Vol. 3. London: Pluto.

Bourne, J. (1980) Cheerleaders and ombudsmen: the sociology of race relations in Britain. *Race and Class*, 21 (4) pp. 331-352.

Bourne, J. (1987a) *Homelands of the mind: Jewish feminism and identity politics.* London: Institute for Race Relations (IRR).

Bourne, J. (1987b) *Towards an anti-racist feminism.* London: IRR.

Bourne, J. (1995) Review of S. Dunant, *The war of the words: the political correctness debate, Race and Class*, 36 (3) pp. 89-91.

Bowe, R. and Ball, S. with Gold, A. (1996) The Policy Process and the Processes of Policy. In J. Ahier, B. Cosin and M. Hales (eds.) *Diversity and Change: Education, Policy and Selection.* London: Routledge.

Bowe, R.and Ball, S. with Gold, A. (1992) *Reforming Education and Changing Schools.* London: Routledge.

Bowles, S. and Gintis, H. (1976) *Schooling in Capitalist America: Educational reform and the contradictions of economic life.* New York: Basic Books & London: Routledge and Kegan Paul.

Boyne, R. and Rattansi, A. (eds.) (1990) *Postmodernism and Society*, London: Macmillan.

Brenner, R. (1998) The economics of global turbulence. *New Left Review*, (229) pp. 1-264.

Brindle, D. (1997) Britain in UN dock on poverty record. *The Guardian*, 17th Nov.

Brindle, D. (1998) Gap between rich and poor widens again. *The Guardian,* 16th Oct.

Brosio, R. A. (1994) *A radical democratic critique of capitalist education.* New York: P. Lang.

Brown, P. and Lauder, H. (1991) Education, Economy and Social Change. *International Studies in the Sociology of Education*, 1.

Brown, S., Duffield, J. and Riddell, S. (1995) School Effectiveness Research: The Policy Makers' Tool for School Improvement? *EERA Bulletin,* March, pp. 6-15.

Brown, S., Riddell, S. and Duffield, J. (1997) *Classroom approaches to learning and teaching: the social class dimension.* Paper delivered to the ECER (European Educational Research Association) Annual Conference, Seville, Spain.

Bruegel, I (1986) The Reserve Army of Labour 1974–7. In Feminist Review (ed.) *Wage Work: A Reader.* London: Virago.

Brunt, R. (1988) Bones in the corset. *Marxism Today,* October, pp. 20-23.

Bryan, B., Dadzie, S. and Scafe, S. (1985) *The heart of the race: black women's lives in Britain.* London: Virago.

Burbach, R. (1998) The (Un)defining of Postmodern Marxism: on smashing modernization and narrating new social and economic actors. *Rethinking Marxism,* 10 (1) pp. 52-65.

Burbach, R., Núñez, O. and Kagarlitsky, B. (1997) *Globalization and Its Discontents: the rise of postmodern socialisms.* London: Pluto Press.

Butler, J. (1990) *Gender Trouble: Gender and the Subversion of Identity.* London: Routledge.

Butler, J. (1998) Merely Cultural. *New Left Review*, 227 pp. 33-44.

Callard, F. (1998) The body in theory, *Environment and Planning D: Society and Space,* 16, pp. 387-400.

Callinicos, A. (1989) *Against Postmodernism: A Marxist Critique.* Cambridge: Polity Press & New York: St. Martin's Press.

Callinicos, A. (1995) *Theories and narratives: Reflections on the philosophy of history.* Durham, North Carolina: Duke University Press.

Carnoy, M. (1998) 'Foreword'. In Paulo Freire, *Pedagogy of the Heart.* New York: Continuum.

Charter, D. (1996) Schools must not blur boundary of culture, says curriculum chief. *The Times*, 8 Feb.

Chitty, C. (1997) The School Effectiveness Movement: Origins, Shortcomings and Future Possibilities. *The Curriculum Journal*, 8 (1) pp. 45-62.

Chodorow, N. (1978) *The Reproduction of Mothering: Psychoanalysis and the Sociology of Gender.* Berkeley: University of California Press.

Chubb, M. and Moe, T. (1990) *Politics, Markets and America's Schools.* Washington: Brookings Institution.

Clarke, J. (1991) *New times and Old Enemies.* London: Harper Collins.

Clarke, S. (1988) *Keynesianism, Monetarism and the Crisis of the State.* Aldershot: Edward Elgar.

Clarke, S. (1991) *Marx, Marginalism and Modern Sociology.* London: Macmillan.

Cliff, T. and Gluckstein, D. (1996) *The Labour Party: a Marxist History.* London: Bookmarks.

Clough, R. (1992) *Labour: a Party Fit for Imperialism.* London: Larkin Publications.

Cohen, P. (1986) *Anti-racist cultural studies: a Curriculum Development Project in School and Community Education.* London: London University Institute of Education.

Cohen, P. (1988) The perversions of inheritance: studies in the making of multi-racist Britain. In P. Cohen and Harwant Bains, (eds.) *Multi-racist Britain.* London: Macmillan.

Cohen, P. (1991) *Monstrous Images, perverse reasons.* London: Centre for Multicultural Education, University of London Institute of Education.

Cohen, P. (1992) 'It's racism what dunnit': hidden narratives in theories of racism. In J. Donald and A. Rattansi (eds.) *'Race', culture and difference.* London: Sage.

Cohen, P. (1997) *Rethinking The Youth Question, Education, Labour and Cultural Studies.* Basingstoke: Macmillan.

Cohen, S. and Moody, K. (1998) Unions, Strikes and Class Consciousness Today. In L. Panitch and C. Leys (eds.) *Socialist Register 1998.* Rendlesham: Merlin.

Cole, M. & Skelton, B. (eds.) (1980) *Blind Alley: Youth in a Crisis of Capital.* Ormskirk: G.W. & A. Hesketh.

Cole, M. (1988a) (ed.) *Bowles and Gintis Revisited: Correspondence and Contradiction in Educational Theory.* Lewes: Falmer Press.

Cole, M. (1988b) From reductionist Marxism and revolutionary socialism to post-Liberal democracy and ambiguity: some comments on the changing political philosophy of Bowles and Gintis, *British Journal of Sociology*, 34 (3) pp. 452-462.

Cole, M. (1992) *Racism, History and Educational Policy: From the Origins of the Welfare State to the Rise of the Radical Right.* Unpublished PhD. thesis: Department of Sociology, University of Essex.

Cole, M. (1998) Casino Capitalism's Last Roll of the Dice? *The Times Higher Education Supplement*, March 20.

Cole, M. (1998) Globalisation, Modernisation and Competitiveness: A Critique of the New Labour Project in Education. *International Studies in Sociology of Education*, 8 (3) pp. 315-332.

Cole, M. and Hill, D. (1996) 'Resistance Postmodernism': Emancipatory Politics for a New Era or Academic Chic for a Defeatist Intelligentsia? In: K. Gill (ed.) *Information Society: New Media, Ethics and Postmodernism.* London: Springer-Verlag.

Cole, M. and Hill, D. (1996b) Postmodernism, Education and Contemporary Capitalism: A Materialist Critique, in M. O. Valente, A Barrios, A Gaspar and V. Teodoro (eds.), *Teacher Training and Values Education*, Lisbon: Association for Teacher

Education in Europe in association with Departamento de Educacao da Faculdade de Ciencias da Universidade de Lisboa.

Cole, M. and Hill, D. (1997) 'New Labour', Old Policies: Tony Blair's 'Vision' for Education in Britain. *Education Australia*, 37 pp. 17-19.

Cole, M. and Hill, D. (1999) Ex-Left Academics and the Curse of the Postmodern. *Education and Social Justice*, I (3) In press.

Cole, M., Hill, D. and Rikowski, G. (1997) Between Postmodernism and Nowhere: The Predicament of the Postmodernist. *British Journal of Educational Studies*, 45 (2), pp. 187-200.

Cole, M., Hill, D. and Shan, S. (eds) (1997), *Promoting Equality in Primary Schools*. London: Cassell.

Connell, R. (1995) Transformative Labour: Theorizing the Politics of Teachers Work. In M. Ginsburg, *The Politics of Educators Work and Lives*. New York/London: Garland Publishing.

Covington, S. (1998) How Conservative Philanthropies and Think Tanks Transform US Policy. *CoverAction Quarterly*, (63) pp. 6-16.

Crichton, M. (1991) *Jurassic Park*. London: Arrow.

Crichton, M. (1995) *The Lost World*. London: Century.

Crook, S. (1990) The End of Radical Social Theory? Notes on Radicalism, Modernism and Postmodernism. In R. Boyne and A. Rattansi (eds.) *Postmodernism and Society*. London: Macmillan.

Curtis, B. (1992) *True Government by Choice Men?* Toronto: University of Toronto Press.

Da Cunha, O. M. G. (1998) Black movements and the 'politics of identity' in Brazil. In S. E. L. Alvarez, E. Dagnino, and A. Escobar (eds.), *Cultures of politics: Politics of culture: Re-visioning Latin American social movements*. (pp. 220-251). Boulder, CO: Westview Press.

Dale, R. (1989) The Thatcherite Project in Education. *Critical Social Policy*, 9 (3).

Davies, A. (1998) The Cheapening of Education, *Fight Racism, Fight Imperialism!*, 143, June-July. BM Box 5909, London, WCIN 3XX, p. 11.

Debord, G. (1977) *The Society of the Spectacle*. Detroit: Black and Red.

Deer, B. (1996) Still Struggling After All These Years, *New Statesman*, 23rd Aug. pp12-13.

Derrida, J. (1994) *Specters of Marx: The State of the Debt, the Work of Mourning*. New York and London: Routledge.

Docherty, T. (ed.) (1993) *Postmodernism: A Reader*. London: Harvester Wheatsheaf.

Donald, J. (1989) 'Interesting Times', *Critical Social Policy*, 9 (3).

Donald, J. and Rattansi, A. (eds.) *'Race', culture and difference*. London: Sage.

Donnelly, C., Nimmo, M. and Convery, P. (1998) *The New Deal Handbook*. London: Unemployment Unit and Youthaid.

Duffield, J. (1998a) School support for lower achieving pupils, *British Journal of Special Education*, 25 (3) pp. 126-134.

Duffield, J. (1998b) *Unequal Opportunities or Don't mention the (class) war*. Paper to the Scottish Educational Research Association (SERA) Conference, Dundee.

Duffield, J. (1998c) Learning Experiences, effective schools and social context, *Support for Learning*, 13 (1) pp. 3-8.

Dunn, R. (1988) Quoted in *Education*, 8 July.

Eagleton, T. (1996) *The illusions of postmodernism*. Malden, Massachusetts: Blackwell Publishers.

Eagleton, T. (1997) Where do postmodernists come from? In E. Meiksins Wood and J. Bellamy Foster, *In defense of history: Marxism and the postmodern agenda.* New York: Monthly Review Press.

Ebert, T. L. (1996) *Ludic feminism and after: Postmodernism, desire, and labor in late capitalism.* Ann Arbor: The University of Michigan Press.

Ehrenreich, B. (1998) Beyond Monica—The future of Clinton's past. *The Nation,* 267 (7) pp. 13-14.

Einstein, A. (1998) Why socialism? *Monthly Review,* 50 (1) pp. 1-10.

Eisner, E. and Peshkin, A. (eds.) *Qualitative Inquiry in Education.* New York: Teachers College Press.

Engels, F. (1978) [1884] *The Origin of the Family, Private Property and the State.* Peking: Foreign Language Press.

Evans, J. and Penney, D. (1994) The Politics of Pedagogy: making a National Curriculum Physical Education. *Journal of Education Policy,* 10 (1) pp. 27-44.

Fekete, L. (1998) Let them eat cake, *Race and Class,* 39 (3) pp. 77-82.

Ferguson, M. and Wicke, J. (eds.) (1994) *Feminism and Postmodernism.* Durham and London: Duke University Press.

Fielding, S. and Rikowski, G. (1996) *Resistance to Restructuring? Post-Fordism in British Primary Schools.* Unpublished Paper, School of Education, University of Birmingham, UK.

Finn, D. (1987) *Training Without Jobs, New Deals and Broken Promises.* London: Macmillan.

Firestone, S. (1970) *The Dialectic of Sex.* New York: Bantam,

Fiske, J. (1991) *Understanding Popular Culture.* London: Routledge.

Flax, J. (1987) Postmodernism and Gender Relations in Feminist Theory. *Signs* 12, pp. 621-643.

Fornäs, J. (1995) *Cultural theory and late modernity.* London and Thousand Oakes: SAGE Publications.

Foster, H (ed.) (1985) *Recordings: Art, Spectacle, Cultural Politics.* Port Townend, Washington: Bay Press.

Foster, H. (ed.) (1983). *The Anti-aesthetic: essays on postmodern culture.* Port Townsend, Washington: Bay Press.

Frankel, B. (1997) Confronting neo-liberal regimes: The post-Marxist embrace of populism and realpolitik. *New Left Review,* (226) pp. 57-92.

Fraser, N. and Gordon, L. (1994) A Genealogy of Dependency. *Signs,* 19, pp. 309-336.

Fraser, N. and Nicholson, L.J. (1988) Social Criticism without Philosophy: An Encounter between Feminism and Postmodernism. In Nicholson (1990) *Feminism/ Postmodernism.* London: Routledge.

Freire, P. (1998) *Pedagogy of the Heart.* New York: Continuum.

Frith, S. (1983) *Sound Effects: youth, leisure, and the politics of rock.* London: Constable.

Fryer, P. (1984) *Staying Power.* London: Pluto.

Gamman and Makinen (1994) *Female Fetishism.* New York: New York University Press.

Gane, M. (ed.) (1993) *Baudrillard Live: Selected Interviews.* London: Routledge.

Gardels, N. (1997) Globalization with a human face. *New Perspectives Quarterly,* 14 (4) pp. 48-49.

Gerwitz, S., Ball, S. and Bowe, R. (1995) *Markets, Choice and Equity in Education.* Buckingham: Open University Press.

Gibson-Garaham, J. K. (1996) *The end of capitalism (as we knew it): A feminist critique of political economy.* Malden, Massachusetts: Blackwell Publishers.

Gibson-Graham, J. K. (1995) Waiting for the revolution, or how to smash capitalism while working at home in your spare time. In A. Callari, S. Cullenberg, and C. Biewener (eds.), Marxism in the postmodern age: Confronting the new world order. New York and London: The Guilford Press.

Giddens, A. (1998) The Third Way. London: Polity.

Gilligan, C. (1983) In a Different Voice: Psychological Theory and Women's Development. Cambridge, MA: Harvard University Press.

Gilroy, P. (1991) There ain't no Black in the union Jack: The cultural politics of race and nation. Chicago, Ill.: The University of Chicago Press.

Gilroy, P. (1993) Black Atlantic: Modernity and Double Consciousness. London and New York: Verso.

Gimenez, M. E. (1995) The production of divisions: Gender struggles under capitalism. In A. Callari, S. Cullenberg, and C. Biewener (eds.) Marxism in the postmodern age: Confronting the new world order. New York and London: The Guilford Press.

Giroux, H. (1983) Theories of Reproduction and Resistance in the New Sociology of Education: a Critical Analysis. Harvard Education Review, 53 (3) pp. 257-293.

Giroux, H. (1988) Teachers as Intellectuals: Towards a Critical Pedagogy of Learning. Granby, Massachusetts: Bergin and Garvey.

Giroux, H. (1994) Living dangerously: identity, politics and the new cultural racism. In H. Giroux and P. McLaren (eds.), Between borders: pedagogy and politics of cultural studies. London: Routledge.

Giroux, H. (ed.) (1990) Postmodernism, Feminism, and Cultural Politics. New York: State University of New York Press.

Giroux, H. A. (1988) Teachers as intellectuals: Towards a critical pedagogy of learning. South Hadley, MA: Bergin and Garvey.

Giroux, H. A. (1992) Border crossings: Cultural workers and the politics of education. London & New York: Routledge.

Giroux, H. and McLaren, P. (1988) Critical Pedagogy, the State and Cultural Struggle. New York: State University of New York Press.

Gitlin, A. (ed.) (1994) Power and Method. New York: Routledge.

Glenn, C. (1987) The Myth of the Common School. Amhurst: University of Massachusetts Press.

Gordon, F. (1995) Workers and Masses, Open Polemic, 11, March 1995. PO Box 1169, London, W3 9PF.

Grace, G. (1991) Welfare Labourism and the New Right: The struggle in New Zealand's education policy. International Studies in Sociology of Education, 1.

Green, A. (1994) Postmodernism and state education. Journal of Education Policy, 9 (1) pp. 67-83.

Green, T. and Whitty, G. (1994) The Legacy of the New Sociology of Education. Unpublished paper presented at the American Educational Research Association, New Orleans.

Greider, W. (1998) The Global Crisis Deepens: Now What? The Nation, 267 (12) pp. 11-16.

Gunn, R. (1992) 'Against Historical Materialism: Marxism as a First-order Discourse', in: Bonefeld, W. et al. (eds.).

Gur-Zeév. I. (1998) Towards a Non-repressive Critical Pedagogy, Education Theory, 48 (4) pp. 463-486.

Habermas, J. (1981) Modernity vs Postmodernity, New German Critique, 2 pp. 3-14.

Habermas, J. (1983) Modernity—an Incomplete Project. In H. Foster (ed.) The Anti-Aesthetic: Essays on Postmodern Culture, Port Townsend, Washington: Bay Press.

Habermas, J. (1990) *The philosophical discourse of modernity: Twelve lectures* (F. Lawrence, Trans.). Cambridge, Mass: MIT Press.

Hall, S. (1988) Brave new world, *Marxism Today,* Special issue October, pp. 24-29.

Hall, S. (1992) Cultural Studies: Two paradigms. In Grossberg, L., Nelson, C., and Treichler, P. (eds.) *Cultural Studies*. New York: Routledge.

Hall, S. (1992) New Ethnicities. In A Rattansi, J. Donald (eds.) *'Race', culture and difference*. London: Sage.

Hall, S. (1998) The Great Moving Nowhere Show: Blair has failed to break with neo-liberalism and thereby squandered a golden opportunity, *Marxism Today*, Nov./Dec. 1998.

Hall, S. and Jacques, M. (eds.) (1989) *New Times: The Changing Face of Politics in the 1990s*. London: Lawrence and Wishart.

Hall, S. and Jefferson, T. (eds) (1975) *Resistance through Rituals: Youth Sunculture in Post War Britain*. London: Hutchinson.

Hall, S., Critchley, C., Jefferson, A., Clarke, S. and Roberts, B. (1978) *Policing the crisis: mugging, the state and law and order.* London: Macmillan.

Hall, S., Held, D. and McLennan, G. (1992) Introduction to Hall, S., Held. and T. McGrew (eds.) *Modernity and its Futures*. Cambridge: Polity Press.

Halpin, D. (1998) Editorial: Getting by through Failing to Deliver Simple Truths. *British Journal of Educational Studies*, 46 (1) pp. 1-7.

Halstead, J. M. (1986) *The Case for Muslim Voluntary-Aided Schools*. Cambridge: The Islamic Academy.

Haraway, D. (1988) Situated Knowledges: The Science Question in Feminism and the privilege of partial perspectives. *Feminist Studies*, 14, pp. 575-599.

Haraway, D. (1991) *Simians, Cyborgs, and Women: The Reinvention of Nature*. New York: Routledge.

Hargreaves, A. (1994) Restructuring restructuring: postmodern and the prospects for educational change. *Journal of Education Policy* 9 (1) pp. 47-66.

Harman, C./Socialist Workers Party (1993) *In the Heat of the Struggle: 25 Years of Socialist Worker.* London: Socialist Worker and Bookmarks.

Harris, K. (1979) *Education and Knowledge*. London: RKP.

Hartley, D. (1993) Confusion in Teacher Education: a postmodern condition? In P. Gilroy, and M. Smith, (eds.) *International Analyses of Teacher Education*, London: Carfax Publishing Company.

Harvey, D. (1989) *The Condition of Postmodernity*. Oxford: Basil Blackwell.

Harvey, D. (1993) Class Relations, Social Justice and the Politics of Difference. In J. Squires (ed.) *Principled Positions*. London: Lawrence and Wishart.

Harvey, D. (1998) The body as an accumulation strategy, *Environment and Planning D: Society and Space*, 16, pp. 401-421.

Harvey, D. (1998) The geography of the Manifesto. In L. Panitch and C. Leys (eds.) *Socialist register: The Communist Manifesto now*. New York: Monthly Review Press.

Hatcher, R. (1998) Labour, official school improvement and equality, *Journal of Education Policy*, 13 (4) pp. 485-499.

Hatcher, R. (1998) Labour, Official School Improvement and Equality, *Journal of Education Policy*, 13 pp. 458-499.

Hatcher, R. (1998) Social Justice and the Politics of School Effectiveness and Improvement, *Race, Ethnicity and Education*, 1 (2) pp. 267-289.

Hatcher, R. and B. Troyna (1994) The Policy Cycle: A Ball by Ball Account. *Journal of Education Policy*, 9 (2) pp. 155-170.

Hatton, D. (1988) *Inside Left, the Story so far.* London: Bloomsbury Publishing.

Hebdige, D. (1979) *Subculture: the meaning of style.* London: Methuen.

Hebdige, D. (1988) *Hiding in the Light.* London: Routledge.

Henwood, D. (1995) The bull's sour 16. *The Nation,* 267 (7) p. 5.

Herrnstein, R. and Murray, C. (1994) *The Bell Curve.* New York: Free Press.

Hewitt, M. (1993) Illusions of Freedom: the regressive implications of 'postmodernism'. In, R. Miliband and L. Panitch (eds.) *Real Problems, False Solutions. Socialist Register.* London: Merlin Press.

Hill, D. (1989) *Charge of the Right Brigade: the Radical Right's Assault on Schooling and Teacher Education in Britain and the USA.* Brighton: Institute for Education Policy Studies.

Hill, D. (1990) *Something old, something new, something borrowed, something blue: schooling teacher education and the radical right in Britain and the USA.* London: Tufnell Press.

Hill, D. (1991a) *What's Left in Teacher education. London: Tufnell Press.*

Hill, D. (1991b) Seven Ideological Perspectives on Teacher Education Today and the Development of a Radical Left Discourse, Sydney, Australia, *Australian Journal of Teacher Education,* 16 (2) pp. 5-29.

Hill, D. (1994) Cultural Diversity and Initial Teacher Education. In G. Verma and P. Pumfrey (eds.) *Cultural Diversity and the Curriculum, Vol. 4. Cross-Curricular Contexts, Themes and Dimensions in Primary Schools.* London: Falmer Press.

Hill, D. (1997) Equality in Primary Schooling: the policy context, intentions and effects of the Conservative 'reforms'. In M. Cole, D. Hill and S. Shan (eds.) *Promoting Equality in Primary Schools.* London: Cassell.

Hill, D. (1997a) Equality in British Schooling: The Policy Context of the Reforms. In M. Cole, D. Hill and S. Shan (eds.), *Promoting Equality in Primary Schools.* London: Cassell.

Hill, D. (1997a) Equality in British Schooling: The Policy Context of the Reforms. In M. Cole, D. Hill and S. Shan (eds.), Promoting Equality in Primary Schools. London: Cassell.

Hill, D. (1997b) Reflection in Teacher Education. In K. Watson, S. Modgil and C. Modgil (eds.) *Educational Dilemmas: Debate and Diversity, vol.1: Teacher Education and Training.* London: Cassell.

Hill, D. (1999) Social Class and Education. In D. Matheson and I. Grosvenor (eds.) *An Introduction to the Study of Education.* London: David Fulton.

Hill, D. (1999a) The National Curriculum as Ideological and Cultural Reproduction. In D. Hill and M. Cole (eds.) *Schooling and Equality: Factual and Conceptual Issues:.* London: Tufnell Press.

Hill, D. (1999b) 'New Labour' and the conservative revolution in teacher education. In Hill, D. and Cole, M. (eds.) (1999b) *Schooling and Equality: Factual and Conceptual Issues.* London: Tufnell Press.

Hill, D. (1999c) Social Class and Education. In Matheson, D. and Grosvenor, (eds) *An Intraduction to the Study of Education.* London: David Fulton.

Hill, D. (ed.) (2000 forthcoming) *Education, Education, Education: Capitalism, Socialism and the Third Way.* London: Cassell.

Hill, D. (ed.) (2000) Education, Education, Education: Capitalism, Socialism and 'The Third Way'. London: Cassell

Hill, D. and Cole, M. (1995) Marxist state theory and state autonomy theory: the case of 'race' education in initial teacher education. *Journal of Education Policy,* 10 (2) pp. 221-232.

Hill, D. and Cole, M. (1996) Materialism and the Postmodern Fallacy: The Case of Education, in J.V. Fernandes (ed.), *Proceedings, of the Second International Conference of Sociology of Education in Portugal,* Faro, Portugal: Escola Superior de Educacao da Universidade do Algarve.

Hill, D. and Cole, M. (eds.) (1999a) *Promoting Equality in Secondary Schools.* London: Cassell.

Hill, D. and Cole, M. (eds.) (1999b) *Schooling and Equality: Factual and Conceptual Issues.* London: Tufnell Press.

Hillcole Group (1997) *Rethinking Education and Democracy: a Socialist Alternative for the Twenty-First Century.* London: Tufnell Press.

Hillcole Group/ed. Clyde Chitty (1991) *Changing the Future: Redprint for Education.* London: Tufnell Press.

Hillgate Group (1987) *The Reform of British Education.* London: Claridge Press.

Hird, M. J. (1998) Theorising Student Identity as Fragmented: some implications for feminist critical pedagogy. *British Journal of Sociology of Education,* 19 (4) pp. 517-527.

Hirom, K., Waller, T. and Cole, M. (1999) Gender. In D. Hill and M. Cole (eds.) *Equality and Schooling: Factual and Conceptual Issues.*

Hobsbawm, E. (1998) The Death of Neo-Liberalism: the present global crisis marks the end of market fundamentalism. *Marxism Today,* Nov./Dec. pp. 4-8.

Hollands, R. (1990) *The Long Transition.* London: Macmillan.

Holloway, J. (1995) From Scream of Refusal to Scream of Power: The Centrality of Work, in: W. Bonefeld, R. Gunn, J. Holloway & C. Psychopedis (eds.) *Emancipating Marx: Open Marxism—Volume 3.* London: Pluto Press.

Hunter, I. (1994) *Rethinking the School.* Boston: Allen & Unwin.

Jacques, M. (1988) *Marxism Today.* Special issue October.

Jacques, M. (1998) Leader: as we move into a new era, New Labour remains firmly stuck in the old one, *Marxism Today,* Nov./Dec. pp. 2-3.

Jameson, F. (1984) Postmodernism or, The Cultural Logic of Late Capitalism, *New Left Review,* 146, pp. 59-92.

Jameson, F. (1991) *Postmodernism.* London: Verso.

Jarvis, D. S. L. (1998) Postmodernism: a critical typology. *Politics and Society,* 26 (1) pp. 95-142.

Jay, M. (1998) *Cultural Semantics: Keywords of our Time.* Amherst: University of Massachusetts Press.

Jenkins, R. (1971) *The production of knowledge at the Institute of Race Relations.* London: Independent Labour Party.

Jessop, B. (1990) *State Theory: Putting Capitalist States in their Place,* Cambridge: Polity.

Johnson, R. (1979) Three problematics: elements of a theory of working-class culture, in J. Clarke, C. Critcher and R. Johnson (eds.) *Working Class Culture.* London: Hutchinson.

Joines, R. (1997) The academic left today. *Political Affairs,* 76 (6) p. 29-33.

Kay, G. & Mott, J. (1982) *Political Order and the Law of Labour.* London: Macmillan.

Kellner, D. (1995) The end of orthodox Marxism. In A. Callari, S. Cullenberg, and C. Biewener (eds.), *Marxism in the postmodern age: Confronting the new world order.* New York and London: The Guilford Press.

Kelly, J. (1992) Postmodernism and Feminism, *International Marxist Review,* 14, Winter 14 pp. 39-55. Paris, Presse-Edition-Communication (PEC).

Kelly, J. (1999) Gender and Equality: One hand tied behind us. In M. Cole (ed.) *Human Rights, Education and Equality.* London: Falmer Press.

Kelly, J., Cole, M. and Hill, D. (1999) Education Theory and the Defense of Marxism. *Education Theory*, in press.

Kelly. J., Cole, M. and Hill, D. (1999 in press) Education Theory and the Defense of Marxism, *Education Theory* (forthcoming).

Kohli, W. (1998) Critical education and Embodied Subjects: Making the Poststructural Turn, *Education Theory*, 48 (4) pp.511-520.

Korten, D. C. (1996) The mystic victory of market capitalism. In J. Mander and E. Goldsmith (eds.), *The case against the global economy and for a turn toward the local*. San Francisco: Sierra Club Books.

Laclau, E, and Mouffe, C. (1985) *Hegemony and socialist strategy: Towards a radical democratic politics*. (W. Moore and P. Cammack, Trans.). London: Verso Books.

Laclau, E. (1991) *Reflections on the New Revolutions of Our Times*. London: Verso.

Lash, S. (1990) *Sociology of Postmodernism*. London: Routledge.

Lather, P. (1984) Critical Theory, Curricular Transformation, and Feminist Mainstreaming. *Journal of Education*, 166 (1) pp. 49-62.

Lather, P. (1991) *Getting Smart: Feminist Research and Pedagogy With/in the Postmodern*. London & New York: Routledge.

Lather, P. (1998) Critical Pedagogy and its Complicities: a praxis of stuck places. *Educational Theory*, 48 (4) pp. 487-497.

Lauder, H. Hughes, D., Watson, S., Simuyi, I., Strathdee, R. and Waslander, S. (1995) *Trading in Futures: the Nature of Choice in Educational Markets in New Zealand*. Smithfield Project. Wellington: Victoria University of Wellington.

Lawton, D. (1975) *Class, Culture and the Curriculum*. London: Routledge.

Lebowitz, M. (1992) *Beyond Capital: Marx's Political Economy of the Working Class*. Basingstoke: Macmillan.

Lenin, V. I. (1965) A Great Beginning. In *Collected Works*, Vol. 29. Moscow: Progress Publishers.

Leys, C. and Panitch, L. (1998) The Political Legacy of the Manifesto. In L. Panitch and C. Leys (eds.) *Socialist Register 1998*. Rendlesham: Merlin.

Liston, D. (1988) *Capitalist Schools: Explanation and Ethics in Radical Studies of Schooling*. London: Routledge.

Livingstone, D. (1997) Searching for the Missing Links: neo-Marxist theories of Education, *British Journal of Sociology of Education*, 16 pp. 53-73.

Livingstone, K. (1987) *If Voting Changed Anything, They'd Abolish it*. London: Collins.

Low Pay Unit (1997) *The New Review*, Nov/Dec, London.

Luke, T. (1998) 'Moving at the Speed of Life?' A Cultural Kinematics of Telematic Times and Corporate Values, in: S. Lash, A. Quick & R. Roberts (eds.) *Time and Value*. Oxford: Blackwell.

Mahony, P. & Zmroczek, C. (1997) *Class Matters: 'Working-class' Women's Perspectives on Social Class*. London: Taylor and Francis.

Malik, K. (1996) Universalism and difference: Race and the postmodernists. *Race and Class*, 37 (3) pp. 1-17.

Malik, K. (1997) The mirror of race: postmodernism and the celebration of difference. In E. Meiksins Wood and J. Bellamy Foster (eds.), *In defense of history: Marxism and the postmodern agenda*. New York: *Monthly Review*.

Martin, H-P. and Schumann, H.(1997) The Global Trap: Globalization and the Assault on Democracy and Prosperity. London: Zed Books.

Martin, J. (1999) Barbarians are at the Gates: Gender, Education and the new Millennium. In M. Cole (ed.) *Human Rights, Education and Equality*. London: Falmer Press.

Marx, K. (1844a) [1992] Excerpts from James Mill's *Elements of Political Economy*. In 'Karl Marx: Early Writings'. London: Penguin Classics/New Left Review.

Marx, K. (1844b) [1977] *Economic and Philosophical Manuscripts of 1844*. Moscow: Progress Publishers.

Marx, K. (1845) [1978] Theses on Feuerbach. In R. Tucker (ed) *'The Marx-Engels Reader'*, New York: W.W. Norton.

Marx, K. (1847a) [1977] Wage-Labour and Capital. In *Selected Works Vol.1*. Moscow: Progress Publishers.

Marx, K. (1847b) [1978] The Poverty of Philosophy. In R. Tucker (ed) *'The Marx-Engels Reader'*, New York: W.W. Norton.

Marx, K. (1852) [1974] The Eighteenth Brumaire of Louis Bonaparte. In *'Surveys from Exile'*. New York: Vintage Books.

Marx, K. (1857) [1973] General Introduction (to the *Grundrisse*). Trans. M. Nicolaus. Harmondsworth: Penguin.

Marx, K. (1858) [1973] *Grundrisse: Foundations of the Critique of Political Economy* (Rough Draft). Trans. M. Nicolaus. Harmondsworth: Penguin.

Marx, K. (1859) [1977] *A Contribution to a Critique of Political Economy*. Moscow: Progress Publishers.

Marx, K. (1863) [1969] *Theories of Surplus Value—Part 1*. Moscow: Progress Publishers.

Marx, K. (1865a) [1977] *Capital, Vol.3*. London: Lawrence & Wishart.

_____ [1978] In R. Tucker (ed) *'The Marx-Engels Reader'*, New York: W.W. Norton.

_____ [1981] Harmondsworth: Penguin.

Marx, K. (1865b) [1977] Wages, Price and Profit. In *Selected Works Vol.2*. Moscow: Progress Publishers.

Marx, K. (1866) [1979] *Results of the Immediate Process of Production*, Addendum to 'Capital', Vol.1. Harmondsworth: Penguin.

Marx, K. (1867a) [1977] *Capital, Vol.1*. London: Lawrence & Wishart.

_____ [1977] New York: Vintage Books.

_____ [1986] Harmondsworth: Penguin.

Marx, K. (1867b) [1977] Preface to the First German Edition of *'Capital' (Vol.1)*. London: Lawrence & Wishart.

Marx, K. (1878) [1978] *Capital, Vol.2*. Harmondsworth: Penguin.

Marx, K. (1992) *Early Writings*. Trans. R. Livingstone & G. Benton. London: Penguin Classics/New Left Review.

Marx, K. & Engels, F. (1846) [1976] *The German Ideology*. Moscow: Progress Publishers.

Marx, K. & Engels, F. (1848) [1978] In R. Tucker (ed) *'The Marx-Engels Reader'*, New York: W.W. Norton.

_____ [1985] *The Communist Manifesto*. London: Penguin.

Maynard, M. (1993) Feminism and the possibilities of a postmodern research practice. *British Journal of Sociology of Education*, 14 (3) pp. 327-331.

McCarthy, C. and Crichlow, W. (eds.) (1993) *Race, Identity, and Representation in Education*. New York: Routledge.

McGreal, J. and Corrigan, P. (1970) *Ideology in 'Colour' and Citizenship*. London: LSE.

McKay, G. (1996) *Senseless Acts of Beauty: cultures of resistance since the sixties*. London and New York: Verso.

McKay, I. (1995/1996) The many deaths of Mr. Marx: Or, what left historians might contribute to debates about the 'crises of Marxism.' *Left History*, (3.2 and 4.1) pp. 9-84.

McLaren, P. (1986) Postmodernity and the Death of Politics: A Brazilian Reprieve. *Educational Theory*, Fall, 36 (4) pp. 389-401.

McLaren, P. (1994) Multiculturalism and the postmodernism critique: towards a pedagogy of resistance and transformation. In H. Giroux and P. McLaren (eds.) *Between Borders: Pedagogy and the Politics of Cultural Studies*. London: Routledge.

McLaren, P. (1995) *Critical pedagogy and predatory culture: Oppositional politics in a postmodern era*. London and New York: Routledge.

McLaren, P. (1997) *Critical Pedagogy and Globalization: Thirty Years After Che*. Keynote Address at the Annual Convention for the National Association for Multicultural Education, Albuquerque, New Mexico, 31st October 1997.

McLaren, P. (1997) *Revolutionary Multiculturalism: Pedagogies of Dissent for the New Millennium*. Boulder: Westview Press.

McLaren, P. (1997a) *Life in schools: An introduction to critical pedagogy in the social foundations of education* (3rd ed.). New York: Longman Inc.

McLaren, P. (1998a) Revolutionary Pedagogy in Post-Revolutionary Times: Rethinking the Political Economy of Critical Education. *Education Theory*, 48 (4) pp. 431-462.

McLaren, P. (1998b) Che: The Pedagogy of Che Guevara: Critical Pedagogy and Globalization Thirty Years After Che. *Cultural Circles*, 3 pp. 28-104

McLaren, P. (1998b) *Life in Schools: an Introduction to Critical Pedagogy in the Foundations of Education (3rd. ed.)*. Harlow: Longman.

McLaren, P. (1999a) Traumatizing capital: Pedagogy, politics, and praxis in the global marketplace. In M. Castells, R. Flecha, P. Freire, H. Giroux, D. Macedo, and P. Willis (eds.) *An introduction to new perspectives in education*. Boulder, Colorado: Rowman and Littlefield.

McLaren, P. (in press) Beyond Phallogocentrism: Critical Pedagogy and its Capital Sins: A response to Donna Lecourt. *Strategies*, 11/12 pp. 34-35

McLaren, P., Fischman, G., Serra, S. & Antelo, E. (1998) The Specters of Gramsci: Revolutionary Praxis and the Committed Individual, *Journal of Thought*, Fall 1998, pp. 9-41.

McLaren, P. and Leonardo, Z. (1998) Dead poet's society: Deconstructing surveillance pedagogy. *Studies in the Literary Imagination*, 31 (1) pp. 127-147.

McNally, D. (1993) *Against the Market: Political Economy, Market Socialism and the Marxist Critique*. London: Verso.

McRobbie, A. (1994) *Postmodern and Popular Culture*. London: Routledge.

McVicar, J. (1979) *By Himself*. London: Arrow.

Meagher, N. (1998) *What do employers require from their young recruits?*, Department of Education, University of Newcastle, St. Thomas Street, Newcastle-upon-Tyne.

Meiksin Wood, E. (1998) The Communist Manifesto after 150 years. *Monthly Review*, 50 (1) pp. 14-35.

Meiksins Wood, E. (1986) *The retreat from class*. London: Verso.

Meiksins Wood, E. (1997) A Reply to A. Sivanandan. *Monthly Review Press*, (48) pp. 21-32.

Meiksins Wood, E. and Bellamy Foster, J. (eds.) (1997) *In defence of history: Marxism and the postmodern agenda*. New York: *Monthly Review*.

Mercer, K. (1990) Welcome to the jungle: identity and diversity in postmodern politics. In J. Rutherford (ed.), *Identity: community, culture, difference*. London: Lawrence and Wishart.

Mészáros, I. (1998) Globalizing capital. *Monthly Review*, 49 (2) pp. 27-37.

Miliband, R. (1991) *Divided Societies*. Oxford: Oxford University Press.

Miner, B. (1998) Target: Public Education. *The Nation*, 267 (18) pp. 4, 6.

Molnar, A. (1996) Giving the Kids the Business: The Commercialization of America's Schools. Boulder, Colorado: Westview Press.

Moody, K. (1997) *Workers in a lean world: Unionism in the international economy*. London: Verso Books.

More, M. (und.) The Post Human Sub-page, referred to in: R. Pepperell, *The Post-Human Condition* (Exeter, Intellect Books), and at: http://www.acm.usl.edu/~dca6381/c2_mirror/xi/entropy.

Morris, B. (1991) *Western Conceptions of the Individual*. Oxford: Berg.

Murray, N. (1989) Anti-racists and other demons: the press and ideology in Thatcher's Britain. In *Racism and the press in Thatcher's Britain*. London: IRR.

Nash, K. (1994) The Feminist Production of Knowledge: Is Deconstruction a Practice for Women? *Feminist Review*, (47) Summer, pp. 65-77.

Neary, M (1997) *Youth, Training and the Training State: the real history of youth training in the twentieth century*. London: Macmillan.

Neary, M. & Rikowski, G. (1999) Deep Possession: Marx, Labour and the Transhuman (forthcoming).

Neary, M. & Taylor, G. (1998) *Money and the Human Condition*. London: Macmillan.

Neary, M. (1997) *Youth, Training and the Training State: the real history of youth training in the twentieth century*. London: Macmillan.

Neary, M. (1998) Situating the Situationists: the most modern discourse, *Radical Chains*, Issue 5, pp. 26-31.

Nederveen Pieterse, J. (1992) *Emancipations—Modern and Postmodern*. London: Sage.

Negri, A.(1988) *Revolution Retrieved, Selected Writings on Marx, Keynes, Capitalist Crisis and New Social Subjects 1967-1983*. London: Red Notes.

Nichol, C. (1997) Patterns of Pay: Results from the 1997 New Earnings Survey. *Labour Market Trends*, November. London: Government Statistical Service.

Nicholson, L. J. (1994) Feminism and the Politics of Postmodernism. In Ferguson, M. and Wicke, J. (1994) (eds.) *Feminism and Postmodernism*. Durham and London: Duke University Press.

Nicholson, L.J. (ed.) (1990) *Feminism/Postmodernism*. London: Routledge.

Nikolinakos, M. (1975) Notes towards a general theory of migration in late capitalism. *Race and Class*, 17 (1) p. 12.

Norris, C. (1992) *Uncritical Theory*. London: Lawrence & Wishart.

Ormer, M., Miller, J. & Ellsworth, E. (1996) Excessive Moments and Educational Discourses that Try to Contain them, *Educational Theory*, 46 (1) pp. 71-91.

Ortner, S. (1998) Identities: The hidden life of class. *Journal of Anthropological Research*, 54 (1) pp. 1-17.

Ozga, J. (1989) Policy Research and Policy Theory, *Journal of Education Policy*, 5(4).

Pakulski, J. (1995) Social Movements and Class: The Decline of the Marxist Paradigm. In L. Maheu (ed.) *Social Movements and Social Classes*. London: Sage.

Pan (1979) *Dictionary of Philosophy*. London: Pan.

Panitch, L. (1998) ''The State in a Changing World': Social Democratizing Global Capitalism'? Monthly Review, 50 (5) pp. 11-22.

Parenti, M. (1998) *America besieged*. San Francisco: City Lights Books.

Parker, S. (1997) *Reflective Teaching in the Postmodern World: A Manifesto for Education in Postmodernity*. Buckingham: Open University Press.

Parmar, P. (1981) Young Asian Women: a critique of the pathological approach, *Multiracial Education*, 9 (5).

Parmar, P. (1990) Black feminism: the politics of articulation. In J. Rutherford (ed.), *Identity: community, culture, difference*. London: Lawrence and Wishart.

Pepperell, R. (1997) *The Post-Human Condition*. Exeter: Intellect Books.

Petras, J. and Polychroniou, C. (1996) Capitalist transformation: The relevance of and challenges to Marxism. In C. Polychroniou and H. R. Targ (eds.), *Marxism today: Essays on capitalism, socialism, and strategies for social change*. East port, Connecticut and London: Praeger.

Petras, J. and Polychroniou, C. (1998) 'Clinton and Volunteerism: The Poverty of American Social Policy at the End of the Century'. *New Political Science*, 20 (2) pp. 223-231.

Phillips, M. (1988) Why black people are backing Baker. *The Guardian*, 9 September.

Postone, M. (1996) *Time, Labor and Social Domination: a reinterpretation of Marx's critical theory*. Cambridge: Cambridge University Press.

Raduntz, H. (1999) *Researching a Hegelian-Marxian dialectic for a theory of Australian Catholic schooling*. Modified version of a presentation at the 1998 Conference of the Australian Association for Education Research (RSD 98259).

Rattansi, A. (1994) Modern racisms, racialized identities. In A. Rattansi and S.Westwood, (eds.). *Racism, modernity and identity: on the western front*. Cambridge: Polity.

Rattansi, A. and Donald, J. (eds.) (1992) Introduction. In *'Race', culture and difference*. London: Sage.

Redhead, S. (1993) *Rave Off*. Aldershot: Avebury.

Rikowski, G. & Neary, M. (1997) 'Working Schoolchildren in Britain Today', *Capital & Class* (63) pp. 25-35.

Rikowski, G. (1990a) *The Recruitment Process and Labour Power*. Unpublished paper, Division of Humanities & Modern Languages, Epping Forest, Loughton, Essex.

Rikowski, G. (1990b) *Labour-Power Once More*. Unpublished paper, Division of Humanities & Modern Languages, Epping Forest, Loughton, Essex.

Rikowski, G. (1992) Work Experience Schemes and Part-time Jobs in a Recruitment Context, *British Journal of Education and Work*, 5 (1) pp. 19-46.

Rikowski, G. (1995) *Education Markets and Missing Products*, Paper presented to the Conference of Socialist Economists, University of Northumbria at Newcastle, 7-9 July 1995.

Rikowski, G. (1996) Left Alone: end time for Marxist educational theory? *British Journal of Sociology of Education*, 17 (4) pp. 415-451.

Rikowski, G. (1997) Scorched Earth: Prelude to Rebuilding Marxist Educational Theory, *British Journal of Sociology of Education*, 18 (4) pp. 551-574.

Roman, L. and Apple, M. W. (1990) Is Naturalism a Move Beyond Positivism? In Eisner, E. and Peshkin, A. (eds.) *Qualitative Inquiry in Education*. New York: Teachers College Press.

Rorty, R. (1980) *Philosophy and the Mirror of Nature*. Princeton, NJ: Princeton University Press.

Rosaldo, M.Z. (1974) Woman, Culture and Society: A Theoretical Overview. In Rosaldo, M.Z. and Lamphere, L. (eds.) *Woman, Culture and Society*. Stanford: Stanford University Press.

Rose, E.J. B. in association with Deakin, N., Abrams, M., Jackson, V., Peston, M., Vanags, A., Cohen, B., Galtskill, J. and Wood, P. (1972) *Colour and Citizenship: a report on British race relations*. London: Oxford University Press for the IRR.

Rosenau, P. (1992) *Postmodernism and the Social Sciences: Insights, Inroads and Intrusions*. Princeton: Princeton University Press.

Rowbotham, S., Segal, L. and Wainwright, H. (1979) *Beyond the fragments*. London: Merlin Press.

Rustin, M. (1989) The Trouble with New Times. In S. Hall and M. Jacques (eds.) (1989) *New Times: The Changing Face of Politics in the 1990s*. London: Lawrence and Wishart.

Rutherford, J. (1990) A place called home: identity and the cultural politics of difference. In J. Rutherford (ed.), *Identity: community, culture, difference*. London: Lawrence and Wishart.

Said, E. (1978) *Orientalism*. London: Routledge.

Said, E. (1993) *Culture and Imperialism*. New York: Vintage.

Sardar, Z. (1998) *Postmodernism and the other: The new imperialism of Western culture*. London and Chicago, Illinois: Pluto Press.

Sarup, M. (1982) *Education, State and Crisis*. London: RKP.

Sarup, M. (1983) *Marxism Structuralism Education*. Lewes: Falmer Press.

Sassen, S. (1998) *Globalization and its discontents*. New York: New Press.

Saville, J. (1994) *The Consolidation of the Capitalist State 1800-1850*. London: Pluto Press.

Searle, C. (1996) OFSTEDed, Blunketted and Permanently Excluded: an experience of English education. *Race and Class*, 38 (1) pp. 21-38.

Searle, C. (1997) *Living Community, Living School*. London: Tufnell Press.

Segal, L. (1997) *New Sexual Agendas*. London: Macmillan.

Seve, L. (1975) *Marxism and the Theory of Human Personality*. London: Lawrence & Wishart.

Shor, I. (1986) *Culture Wars; School and Society in the Conservative Restoration 1969-1984*. London: Routledge Kegan Paul.

Sivanandan, A. (1974) *Race and Resistance: the IRR story*. London: IRR.

Sivanandan, A. (1976) *Race, class and the state*. London: IRR.

Sivanandan, A. (1982a) Introduction. In *Patterns of racism*. London: IRR.

Sivanandan, A. (1982b)) Introduction. In *Roots of racism*. London: IRR.

Sivanandan, A. (1982c) *From resistance to rebellion: Asian and Afro-Caribbean struggles in Britain*. London: IRR.

Sivanandan, A. (1983) Challenging racism: strategies for the 1980s, *Race and Class*, 25 (2) pp. 1-11.

Sivanandan, A. (1985) RAT and the degradation of black struggle, *Race and Class*, 26 (4) pp. 1-33.

Sivanandan, A. (1987) Race, class and Brent. *Race and Class*, 29 (1) pp. 73-77.

Sivanandan, A. (1990) All that Melts into Air is Solid: The Hokum of New Times. *Race and Class*, 31 (3) pp. 1-30.

Sivanandan, A. (1995) La trahison des clercs. *New Statesman*, 14 July, pp. 20-21.

Skeggs, B. (1991) Postmodernism: What is all the fuss about? *British Journal of Sociology of Education*. 12 (2) pp. 255-267.

Skeggs, B. (1997) *Formations of Class and Gender*. London: Sage.

Sloterdijk, P. (1988) *Critique of Cynical Reason*. London: Verso.

Sly, F., Price, A. and Risdon, A. (1997) Women in the Labour Market: Results from the Spring 1996 Labour Force Survey. *Labour Market Trends*, March. London: Government Statistical Service.

Sohn-Rethel, A. (1978) *Intellectual and Manual Labour: a critique of epistemology*. London and Basingstoke: Macmillan.

Spivak, G. (1976) translation of J. Derrida, *Of Grammatology*. London: John Hopkins University Press.

Stabile, C. A. (1995) Feminism without guarantees: The misalliances and missed alliances of postmodernist social theory. In A. Callari, S. Cullenberg, and C. Biewener (eds.), *Marxism in the Postmodern Age: Confronting the New World Order*. New York and London: The Guilford Press.

Stevens, M. (1991) *Japan and Education*. London: Macmillan.

Stronach, I. and MacLure, M. (1997) *Educational Research Undone: the Postmodern Embrace*. Buckingham: Open University Press.

Subversion (1998) 23rd June. Dept. 10, 1 Newton St., Manchester, M1 1HW.

Taaffe, P. and Mulhearn, T. (1988) *Liverpool: a City that Dared to Fight*. London: Fortress Books.

Teeple, G. (1995) *Globalization and the decline of social reform*. New Jersey: Humanities Press.

The Guardian (1998) Brain implants allow patients to work computer by thought-power, *The Guardian*, 15th October 1998, p. 7.

Thornett, A. (1998) *Inside Cowley*. London: Porcupine Press.

Trigg, R. (1988) *Ideas of Human Nature: An Historical Introduction*. Oxford: Blackwell.

Trotsky, L. (1973) *Women and the Family*. New York: Pathfinder Press.

TUC (1947) *Annual Conference Report*. London: Trades Union Congress.

Tucker, R. C. (ed.) (1978) *The Marx-Engels Reader*. New York: W.W. Norton and Co.

Unger, R., Mangabeira, and West, C. (1998). Progressive Politics and What Lies Ahead. *The Nation*, 267 (17) pp. 11-15.

Urry, J. (1995) Rethinking Class. In L. Maheu (ed.) *Social Movements and Social Classes*. London: Sage.

Usher, R. and Edwards, R. (1994) *Postmodernism and Education: different voices, different worlds*. London: Routledge.

Virilio, P. (1995) *The Art of the Motor* (trans. J. Rose). London, Minneapolis: University of Minnesota Press.

Vogel, L. (1983) *Marxism and the Oppression of Women: Towards a Unitary Theory*. London: Pluto Press

Wainwright, H. (1994) *Arguments for a New Left: Answering the free market right*. London and Cambridge, USA: Blackwell Publishers.

Waite, G. (1996) *Nietzsche's Corps/e: aesthetics, politics, prophecy, or, the spectacular technoculture of everyday life*. Durham and London: Duke University Press.

Walford, G. and Miller, H. (1991) *City Technology College*. Milton Keynes: Open University Press.

Walker, P. (ed.) (1979) *Between Labour and Capital*. Brighton: Harvester Press.

Walkerdine, V. (1990) *Schoolgirl Fictions*. London: Verso.

Walkling, P. and Brannigan, C. (1986) Anti-sexist/anti-racist education: a possible dilemma, *Journal of Moral Education*, 15 (1).

Weedon, C. (1987) *Feminist Practice & Poststructuralist Theory*. Oxford: Blackwell.

Wexler, P. (1992) *Becoming Somebody*. Lewes: Falmer.

White, M. (1999) Blair hails middle class revolution. *The Guardian*, 15th Jan.

Whitty, G. (1985) *Sociology and School Knowledge: Curriculum Theory, Research and Politics*. London: Methuen Books.

Whitty, G. (1986) Education policy and the inner cities. In Lawless, P. and Raban, C. (eds.) *The Contemporary British City*. London: Harper and Row.

Whitty, G. (1989) The New Right and the National Curriculum—state control or market forces? *Journal of Education Policy*, 4 (4).

Whitty, G. (1991) Recent Educational Reform: Is it a Postmodern phenomenon? Conference Paper to Conference on Reproduction, Social Inequality and Resistance, Germany: University of Bielefeld.

Whitty, G. (1993) Education Reform and Teacher Education in England in the 1990s. In P. Gilroy and M. Smith (eds.) *International Analyses of Teacher Education.* London: Carfax.

Whitty, G. (1997) Creating Quasi-Markets in Education. In Apple, M. W. (ed.) Review of Research in *Education,* 22. Washington: American Educational Research Association.

Whitty, G. (1998) Citizens or Consumers? Continuity and Change in Contemporary Education Policy. In Carlson, D. and Apple, M. (eds.) *Power/Knowledge/ Pedagogy* Boulder: Westview Press.

Whitty, G. (1998) New Labour, Education and Social Justice, *Socialist Teacher,* 65.

Whitty, G. and Menter, I. (1989) Lessons of Thatcherism: Education Policy in England and Wales, 1979-88. *Journal of Law and Society,* 16 (1).

Whitty, G., Edwards, T. and Gewirtz, S. (1993) *Specialisation and Choice in Urban Education.* London: Routledge.

Whitty, G., Halpin, D., and Power, S. (1997) *Devolution and choice in education: The school, the state and the market.* Buckingham: Open University Press.

Whitty, G., Powers, S. and Halpin, D. (1998) *Devolution and Choice in Education: The School, the State and the Market.* Milton Keynes: Open University Press.

Willis, P. (1990) *Consuming Passions.* Milton Keynes: Open University Press.

Wolff, R. and Resnick, S. (1986) Power, property, and class. *Socialist Review,* 16 (2) pp. 97-124.

Wolpe, A M. (1988) 'Experience' as analytical framework: does it account for girls' education? In M. Cole (ed.) *Bowles and Gintis Revisited: Correspondence and Contradiction in Educational Theory.* Lewes: Falmer Press.

Workers Vanguard, Box 1377, GPO, New York, NY, 10116.

Wright, T. and Carter, M. (1997) *The People's Party: The History of the Labour Party.* London: Thames and Hudson.

Wyn, J. and White, R. (1997) *Rethinking Youth.* London: Sage.

Yeatman, A. (1990) A feminist theory of social differentiation. In L. Nicholson (ed.) *Feminism/Postmodernism.* New York: Routledge.

Zeichner, K. and Liston, D. (1987) Teaching Student Teachers to Reflect, *Harvard Educational Review,* 57 (1) pp. 23-48.

Zipin, L. (1998) Emphasising 'Discourse' and Bracketing People. In Popkewitz, T. and Brennan, M. (eds.) *Governmentality Through Education.* New York: Teachers College Press.

Zukin, S. (1991) *Landscapes of power: From Detroit to Disneyland.* Berkeley, Los Angeles, and Oxford: University of California Press.